DESIGN IN THEORY AND PRACTICE

I0427084

BY

ERNEST A. BATCHELDER

AUTHOR OF "PRINCIPLES OF DESIGN"

New York

THE MACMILLAN COMPANY

1927

COPYRIGHT, 1910,

BY THE MACMILLAN COMPANY.

———

Set up and electrotyped. Published July, 1910. Reprinted
April, 1912; July, 1914; December, 1915; April, 1917;
December, 1918; March, 1920; May, 1927.

Norwood Press
J. S. Cushing Co. — Berwick & Smith Co.
Norwood, Mass., U.S.A.

PREFACE

IT is the aim of this book to be helpful, — not only to teachers and students who may be directly interested in the subject, but to the many others who feel the lack of a criterion or standard to assist them in forming a judgment in questions of design. Though the book is written primarily for workers, I have endeavored to tell the story in such way that it may be of interest to the general reader. A judgment is of little value unless it can be backed with a logical reason. If we would judge wisely and discriminate well, it must be from a more stable basis than personal whim or fancy. To fully appreciate a piece of constructive work, it is necessary to put one's self as nearly as is possible in the place of the worker, study the environment in which he worked, the conditions that confronted him in a solution of his problem, the technical limitations and possibilities through which his idea took definite form and from which his design derives character and style. Hence we may consider as pertinent any serious discussion which aims to define the principles of design and their practical application, touching upon a more sane, more artistic production, on the one hand, and a more intelligent, more discriminating judgment on the other.

The purpose of the book is best accomplished by the presentation of a series of problems. We learn by doing. In setting mind and hand to the solution of a definite problem, we meet and overcome questions which no amount of reading can foresee. We may attend lectures and indulge in critical discussions of design in terms of language; we may become well versed in the history of art, and in biographical data pertaining to the lives of artists; yet find ourselves far removed from any true appreciation of the work of the past, or quite at a loss when confronted by a simple problem in constructive design demanding artistic invention.

Our problems lead from the simple, constructive use of lines and forms under clearly defined limitations to work involving considerable invention, fine feeling, and freedom of execution. They begin with the geometric and work toward Nature; with the abstract, coming gradually into closer relation with the constructive questions discussed in the different chapters of the book.

The work is in no sense an effort to formulate a system or method for teaching design. Rather, it is a presentation of a few among many problems that have gradually developed during several years of teaching and practice. Many have found this work helpful, and its appearance in a series of magazine articles (*The Craftsman*) has aroused sufficient interest to justify its publication in book form. Through the courtesy of the editor of *The Craftsman*, material has been also selected from articles contributed to that magazine subsequent to the original series.

The teacher of design in America must meet conditions quite different from those found in the Old World. Each country abroad has distinctive national traditions. We have no traditions; in which fact is our best hope. Our salvation is to be sought not in borrowing from Europe, but in boldly striking for an elementary basis on which to build, in digging for bed rock on which to raise our superstructure. The student abroad is at all times within easy reach of museums and galleries, of churches and monuments, through which the development of the art of his own and other countries may be traced, and which offer facilities for comparative study not open to most students in America. Books, photographs, even casts, are insufficient to stimulate the imagination or develop the thought and fine feeling essential to fine work; much less do they furnish a clew to work expressing something of American life and character.

Throughout the book the simplest type of technique with brush and pencil has been adhered to. It is not even brush-made design that is sought; for there may be a distinctive style imparted to a design through the manipulation peculiar to the brush. The sole purpose here is to make the worker *think in terms of design,* whatever medium or technique he may choose to employ. Skill in rendering with various mediums, charcoal, pencil, water and oil colors, contributes much to the problems given. But a book is no place for the teaching of technique.

Color has not been touched upon because it must, perforce, deal largely with diagrams and theories. To talk about color, or write about it, is very unsatisfactory, to writer and reader alike. Color can be discussed only through definite examples; and reproductive processes are so inadequate to convey the precise meaning intended that it has seemed best to leave color entirely out of consideration.

The following list of materials will be found serviceable: Drawing board; thumb tacks; some squared, engine-ruled paper; some transparent Japanese watercolor paper; a bottle of waterproof, black India ink; an H.B. pencil; two brushes — No. 2 for lines, No. 7 for washes; a tube of charcoal gray paint; an eraser.

One unused to these tools and materials will find some practice necessary here quite as much as if one were to attempt designing in terms of wood or metal.

Some command of technique is essential to an acceptable expression of any idea.

My thanks are due to pupils who have generously furnished so much of the illustrative material used in the book, — to them and many others who have contributed more through their own thought and effort than the writer can hope to acknowledge.

ERNEST A. BATCHELDER.

PASADENA, CALIFORNIA.

TABLE OF CONTENTS

LIST OF ILLUSTRATIONS

LIST OF PLATES

DESIGN IN THEORY AND PRACTICE

Design in Theory and Practice

CHAPTER I

INTRODUCTION

" Though we travel the world over to find the beautiful, we must have it with us or we find it not." — EMERSON.

LET us give emphasis to one point at the start. The ability to design is not a secret that Nature has vouchsafed to genius alone. It is quite as much a matter of persistent work as of fortuitous inheritance. Indeed, there is so much of common sense and orderly thought involved in the process of building up a design that a resignation to failure is often an unconscious admission of one's own lack of persistence and energy. There is no vest-pocket guide through which one may find a short cut to distinction ; no rules or recipes which one may employ in lieu of personal thought and effort. To be sure, we cannot all produce work of equal merit and interest. To bring to that which we do accomplish some measure of understanding and appreciation is at least worth while. Work always rises to the level of the worker — never higher. To give thought, that one may do common things uncommonly well, is the first essential toward the achievement of important things.

A great deal of the most interesting creative work left to us from the past was done at times when designing was more or less an instinctive process. It was instinct rather than reason that guided the primitive worker at all times. That is to say, he designed from the heart, not from the head. He made no effort to analyze motives or define principles; his work was an unconscious response to the needs, the thought, and the life about him, to the environment in which he lived. The same may be said of peasant work, and of a considerable part of mediæval crafts work. With us designing is an intellectual process, self-conscious, self-critical at all times. We cannot, if we would, escape the traditions and precedents of the centuries preceding us; nor is there in the complex of our own life a thought or feeling sufficiently dominant to shape our work into a distinctive character or style. More than ever before, each individual is a " style " unto himself. Instead of playing many variations of a single tune we play many tunes with a variety of instruments.

It becomes the function of a teacher to point out the way and call attention to the beauty of the scenery,— not to drive or push. It is very likely that there is no particular merit in any system or method for teaching design. In fact, the term *design* implies a wide margin of freedom for individual thought and effort. Work that is helpful to one pupil may not be for the best interests of another. A soil in which the rose will thrive is not necessarily good for the lily. To devise a " system " applicable by all and to all is farthest from the teacher's purpose. He may devise problems working from the simple to the complex, from the known and obvious to the unknown and difficult; but the value of the problem is in the thought it frames, the principle it defines, the stimulus it furnishes.

We study design, then, to stimulate the imagination and arouse latent ideas, to develop original thought, to strengthen judgment, and to acquire the power to express ourselves through the terms and materials employed in a way that shall be, at least, clear and coherent.

By imagination is meant the active, creative faculty of the mind, not the passive state of mind that builds day-dream castles on a summer's holiday. It was a creative imagination that dared the cantilever bridge.

By original thought is meant the simple, straightforward means to an end, the logical reasoning from a premise of accepted conditions. There is no virtue in originality for the sake of being different.

Mr. Ruskin has said that " drawing may be taught by tutors; but design only by heaven." In other

words, we may be taught to observe things placed
before us, and to make an adequate, if not an artistic,
representation of what we see.   In the representation
of a chair, for instance, we may prove that a certain
line is right or wrong; it admits of demonstration.
But in designing a chair we pass beyond questions
of right or wrong into fields where other distinctions
must be sought.   A design for a chair may be interesting or uninteresting, worthy or unworthy ; but no man
shall say this design is right; that design is wrong.
A chair must be comfortable to sit in, strong and
durable in all its parts.   These demands alone
necessitate certain constructive elements — seat, legs,
back, rungs, possibly arms.   In the adjustment
of these constructive elements we have the first
step involved in the problem.   Thus far distinctions
of right and wrong may admit of demonstration.
Now supposing it is the intention to make a beautiful
chair : The first clew will be furnished by the various
constructive elements ; in the adjustment of the lines
and proportions demanded by utility.   But in the
refinement and enrichment of those lines and proportions we are faced by a problem answered only in
part by utilitarian demands.   The chair may be struc-
turally adequate, but stupid and altogether uninteresting
in design.   For the rest we must possess that subtle
faculty commonly called good taste.   It requires a

sound judgment, an appreciation of fundamental principles, a criterion or standard, whether of natural intuition, or acquired through long years of training and experience, which will lead us unerringly to the interesting expression of an idea. To stimulate and develop the creative faculty demanded in the production of a design for a chair is quite a different task from developing the faculty of observation required to make an adequate representation of a chair.

To design is to give tangible and definite expression to an idea. The term *design* implies an interesting, possibly a beautiful, at least an orderly, rendering of this expression. It may seem superfluous to say that we must first have an idea! Yet it is the very paucity of ideas, the lack of imagination, that forms the first stumblingblock in the path which leads into our subject. In this age of acute specialization we are so dependent upon others for the things which we gather about us in daily life that few of us know the joy of creative work, of planning, building, completing things. Where, indeed, can one who uses no tools, practices no craft, attempts no creative work, expect to evolve ideas or find a stimulus to the imagination?

The beautiful things which we treasure so carefully in our museums and galleries were designed and executed by men with tools in their hands in those bygone days when art was not afraid of the grime and soot, the din and clatter of a workshop. To such men ideas came without conscious effort and were given expression in terms of wood, metal, stone, and paint as part of the day's work. There were no artists then; nothing but craftsmen — some better than others. No one thought of studying design; much less of teaching it. Good taste and sound judgment came as a matter of course during the long years of apprenticeship at the bench. The principles of design were felt intuitively; but through succeeding generations of imitation and adaptation we have too often lost sight of principles and borrowed mere outward forms and symbols. We have drawn upon ideas which were once fresh, real, and significant because they embodied in their expression something of the thoughts and feelings of the times in which they were used, but which now appear as misapplied finery.

What is beauty? How are we to know it when we have achieved it? Things may be pretty, rich, stylish, elegant, and still lack all the essential elements of beauty.

Beauty is undefinable, though it is universal. It has no style or period or country. It may appear in an Indian basket woven under the heat of an Arizona sun by one whose life has known no other horizon than the line of the desert mesa tops; it may be found above the plains of Athens in a form so enduring that time, war, and pillage have been unable to efface it.

If beauty is undefinable, we may at least learn something of the various ways in which it manifests itself. As we may know a man by the character of his acquaintances, so may we learn to recognize the beautiful in design through the associations with which it has always been found. The beautiful thing, whatever it may be, is invariably sane and orderly in arrangement, clear and coherent in expression, frank and straightforward in an acceptance of all the conditions imposed by questions of use, environment, construction, tools, materials, and processes. All of these things we may analyze; we may reduce them to simple terms for purposes of study, and endeavor to establish definite principles for our guidance. Then, from simple beginnings through a process of experiment and comparison, a never ending process, we may hope to express ourselves in an orderly, consistent way. "We try for order and hope for beauty."

Where to begin; how to begin. These are questions which interest the student. "Go to Nature," one man says. " There you will find your inspiration and there you will discover all the clews to consistent ornament." Will you, though? Nature is indeed necessary to the designer, but not to the design.   Nor is it necessary to point to a justification in Nature for all that we do in design.   One is reminded of the old Spanish proverb, " He who would bring home the wealth of the Indies must take the wealth of the Indies with him."   What do you expect to find in Nature ? What message do you expect she has for you ?   You may be sure she will return to you just what you take to her ; nothing more.   It is like seeing faces in the fire.   To one the fire is living ; the flames dance and laugh and whisper.   To another the fire is merely a bed of sputtering coals shedding light and heat through the process of combustion.   To each the fire is a reflection of the individual mind.   Nature will not furnish you with an imagination, or teach you how to use the wealth which she places at your hand.   These must originate with you.   If you have them not, you might as well seek the pot of gold at the end of the rainbow as to expect help from Nature.   When you have learned to think in terms of line, form, and tone, and have studied the possibilities and limitations of the problem which you are trying to solve, you may then turn to Nature for suggestions and assistance.   She will never fail you.

"Go to Historic Ornament," another says.   " In the various historic styles you will find the key to good ornament."   And so we continue to build Gothic

churches, and Greek convention halls, and Queen
Anne cottages. Many of our designers boast of an
ability to design anything from a chair to a house in
any given period or style of ornament without an error
of detail. What we most need are workers who can
approach each new problem unhampered by tradition,
though open minded to any structural suggestions
which the past may offer, seeking to express without
affectation, in a clear, straightforward way, something
of our lives, our times, and our environment. It is a
superficial study of Historic Ornament, a familiarity
with so-called styles and periods, that has given us the
characterless bog of modern work. We have filled
our heads with beautiful details, as we would gather
chips in a basket. Is it not odd that we should resent
plagiarism in literature and music, but complacently
accept it as necessary in design? We are sometimes
told that originality is no longer possible or desirable;
that our best things have already been done for us;
that a readjustment of borrowed details is sufficient.
But do we not mistake the meaning of originality? It
may result from a determination to be unique, eccentric, different; but we may be quite as original without
departing from paths of order, simplicity, and frankness.

PROBLEM. The first interest, and, in the final analysis, the true strength of a design is to be found in
the structural relation of its various elements. First

of all there should be such an adjustment of the space and mass relations that the effect, as a whole, will be of interest.   To this end there should be a dominant space or mass, with other spaces and masses subordinate.   Within these big relations the details should be so disposed that the first interest will be justified and retained upon closer examination.   The observer proceeds from an impression of the whole to a study of the parts; the designer must put parts together with the effect of the whole in mind

By space is meant the part of the design that is left untouched.   In Figure 1 the space is the plain weaving of the basketry; in Figure 2 the spaces in each design are the spots of white, untouched paper, bits of silence left as a background.   These background spaces, whether you choose or not, become an integral part of the design.

By mass is meant that portion of the design which is generally referred to *as* the design; namely, decoration or ornament, whatever it may be.   In Figure 1 the darker areas of weaving form the mass; in Figure 2 the concentration of lines in each design furnishes a mass which, contrasted with the space, produces the first effect, a spotting of light and dark.   By a dominant space or mass is meant a space or mass that is dominant in the design by reason of its tone, measure, or shape.

In Figure 2, — ii, iii, iv, v, — we find an interest in the big, simple spotting of the designs. By way of comparison, vi, *as a line design*, lacks force and strength.

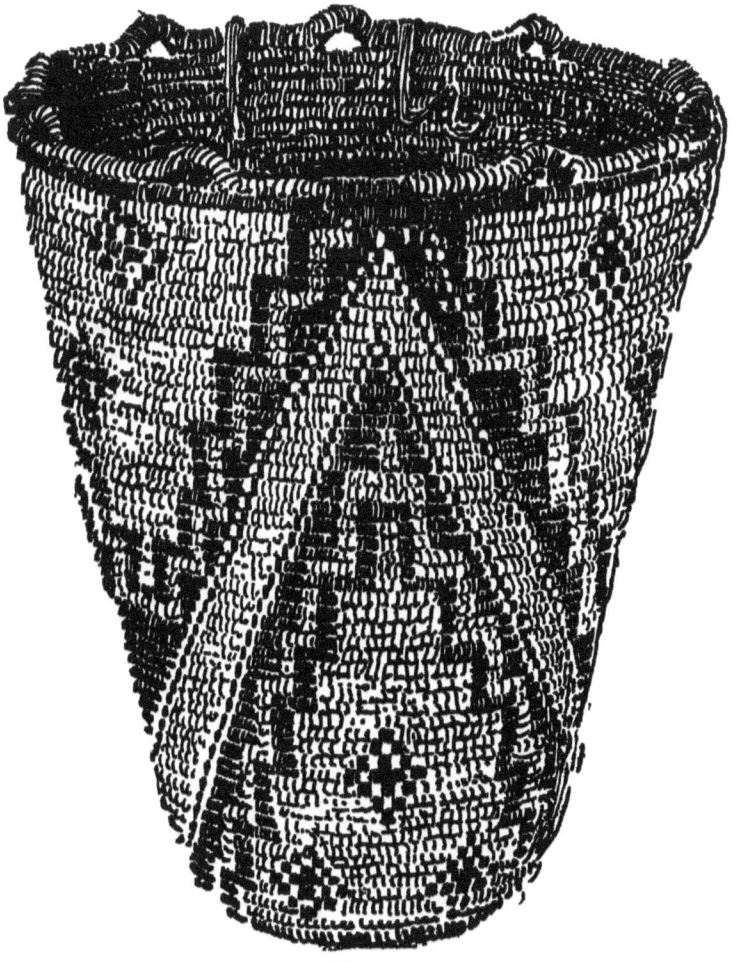

FIG. 1.

We may feel that we are beginning to exercise some command over our materials and tools when we can adjust these relations of space and mass at will; alter

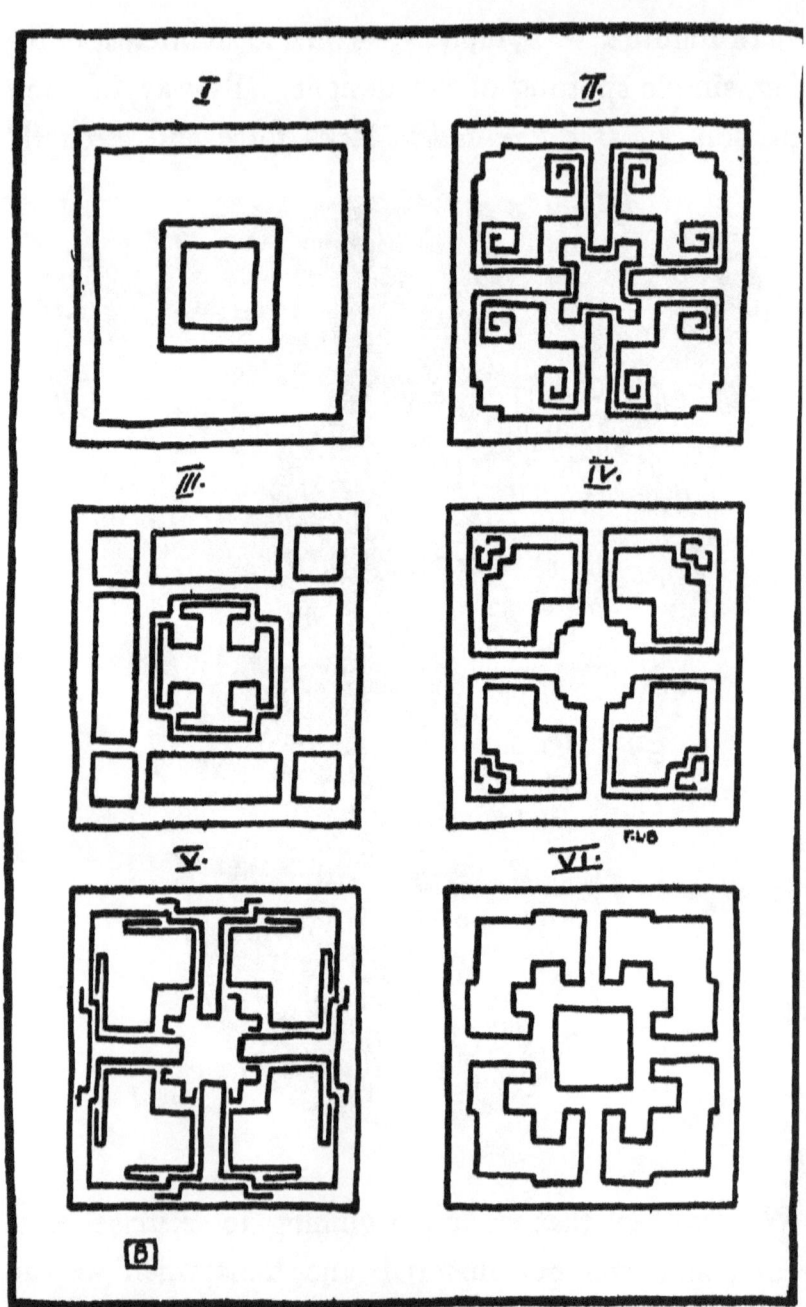

FIG. 2.

their tones, measures, or shapes to conform to the idea we wish to express.

As a first effort in design we shall find our resources sufficiently taxed by a limitation to straight lines, vertical and horizontal. Stretch a piece of transparent paper over the squared underlay; draw with light pencil lines a four-inch square with another square one quarter inch inside the first. Draw in the center a third square two inches in diameter with a fourth a quarter inch inside of this. We shall then have a result similar to Figure 2, i. It is hardly necessary to say that a rectangle of any other dimensions is quite as well adapted to the purpose. From this starting point, under the limitations imposed, we will endeavor, by means of contrasting areas of light and dark, to break the square into an interesting space and mass spotting. It will be found that a tone of dark is formed by the association of two or more lines. Draw a number of lines on a piece of paper, and when seen from a distance of a few feet they will give the appearance of a flat tone of gray paint. This tone may be darkened by increasing the widths of the lines, or by bringing them into closer association. A graphic illustration of this is furnished in Figure 3, three renderings of the same motif in different tones. It is apparent that the choice of line is an important factor to be considered; and it generally happens that a first effort lacks character through the choice of a thin, weak line.

Like every problem in design, this one may be solved in a way that is merely adequate, though totally devoid

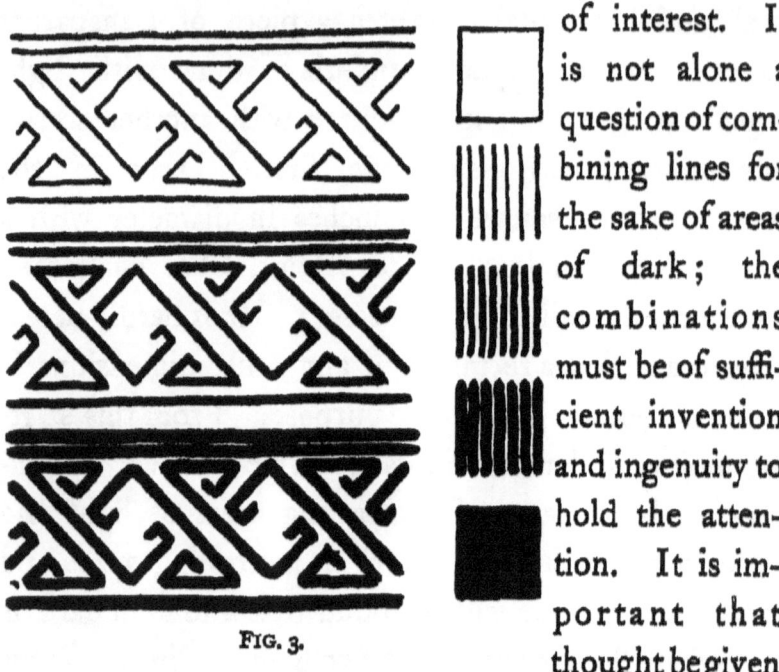

of interest. It is not alone a question of combining lines for the sake of areas of dark; the combinations must be of sufficient invention and ingenuity to hold the attention. It is important that thought be given

FIG. 3.

to the amount of parallelism and opposition of the lines that make the measures of dark. Long lines parallel with the outline of the rectangle tend to strengthen the design; but too many parallel lines result in monotony. There should be a spice of variety through the opposition of lines; but too many sharp oppositions may bring confusion.

Now let us see if we can throw a dominant tone or mass of dark on to the diameter (Figure 2, ii), into the

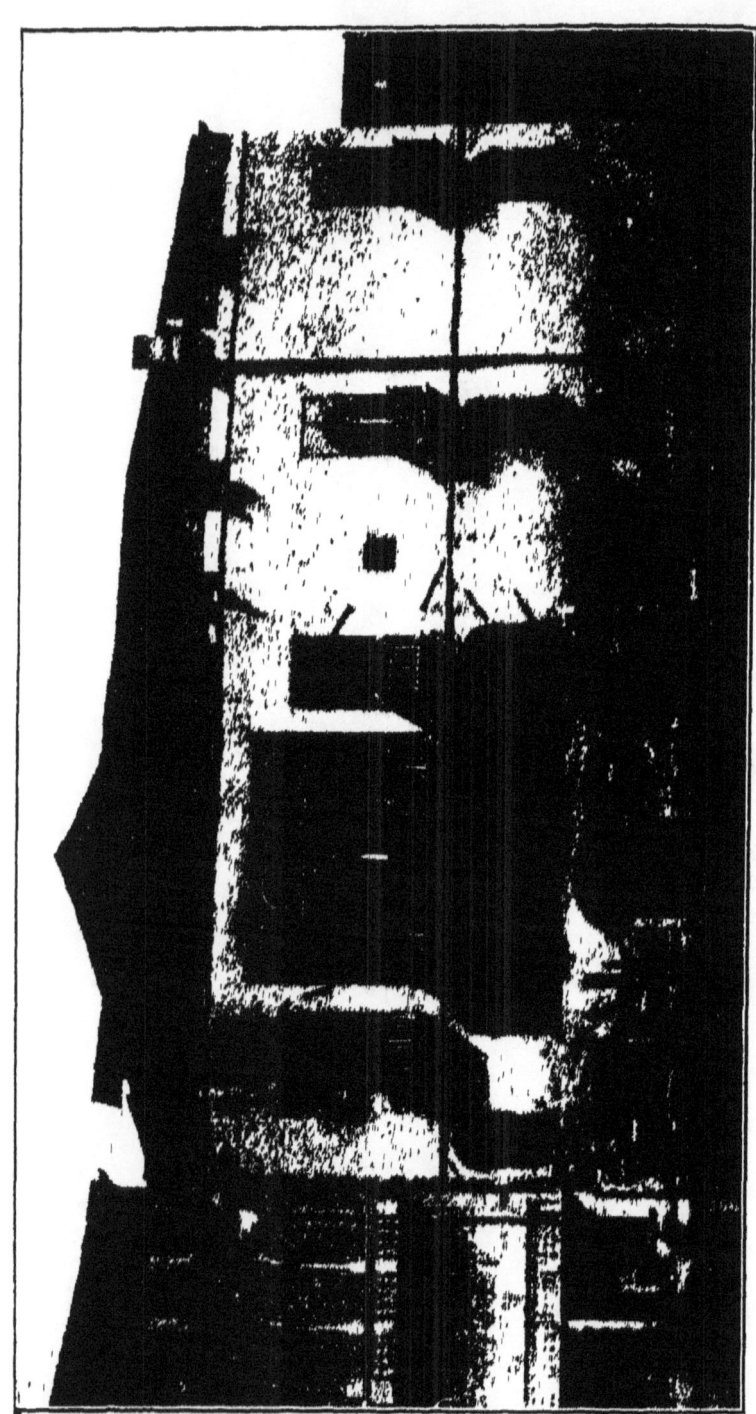

PLATE 1.

PALAZZO SAGREDO, VENICE.

center (iii), to the corners (iv), or to the outer sides of the square (v), and retain withal a contrasting area of space or silence.

In order that a right start may be made, Figure 4 is added to show a possible development of such a problem. It is the purpose to throw the dominant mass of

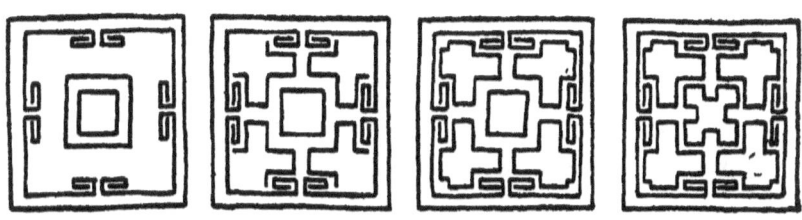

FIG. 4.

the design to the outer sides of the square. This is accomplished at once in the first instance; but there is lack of interest elsewhere. In the second the big space is broken and the different elements bound together. In the third more interest is given to the corners, in the fourth to the center; but all parts are kept subordinate to the idea with which the problem started.

In Plate 1 is the finest possible adjustment of space and mass relations. As a work of art it is more important than anything we may expect to achieve; but it is a question of degree, not of kind.

CHAPTER II

The Utilitarian Basis

"Nothing made by man's hand can be indifferent; it must be either beautiful and elevating, or ugly and degrading." — WILLIAM MORRIS.

IT is not within the province of this book to impart specific information for the working of wood, metal, leather, etc. On the other hand, in treating design as theory and practice it is not the thought to work out paper-made patterns which may, perchance, be applied to some constructive problem. There is peculiar significance in the little word *study*. We do not study design, or music, or law for immediate application and profit. We study to acquire understanding and power. In design we may seek to define on paper the principles governing line, form, and tone composition from a purely æsthetic point of view. In a line parallel with this development we may seek to define those principles which give to constructive design vital, intimate, organic character. But the technical knowledge itself should be sought in a shop, not in a book. In the happy union of technical skill with invention, imagination, refined feeling is the end to be devoutly wished for in the work of the future craftsman.

The evolution of a constructive design was briefly touched upon in the first chapter. It would be well to enumerate the most important points in a concise statement. There comes first, of course, an *idea*, arising, it may be presumed, from a desire to own or make an object of utility, convenience, or luxury, possessing some claims to beauty. Given a clearly defined idea, *use* and *environment* will lead one to a determination of the general form and dimensions. Practical considerations will lead also to a definition of the *essential constructive elements* and, primarily, to a choice of *materials*. The materials will naturally indicate the *tools* to be employed. But with all these factors entering into the problem we may achieve nothing more than a merely adequate expression of the idea. To give beauty to the product we must seek a *refinement* of the construction through an adjustment of the relative proportions of the parts to each other and to the whole. Then comes, if employed at all, *enrichment* on the basis of all that has preceded. Texture, color, finish — these, too, contribute to the beauty of the whole.

As a formula the above is useless. It means nothing until it becomes a habit through practice. Nor

c

must it be assumed that the steps above enumerated follow one upon another in the precise order named at all times and under all conditions. The enrichment does not necessarily await its turn until all other questions have been solved. Each point mentioned furnishes a clew to the designer in the development of his product; but, alas! only a clew. There are many crossroads between the idea and a beautiful expression of it, many opportunities for the unwary to go astray.

Mere adequacy is not beauty. The present generation is abundantly endowed with practical sense, leading to the remarkable mechanical inventions of our time. To pursue an idea through the practical phase alone may lead to a locomotive, a linotype, a machine gun; in other words, to the highest degree of efficiency. Complete efficiency may excite our admiration; but beauty springs from an impulse that craves more than efficient service.

Let us examine the work of a master craftsman who followed this impulse for beauty from the clews suggested by utilitarian demands. There may be more important works of art than the little implement in Figure 5, fashioned by an Indian of the northwest coast of America; but in his own primitive way he has furnished for us a valuable lesson in fundamentals. The simpler the lesson, the clearer the precept. It is a scraper for cleaning hides! This may stand for the idea,—a real need, something useful. With the need for a scraper established, utility at once defined the general form and the constructive elements, a blade of iron, a handle of wood, the two bound together with thongs of rawhide smeared with pitch. A man who is

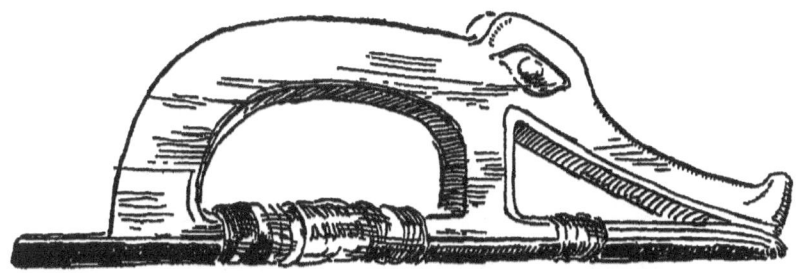

FIG. 5.

making a tool for his own use may be depended upon not to ignore the practical questions of his problem; but the impulse for beauty with which Nature saw fit to endow this Indian was of the kind that seeks expression in daily life and work. A few thoughtful touches of a knife, and an otherwise useful tool becomes an object of extreme interest, insistent in its personality. Being a hunter, this man's thought naturally turned to a beast-like motif as the elements of his design began to define themselves. The form of the creature is governed strictly by the function which it has to perform as a handle; each part, body, legs, and the long snout running out for a brace, is shaped for efficient service; and if you take the scraper in hand, you will find your thumb inevitably seeking a little hollow made for it between the ears. A far less skillful designer might have carved a far more realistic beast, and yet failed to achieve the very things which give distinction to this simple piece of craftsmanship. The more one studies it from every possible point of view, the more consistent and satisfying it becomes.

Now while it was said that mere adequacy is not beauty, it may likewise be said that adequate service is not incompatible with beauty. The assumption that art is a luxury, expensive, is the logical argument of an age that looks upon art as something apart from daily life, to be donned on occasions like a Sunday coat. We say that labor is too dear, time is too valuable, to bring art into the shop and factory to-day. And yet, has labor no other compensation than money? And is time so very valuable, after all, when spent in the production of a thoughtless product, of inutilities, of novelties and fads, out of fashion and consigned to the scrap heap almost as soon as made? We may feel sure that our Indian valued his simple scraper, would fight for it in fact, because it has those requisites which make possession worth while, — efficient service, good workmanship, thoughtful design, personality.

In Figure 6 are two ladles from the island of Java. In the first, adequacy alone was sought. Yet we find in the second that the very impulse which led the worker to a refinement of line and form has resulted in a more serviceable ladle. That form of bowl which seems most useful is the same form that might be chosen for beauty's sake alone; the curve of greatest efficiency chosen for the handle is just the curve that a

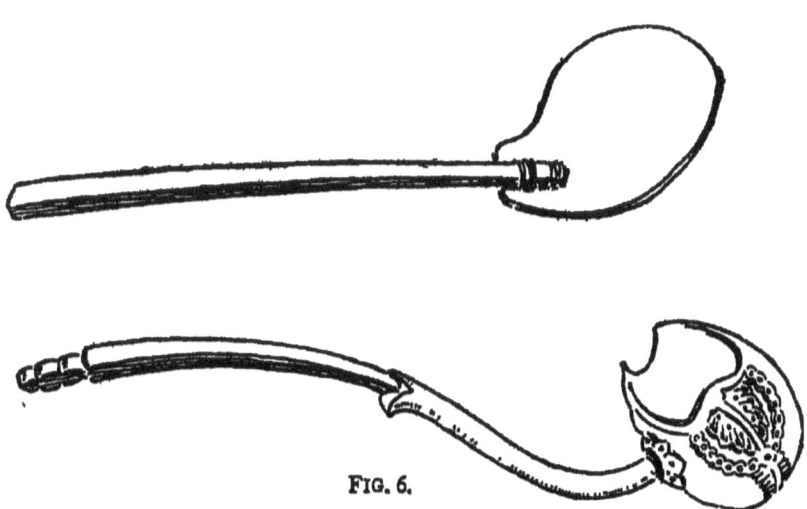

FIG. 6.

refinement of that functional element would bring one to. Here, too, may be noted in the position and character of the enrichment an organic development emphasizing, but in no wise impairing, the function of the different parts of the object. The most interesting ornament is that which seems to just happen, as in this ladle, naturally, logically, as if there were nothing else to do under the circumstances; as if the fancy of the designer could not resist the final touch, giving personal interest to that which was already beautiful in the broadest sense of the word.

The question of utility, of adequate service, arises

as the first point for discussion in determining the general form and essential elements of a constructive problem. Any effort to achieve beauty by ignoring in the slightest degree the demands of adequate service in the object as a whole, or in any of its parts, to the last detail, must be condemned as a misdirected effort. If you are not clear as to what constitutes beauty, are not sure of your own judgment in such matters, be satisfied to bring your fund of common sense to bear upon the one question of adequate service; beauty will take care of itself. We may at least commend the work of the man who invents or makes a useful implement or utensil; but the man who impairs the usefulness of an article by trying to make it beautiful has wasted time and effort. In the work of the master craftsmen the demands of utility were faced squarely.

The historic development of any constructive problem will serve to illustrate the utilitarian basis of design. Let us choose the lighting problem as typical (Figure 7). The idea may be stated in a single word, *light*.

There was a time when men used fatty oils for purposes of lighting. The conditions of the problem demanded a receptacle for the oil, an opening for the wick, a base sufficiently large to give stability, with a handle for convenience in carrying (i). Sometimes the vessel was suspended from chains (ii), in which

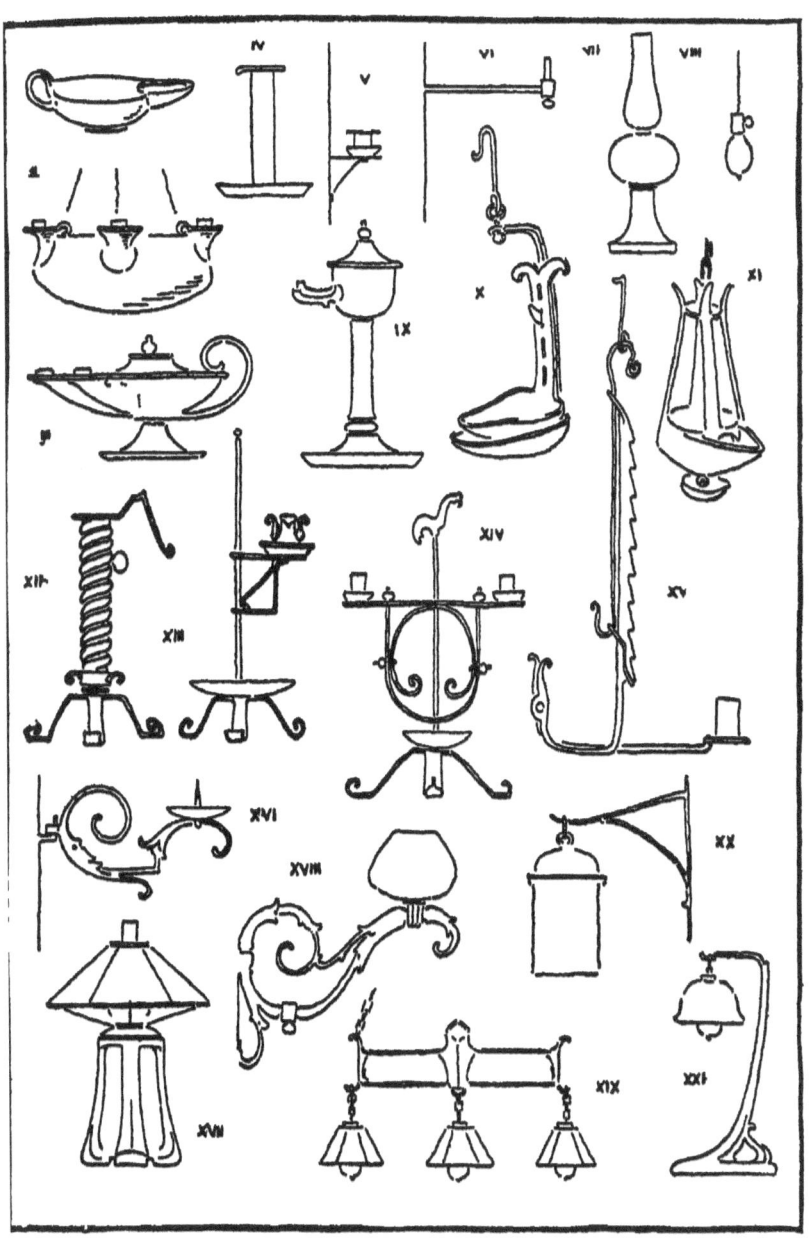

FIG. 7.

case facilities for attaching the chains would naturally take the place of a handle. In the ruder types the vessel was merely a shallow dish with open top; in examples of more careful workmanship (iii) a light of finer quality was gained by decreasing the size of the opening to compress the wick. We may well suspect there was a dripping of oil from those lights. A means for catching this drip of oil would form another structural element demanded by utility, as in ix, x, xi.

It is seen that in meeting the problem of lighting with oils several different forms of lamps were devised; the structural elements were defined in various ways. But whatever the refinements or enrichments, the designers started from the same point, — efficient service.

Then candles were invented and the forms devised for oil lamps became obsolete. Candles presented new elements from which the designers took their clews. A socket or spriket for holding the candle in an upright position must be provided, with a pan to catch the drip from the tallow, and a stable base as before. Candlesticks appeared in an infinite variety of forms (xii, xiii, xiv), from the simple iron holder of the kitchen to the elaborate chandeliers of the cathedral. Sconces and brackets were fashioned for the walls (xv, xvi); lanterns were made of horn, glass, or metal to protect the flame from the wind. But the point is this, — that in whatever form the candle appeared utility defined structural elements quite unlike those of the oil lamps that preceded.

Later came gas, an illuminant conveyed through hollow tubes, a new method of lighting which overturned the forms in common use (vi, xviii). Least interesting of all were the designs for gas fixtures, partly due to the rigid, uncompromising limitations imposed, partly to the fact that gas appeared at a time when designing for industrial purposes was at a particularly low ebb.

Then another kind of illuminating oil was discovered, more inflammable than the first, though presenting structural elements somewhat akin to those of the earlier problem (vii, xvii). A tight vessel was necessary, and a more ingenious burner assured a steadier and more serviceable light. And now we have electricity, unlike any of the other methods of lighting, in which a glass bulb attached to a wire offers varied possibilities for the designer's invention.

Now it would seem that common sense alone would lead a designer to recognize in each method of lighting the demands for a distinctive treatment — that olive-oil lamps are unsuitable for candles ; that candlesticks are not appropriate for gas, and that a pendent electric bulb differs in all essentials from the others. With the utilitarian basis as a starting point we would inevitably establish different structural elements for refinement and enrichment. Yet a visit to any store where lighting fixtures are sold furnishes evidence of the inability of modern commercial designers to grasp even the simplest elementary condition of constructive design.

With what patience can one discuss such things as are shown in Figure 8! These are not imaginative sketches — would that they were! They are literal notes from the "elegant" stock in trade of a single store. Numbers i–ii were excusable in the early days of kerosene and electricity. From a study of the history of design the following statement may be made: The invention of new materials and methods has at various times rendered obsolete the forms in common use; but whenever new materials or methods have been introduced, the designers have for a time been strongly influenced by the forms with which they are familiar. The possibilities of the new materials and methods are not realized at first. In the early days of the electric light it was a natural solution of the problem to attach the bulbs to the gas burners in common use. But such a treatment is no longer excusable. Still less excusable is the treatment of the gas burner in iii or the candlestick in iv; and what must be the mental state of any man who will screw a handled candlestick to the top of a newel post with a Welsbach gas burner for a light! Consider, again, the mental processes involved in the designing of vi–vii, in

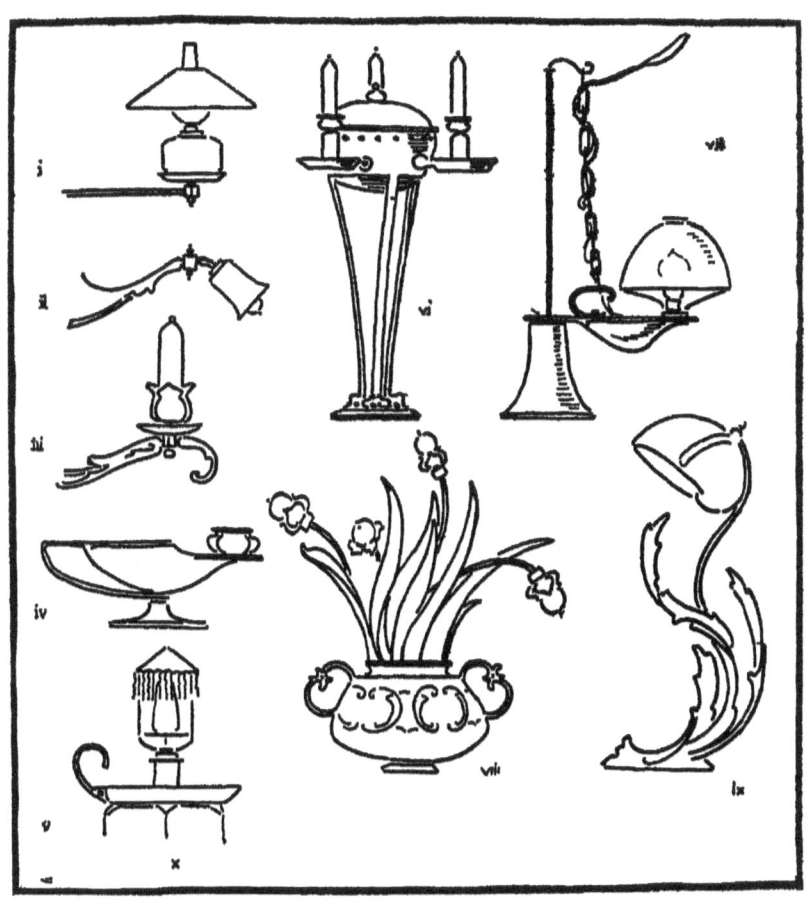

FIG. 8.

which the designers have ignored every logical solution of the problem to go blindly groping back into the past in search of forms which have no possible functional relation to the problems of lighting which they are trying to solve. In viii and ix the designers turned to Nature for assistance; but as they took nothing to Nature they received nothing in return. A sea shell may be beautiful in itself; but what excuse of consistency can one find for dangling it at the top of a tube with leaves, suggesting floral or vegetable growth !

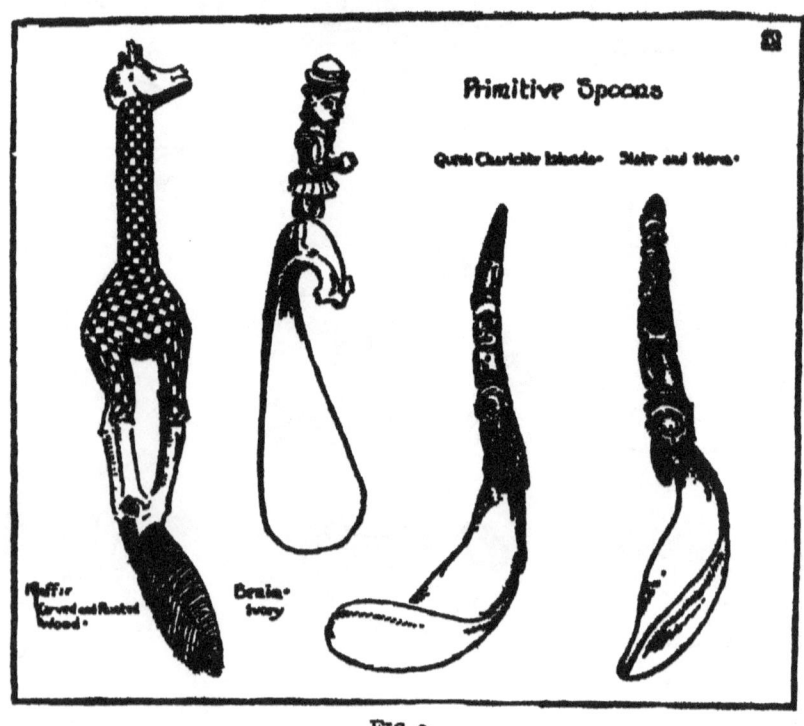

FIG. 9.

It is interesting and profitable to carry the study of utility through a series of the same simple utensil, involving the same functional elements as expressed under different environments and conditions. Figures 9, 10, 11 indicate the thought. How distinctive is

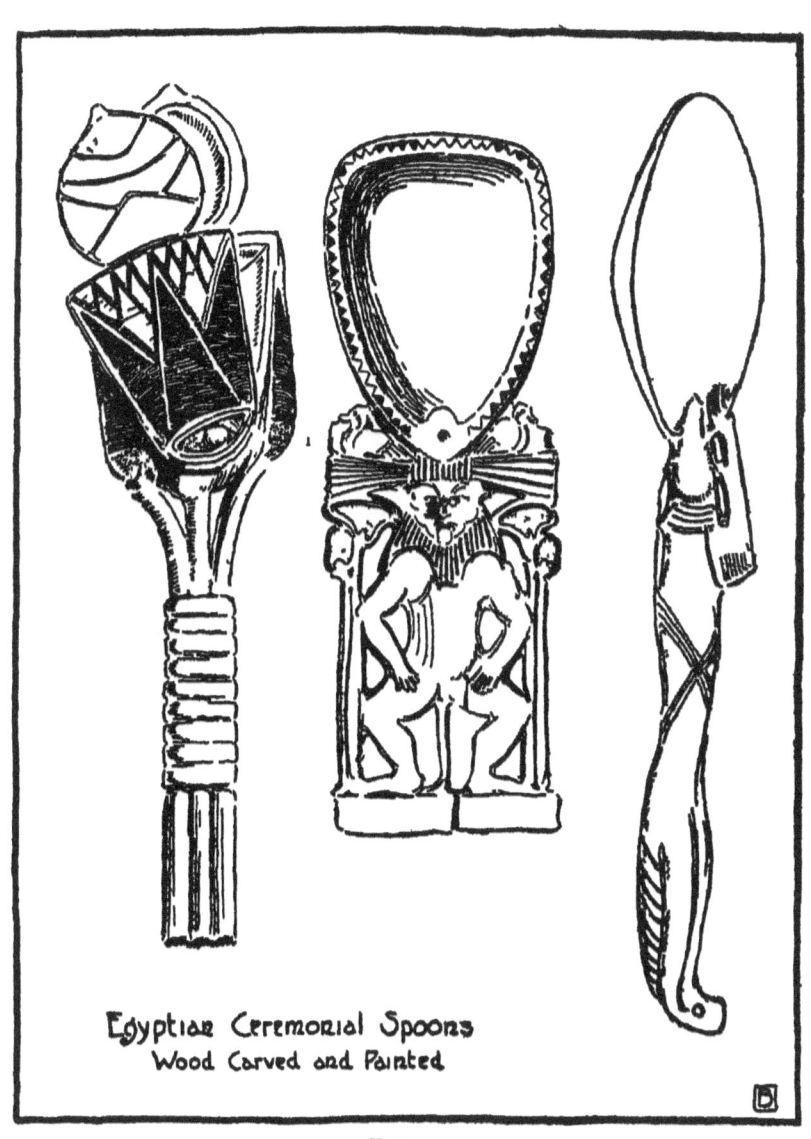

Egyptian Ceremonial Spoons
Wood Carved and Painted

FIG. 10.

that which counts for art in each spoon shown. On
the utilitarian basis of handle and bowl each spoon
stands as a clear index to the thought and character of

the one who fashioned it, and to the environment in which his work was accomplished.

PROBLEM. — Let us clinch the thought of space and mass arrangement by the solution of another problem which represents the same material in a slightly differ-

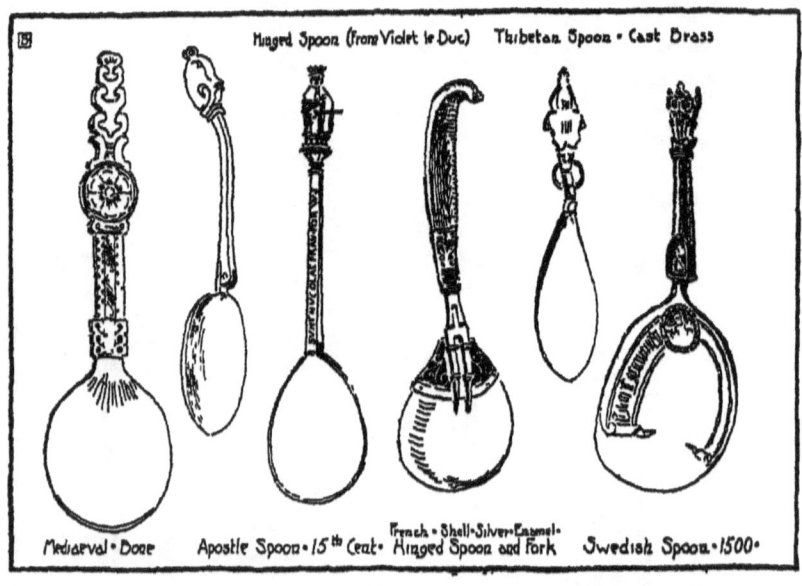

FIG. 11.

ent form, — the repetition of a line motif through a border. As a limitation we will use vertical and horizontal lines as before, and in addition, if so desired, lines at 45° right and left oblique. As this is a purely abstract problem, the width of the border may be left to define itself as the motif develops.

There is the same element of invention involved in the combination of lines as before and the same

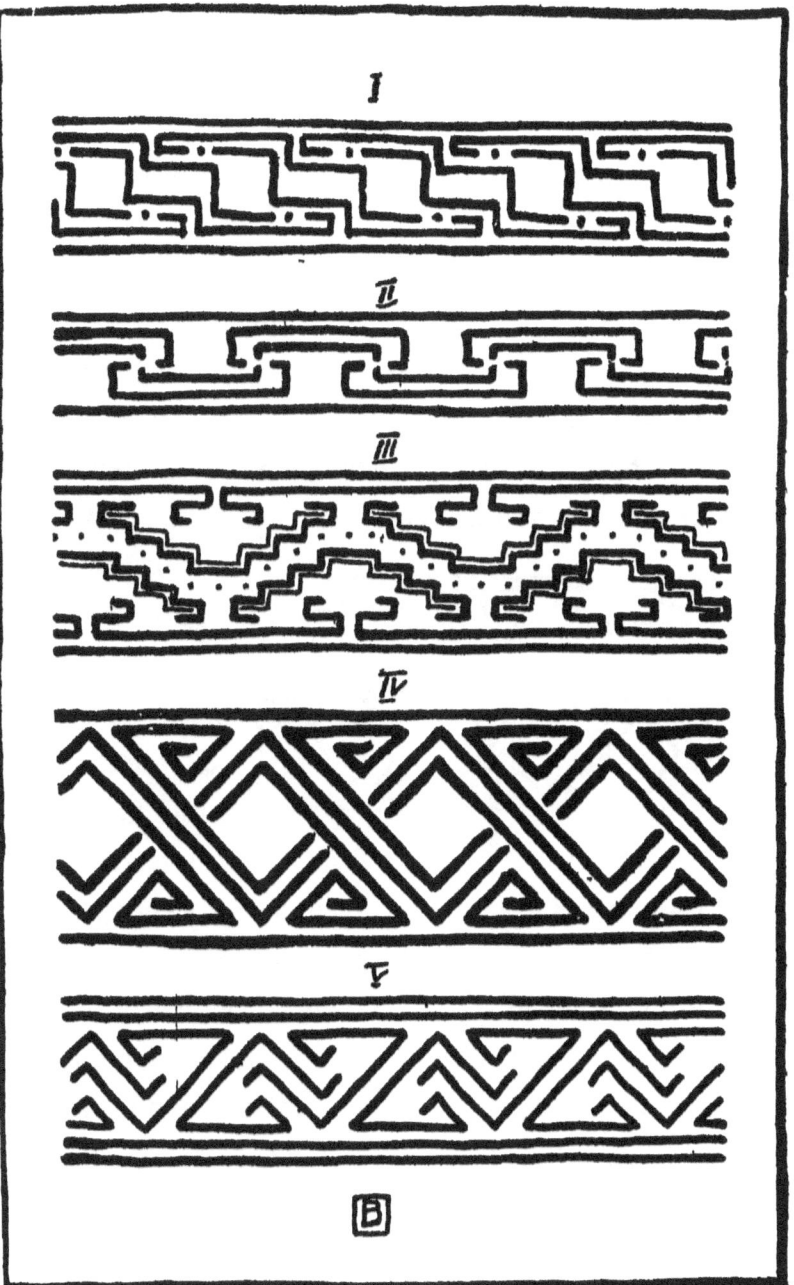

FIG. 12.

question of space and mass adjustment. Fill in the spaces in any one of the designs in Figure 12 and note the immediate loss of effect.

In a solution of this problem we are brought to another important consideration. The mere repetition of a unit at regular intervals is, at the best, a mechanical process; we can hardly distinguish it by calling it designing. But by interrelating or binding together the various units of repeat in such way that each unit supports or completes its neighbors we are really beginning to exercise a faculty for designing. By way of illustration, in Figure 13 there is no particular merit in the regular repetition of a line motif or a geometric figure.

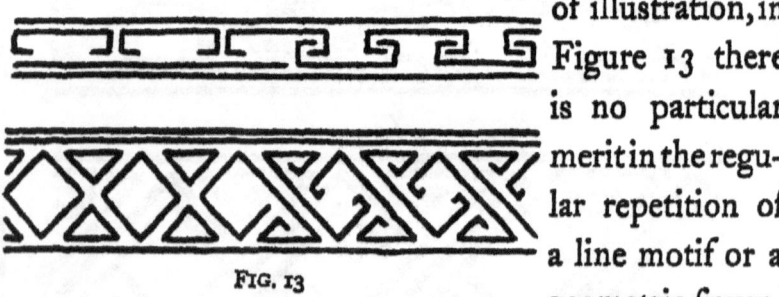

FIG. 13

Each unit stands severely by itself, scarcely on speaking terms with its neighbors. But in the second section of each border a constructive character has been imparted to a solution of the problem; the results possess a unity or wholeness in which the units are interrelated or bound together. We no longer think of each unit as having a separate identity. The construction of a design in the way here indicated is not unlike the framing of a house; each stick of timber must be thoughtfully adjusted,

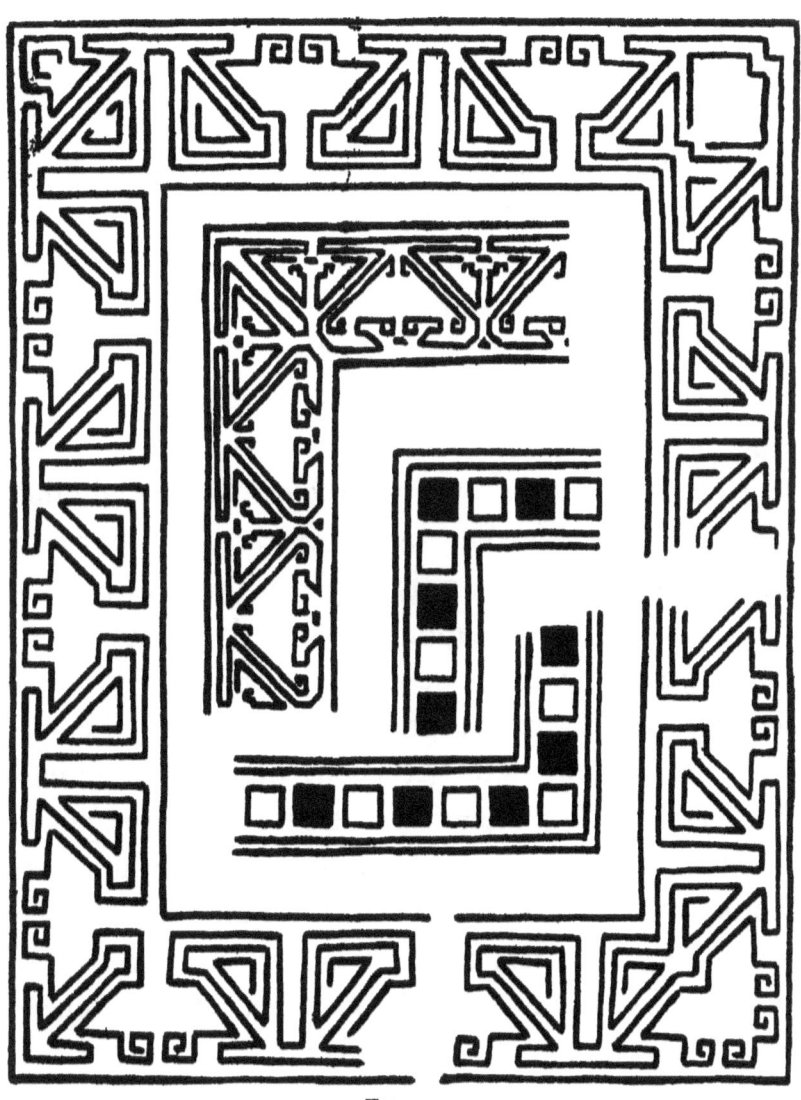

FIG. 14.

made to perform its function in the whole, and in the relation of the timbers, one to another, depends the strength and stability of the structure.

D

Figure 12 shows several expressions of the idea. In the evolution of a piece of work of this character there must be many experiments and comparisons, and a final choice of the best expression. The result is not complete until we feel that no line, space, or mass can be altered without destroying the unity of the whole. A few trials will be sufficient to demonstrate the importance of each line and area; the slightest change at any point results in an entire change of effect or spotting in the whole.

As a continuation of this problem, and as another test of constructive skill, see if you can turn your border about a corner at right angles without disturbing the space and mass relations of the design (Figure 14). In application there are several ways in which a corner may be treated; in the present instance one thought alone is in view, — to get about the corner without tripping or calling attention to the corner through the emphasis of either space or mass; the continuity of the various lines and forms should be unbroken. The corner may be turned on the mass or on the space, as indicated by the two small examples. In the outer border of this figure four different ways of turning the corner, as indicated in the problem, are shown.

CHAPTER III

ELEMENTARY ÆSTHETIC PRINCIPLES

"Not all the mechanical or gaseous forces of the world or all the laws of the universe will enable you either to see a color or draw a line without that singular force anciently called the soul." — RUSKIN.

LET us now outline in a purely elementary and abstract way a definition of three important æsthetic principles. These principles will be given application through practice, though it seems well to indicate at this point various ways in which they manifest themselves.

To secure unity in a design the student seeks: (1) to lead the eye through all the details of the design; (2) to impart to the design a sense of equilibrium or repose; (3) to give to the various terms and elements employed some common factor.

First of all comes rhythm, which may be defined as "joint action or movement." The simplest manifestation of rhythm is through the regular repetition of an unique shape. In such a repetition there may be no actual sense of movement in any particular direction; nor is direction necessarily implied by the term *rhythm*,

35

as it will be used. This type of rhythm is often
spoken of as the " principle of repetition."   But the
idea of repetition, like alternation and variety, is not in
itself a principle.   Repetition, to bring order to the
elements of a design, must be regular.   The reason
for a *regular* repetition is to enable the eye to find a

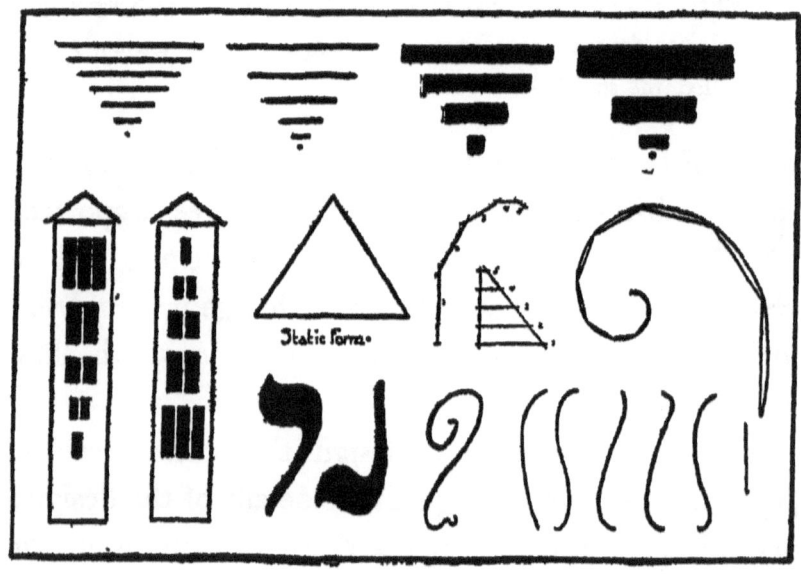

FIG. 15.

way through all the details of a pattern.   Rhythm, in
the sense of "joint action," is a broader term ;—
although it may be said that there is little to be
gained in a discussion of words to be applied to the
practice of design.   The thought involved is the same
whichever word may seem most appropriate.   The
regular repetition of a form occurs in the earliest efforts

of primitive people in design. So susceptible are some of the African negroes to the regular repetition of sounds that the beating of a stick on a convenient surface will start a rhythmic response in the nature of a dance.

Another simple type of rhythm occurs through the interrelation of details in an increasing ratio of measures from small to large. This may be termed measure rhythm. It is this type of rhythm which forms the basic principle of nearly every campanile in Italy, and gives beauty to that curve which Mr. Ruskin named the Infinite

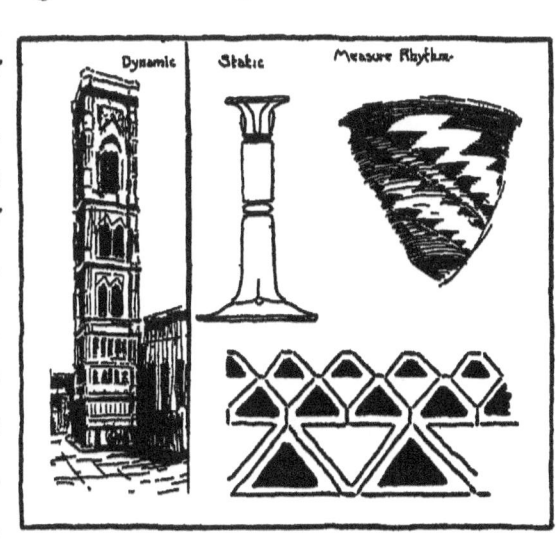

FIG. 16.

Curve. In the case of the campanili (Figures 15, 16) it may be doubted that the builders started with the *idea* of expressing measure rhythm in their structures. Constructive logic alone would lead them to increase the voids at the expense of the solids with the upward growth of their towers. The opposite course would tend to lessen the stability of the structures. But the builders were doubtless conscious of the upward aspira-

tion of their campanili gained through the regular increase in the measures of the openings.   The effect
of this rhythm of measures was often enhanced, as in
Giotto's campanile, by a corresponding increase of enrichment.

In Plate 2 we have another method of imparting a
distinct movement to the details of a design, — a
gradation of values from light to dark.   Here the
movement is downward from the light attractive force
of the higher values to the strong attractive force of
the lower values.   This type of rhythm is employed
more frequently by the painter than by the designer.

The construction of good curves is a test of one's
feeling for rhythm.   A few general hints may be
offered, and their observance should enable one to
venture beyond the commonplace without becoming
entangled in the bizarre and fantastic.   By calling
geometry to our aid certain types of curves may be
plotted; yet in practice we are thrown back upon our
" curve sense," if it may be so expressed.   Our equipment may be increased by the purchase of a number
of the " French curves," so called; but the best advice
is — don't.   In these mechanical aids there is no clew
to the why, when, and where of curves.   It were
better to cultivate a curve sense through diligent study
and practice, and then place dependence upon that
most remarkable of all instruments, the human hand.

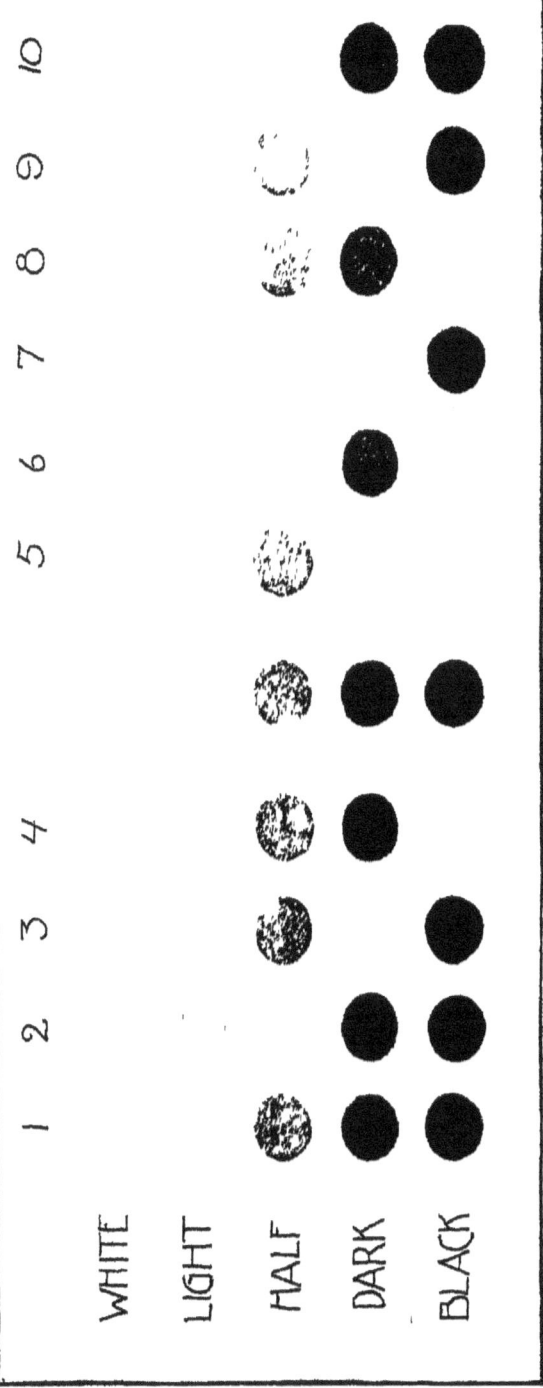

PLATE 2.

VALUE SCALE WITH POSSIBLE COMBINATIONS.

Mr. Ruskin, in "Modern Painters," calls the circle the "finite curve." Any section of a circle, if completed, returns upon itself; a segment from one portion is the same in shape as a segment from another portion. The circle has unity, but lacks variety.

There is another kind of curve which Mr. Ruskin calls the "infinite curve" — more subtle and with greater beauty than the circle. It is the curve that Nature most loves, which she seems ever striving to attain. Seek where you will, from the blade of grass to the shells on the beach, you will find this "infinite curve," the curve of living, growing things, of force and vitality. With T-square and triangle one may be readily plotted on an arithmetic or geometric sequence of lines and angles. As an illustration of the former Figure 15 will serve our purpose. Here the lengths of the segments increase in rhythmic measures, the angles remaining the same. We may be sure that a curve passing through these angles will be a beautiful curve. The angles might also increase in acuteness, or *vice versa;* the possible combinations are many. The curve may unfold itself to the end of time; it will never return to its starting point. In such a curve there is variety with unity.

There are, of course, other curves that may be plotted with instruments, such as the curve of the ellipse, the oval, the cycloidal curve. But the impor-

tant thing is to appreciate *why* the infinite curve or
"curve of force" is beautiful.   It is not to be inferred
that this curve is always best in practice; the choice
of a curved line, and its relation to the other lines of a
design, brings one back to the "curve sense" which
may be cultivated through thoughtful observation and
practice.   A comparative study of the profiling of
moldings in the work of the Greek and Gothic
builders, of the designers of the Renaissance and
Japan, of the lines and forms from Nature's storehouse — such study may contribute much to the culti-
vation of the feeling for appropriate curves.   It is a
live curve that interests us most, sometimes approaching a straight line, again swinging full and clear;
sometimes reversed, ever subtle and varied in its
course.   It may be an "eccentric" curve; but if it is
to be beautiful, it must never be uncertain or lacking
in firmness.   A curve has rhythm and balance, is
subject to the laws of proportion.   There is no better
device for charting its course than the hand, with an
eye for compass and a clear head at the top.

Thus it will be seen that the principle of rhythm is
one over which the designer must have intelligent and
complete control in the orderly adjustment of the
many attractive forces with which he is working.   He
may emphasize the movement, check it, or subordinate
it to other demands, divert it to or concentrate it in

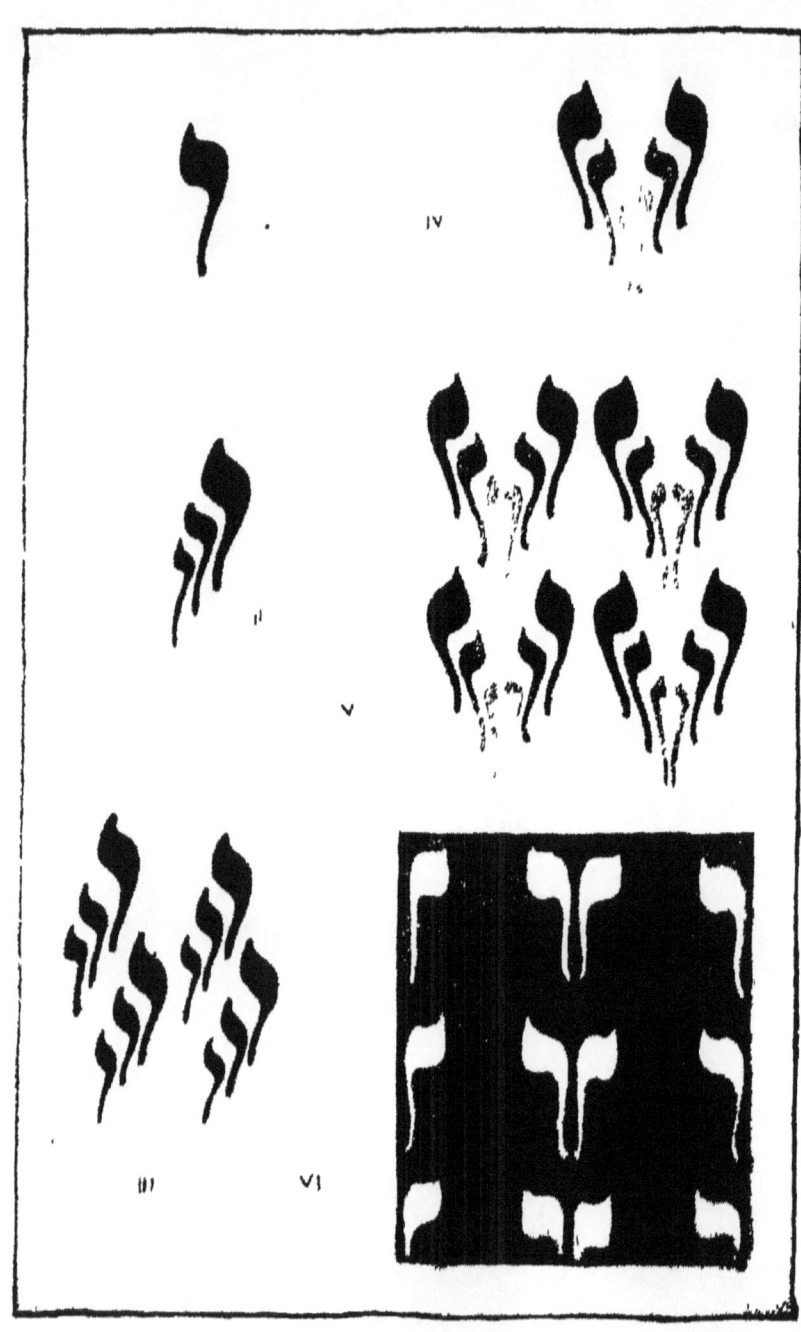

PLATE 3.

ABSTRACT RHYTHM AND BALANCE.

any portion of the design to which it may seem desirable to give dominant interest. The movement may be so apparent that even a casual observer will note its presence ; or it may be so subtle that it baffles analysis. There may be, indeed, no actual feeling of movement, —merely such interrelation of parts that the details hold together as a unity.

In Plate 3 is a rhythmic motif. Its rhythm is due partly to the increase of measure from bottom to top, and partly to the reciprocal relations of the contour lines. It is what may be termed a dynamic shape, in which all forces combine to pull the eye upward. The Italian campanili are dynamic in character ; the Egyptian pyramids are static ; the one suggests an upward aspiration ; the other immovability. The eye naturally moves upward. A downward movement of attractive forces may count for stability in a structural form, or may serve to counteract, to some extent, the strength of the upward movement. In a reversal of this shape (Figure 15) it requires a conscious effort for the eye to move downward ; and one naturally feels, in this instance, that the unit is bottom side up. In Plate 3, ii, the upward movement of the spot is emphasized and hastened by a repetition with gradation of measures. In iii the regular repetition of this rhythmic unit furnishes an instance in which movement, for its own sake, is made the dominant feature of the result. But this little design serves to illustrate the assertion that rhythm alone is not enough. The need is felt for rest and repose in the result. In iv still further emphasis is given to the dynamic character of the unit by the addition of a tone gradation; but here there is a restraint imposed upon the restless activity of the attractive forces composing the unit. In this balance of two equal forces the eye unconsciously seeks a point or line of equilibrium between them. It will be found, then, that in iv, while the forces counting for movement are stronger than in iii, there is a counteracting influence at work to impart some element of repose to the result.

In this symmetrical adjustment of attractive forces we have the simplest and most obvious manifestation of balance, an arrangement in which equal forces are opposed on a point or line of equilibrium. This type of balance is so generally understood and recognized that it seems hardly necessary to give it definition. But, in a definition of the principle of balance, it is well to consider symmetry as its simplest manifestation. Symmetry involves an opposition of *equal and similar* attractive forces on a line or about a central point. In the case of an opposition on a central line, vertical rather than horizontal symmetry is generally implied. Radial symmetry is not in itself necessarily pleasing. It often represents a pulling apart of contending forces.

More important than radial symmetry are the rhythmic connections employed to bind these contending forces into unity.

In the earliest extant artistic remains of the human race, symmetry appears as a basis of ornament. In his efforts toward an art expression, man endeavored to arrange or dispose his ideas in an orderly way. The first manifestations of order appear through regular sequence and alternation, and through symmetry. And in the entire development of primitive art, from the least important productions to the carving of an idol, there is ever present a keen sense of appreciation for the beauty of symmetry. In Nature symmetry appears as the constructive basis in organic and inorganic life, from the crystal to the human figure.

But in Nature, as well as in a more finely organized system of design, actual symmetry often gives place to a more subtle type of balance. In Figure 17, the second example, the effect of symmetry is retained in a motif in which

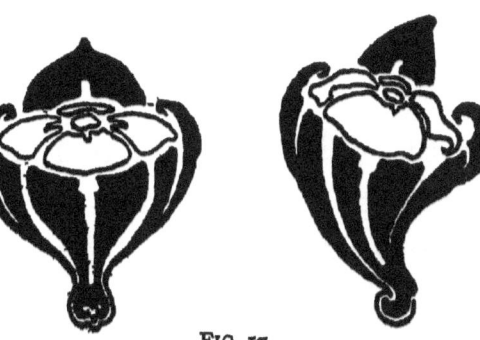

FIG. 17.

the attractive forces involved are the same in tone and measure but unlike in shape. In any discussion of balance in design it is desirable to revert to the laws of physical balance; the underlying principles are the same. In symmetry the opposing attractive forces are the same in line, form, and tone (Figure 17). Now, how may we balance oppositions which exert unequal attractive forces? In Figure 18, i, the actual symmetry is de-

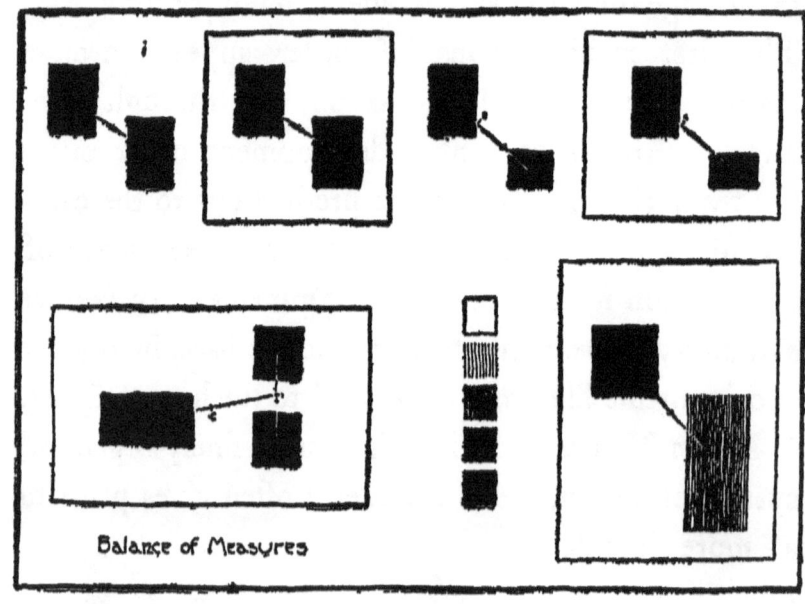

Balance of Measures

FIG. 18.

stroyed. If these were physical forces, they would be balanced by drawing a line to connect their centers. Then we would seek on this line the point of equilibrium. In ii one of the measures of the opposition of forces has been doubled. The attractive forces of the two spots may be expressed by the formula one-two. To balance them we would divide the line connecting centers into

three equal parts, the sum of the forces exerted, and re-
versing the ratio give to the larger spot one third of the
line and to the smaller spot two thirds.   In iii are three
spots exerting attractive forces which may be expressed
by the formula, one-, one-two. The point of equilibrium
may be found by balancing two of the spots, then by
balancing these two with the third, as indicated.   In iv
another factor enters into the problem ; the tone of one
of the spots has been changed, and in consequence its
attractive force is decreased.   There may be a mathematical formula for determining the point of equilibrium, but its complications are so many and its results
of such doubtful value that it is unwise to pursue the
mathematics of it further.   It is readily seen that the
principle is the same, but that mathematics gives way
to judgment.   In balancing attractive forces differing
in tone, in measure, and in shape, we are thrown still
more upon judgment and sensitive feeling in estab-
lishing a point of equilibrium.   But if we were to
inclose varied attractive forces within a rectangle, we
would see to it that the balance point of the attractive
forces coincides with the center line of the inclosing
form.

Now we have to consider still another type of balance, related only indirectly to the definition above, —
a balance of the values of our scale.   In balancing
lines and forms we were concerned chiefly with the

physical law of balance; but in balancing contrasts of values and colors we pass beyond any possible assistance from mathematics to questions decided only by careful discrimination and sensitive feeling.

We sometimes speak of a balance of two tones, as in Plate 4, i, having in mind the distribution and the approximately equal quantities of the tones. In the same way we sometimes speak of a balance of several tones, referring to their relative measures and distribution. But this is, in reality, the same idea that was discussed in a preceding paragraph. In a more direct sense quantity is not an essential factor in a *tone* balance. It is more a question of contrasts. In ii of this same plate is a balance of value contrasts. The two ends of the scale have equal contrasts on a middle ground. The white is just as much lighter than that ground as the black is darker. In Plate 5, i is another balance of values. The contrast of dark on the middle ground is balanced by the contrast of light on the same ground. In ii, the balance is deliberately upset in order to give dominant interest to the flowers. Their attractive force is materially increased by giving them a much stronger contrast on the background. In Plate 3, vi there is a pleasing adjustment of the tones of the design, gained through a rhythmic interrelation of the details and a balance of values on a middle ground. This combination of rhythm and

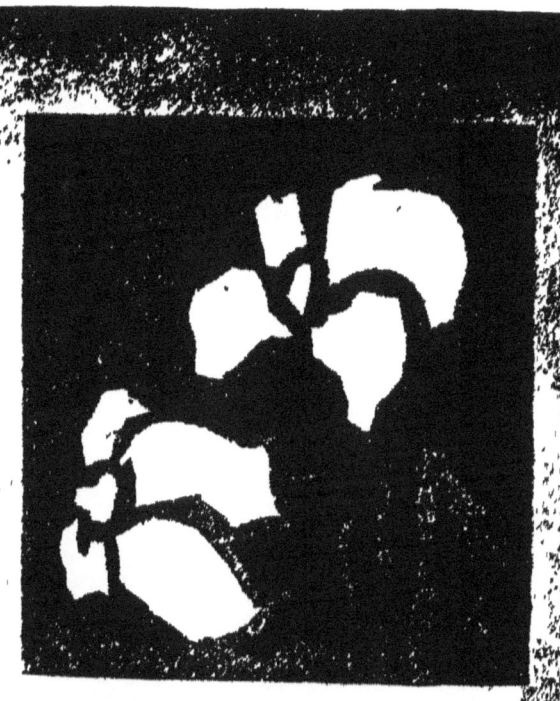
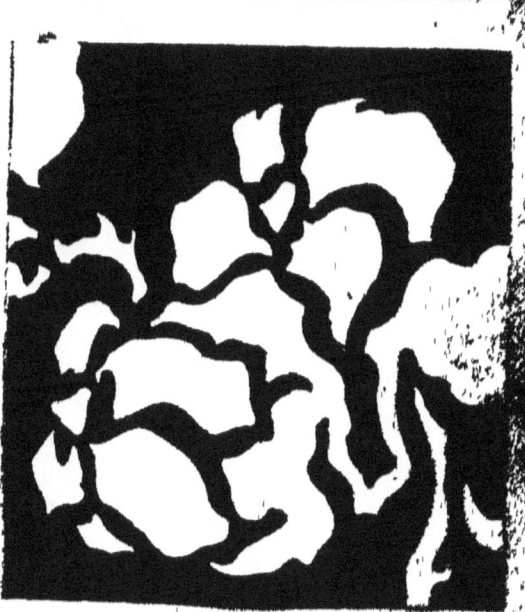

PLATE 4.

TONE BALANCE.

balance gives the most satisfactory rendering shown of the little motif indicated in i of this plate.

Balance, then, like rhythm, should be carefully considered by the student in order that he may work with definite aim and purpose, with a complete command over the terms in which he essays to express himself.

Harmony is a broader term than either rhythm or balance; it may in fact involve one or the other, or both, of these terms. It consists in shunning differences too pronounced, contrasts too startling; in giving to the various elements of a design something in common. Uniformity of · details in tone, measure, and shape might be defined as a perfect harmony. But uniformity is assuredly not the most pleasing manifestation of harmony. The eye craves contrast, variety; how far to go, where to stop, is the problem of the designer. Theoretically an octagon and a circle would be more harmonious in the element of shapes than a square and a circle. But it may be that the contrast offered by the square and circle is of more interest than the former combination. In Figure 19 the first example offers extreme contrasts between the border and field. It would seem here that the differences are too pronounced. In the second example a border has been designed that is more harmoniously related to the field; the similarities are more noticeable than the differences. It is unwise, then, to attempt to define harmony through any formula, or general statement; it is a question that comes home to each problem on its own merits. Incongruous elements may be har-

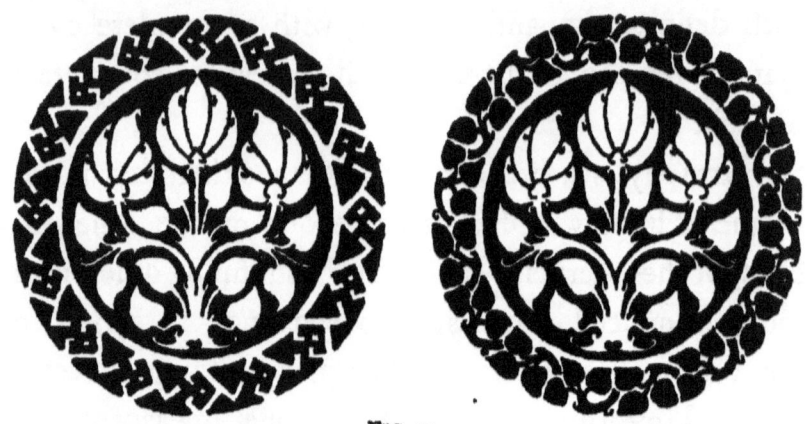

FIG. 19.

monized through association in rhythm and balance in which their separate identities are lost and the eye grasps them as a whole.

A question of harmonious measures brings one at once to the discussion of proportion.* In a question of tones one may say, from an abstract point of view, that the second example in Plate 4 achieves the idea of both balance and harmony. Black and white, the extremes of value, is the most severe test one can give to a design. In Plate 5 the first example represents a more complete harmony of values than either of the two preceding; as values they have more in common.

A style or period in art may be recognized, in a

* Chapter VII.

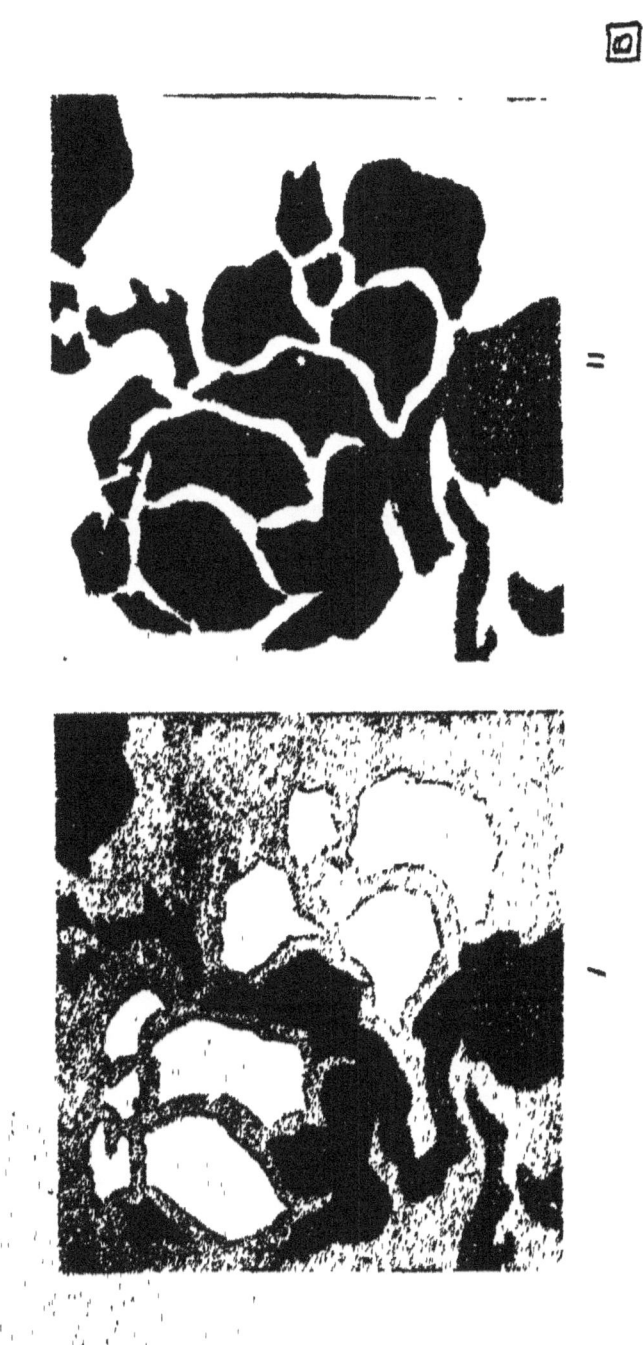

PLATE 5.

TONE BALANCE.

broad way, as a manifestation of harmony, — the recurrence of a type, the persistence of similar ideas and forms under varying conditions. It is this that distinguishes Greek from Gothic, and Japanese from either of the others. There is, too, the harmony of association in the forms and motifs employed. One would not attach roses to thistle leaves, or highly conventionalized flowers to a naturalistic stem. Much of the beauty of primitive work is due to the harmony between the idea, the materials, and the forms employed. Primitive art is directly related to and expressive of primitive thought and needs.

It may be pertinent to remark that, however thoroughly one may study an abstract demonstration of principles, there must enter into any design a quality which is beyond analysis and which can be imparted from one to another only in an indirect way. That is the touch of individuality, the personal quality that clothes dry bones with life, vitality, and interest. To understand the essential principles of design is one thing; but this understanding is merely a means to an end. In any work that is worth while there must enter a live and vigorous imagination, a freedom and spontaneity, without which a design becomes formal and deadly uninteresting. We may call it the play impulse, if we choose, an evidence of pleasure and joy in the work that comes from under one's hand. In

E

nearly all primitive work, and in the work of the mediæval craftsmen, there is ample evidence of this play
impulse.   In the work of these men there appears a
quaint and whimsical grotesque quality that is irresistible in its appeal.   We come upon it in the most un-
expected places, in the basket or on the carved idol,
on the front of the altar or on the carving of the choir
screen; no place is entirely free from it.   There
seems no good reason why a design should not enter-
tain us, even amuse us, and yet be as serious in its
aim and purpose as if we were to approach the subject
in a spirit of bespectacled wisdom.

PROBLEM (Figure 20).   This problem is one of
space and mass composition with an interrelation of
parts, like those preceding it, except that we are now
working directly in areas instead of in lines.   It was
said that the background or space is just as important
as the mass of the design.   You will note the renewed
force of the statement if you will try to think of the
borders in this plate; — first, as designs of black on a
white ground, then as designs of white on a black
ground.   The interest is in the unity of black-and-
white elements.   If the whites are left to chance and
become mere holes, due to the repetition of a black
unit, the interest decreases.   Each element should
strengthen and support the other.   In the first two
problems variety with unity was sought in the positions

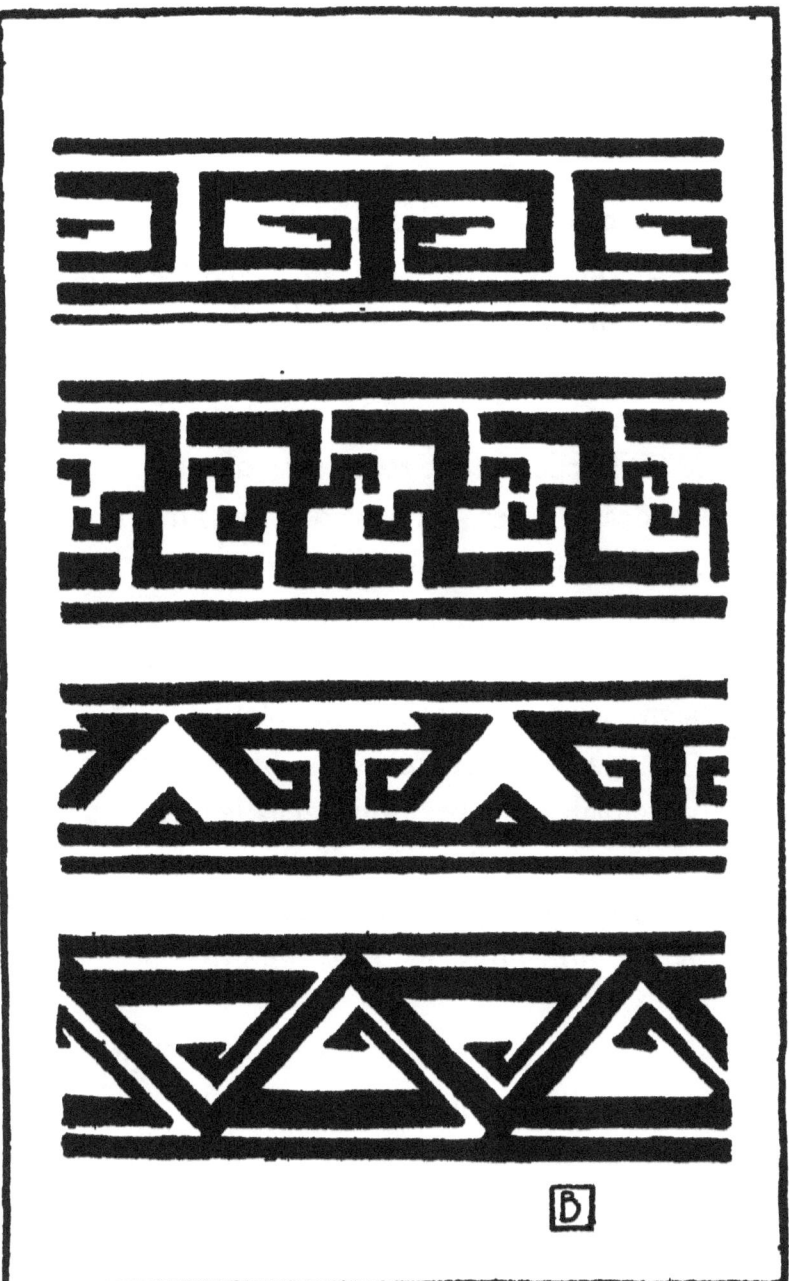

FIG. 20.

and directions of lines ; here it is variety in the shapes
and measures of the areas employed. Avoid the monotonous single unit of measure found in the Greek
fret; avoid with equal care an extreme in the other
direction, a confusion of forms which the eye finds it
difficult to relate. Any one can achieve an example
of variety ; in itself it has no special virtue. The skill
of the designer appears in combining varied elements
into a consistent whole. The mind finds a certain
sense of satisfaction in the recurrence of a unit of measure in a design; yet the unit of measure need not
assert itself in a way that is stupidly obvious.

In the present problem it becomes a process of
spotting out areas of white with black, or *vice versa*, as
the design progresses toward completion. It will no
doubt take a number of trials before that subtle,
scarcely definable quality which challenges and holds
the interest is secured. The result should be a carefully tuned symphony of space and mass, under limitations as to directions of lines imposed in the last
problem.

It is notable that the second border in Figure 20 is
reminiscent of the Chinese frets, while the other three
have more the character of Indian designs. And why
should this not be so ? It is quite probable that if we
work under similar limitations toward similar ends, we
may come to conclusions not unlike those that others

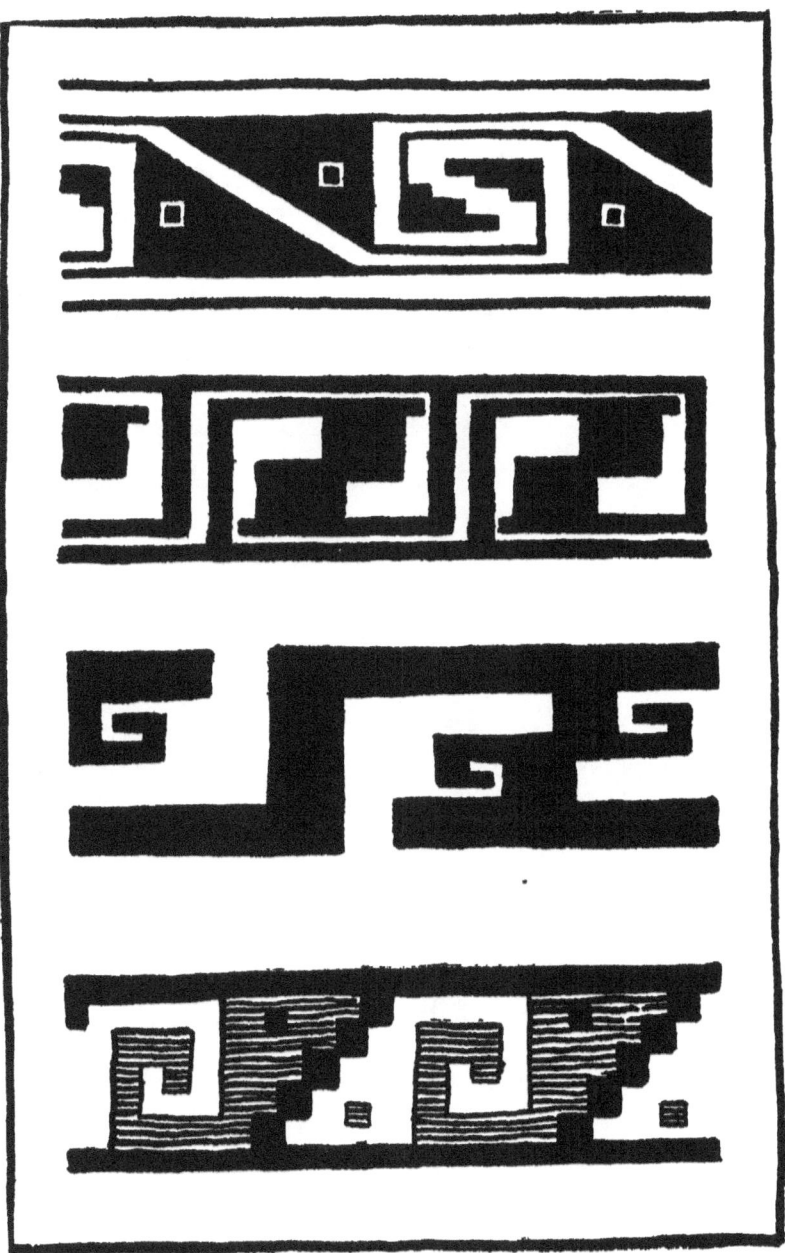

FIG. 21.

have achieved.   Yet our work may be none the less " original " in the true sense of the term.

In Figure 21 are examples of work from Indian weavings quite similar in character to our problem. The American Indians, in their blankets, baskets, and pottery, developed a remarkable feeling for space and mass relations ; their work was invariably strong, virile, insistent.   We are surely loath to credit a poor old Indian woman with more artistic invention than we can claim for our own efforts !

CHAPTER IV

Constructive Designing

"Romance and sentimentality had no part in the creation of Gothic Architecture; it was molded to the forms under which we find it by carefully satisfying social and individual requirements and diligently observing the stern necessities of convenience and economy." — Jackson.

IN the concrete expression of an idea the designer finds that the trail leads through principles of two closely related kinds, — the æsthetic and the practical. The former deals with composition, refinement, enrichment, texture, color, finish, etc.; the latter with utility, construction, tools, materials, processes, etc. But in practice there cannot be, or should not be, in the mind of the designer any conscious distinction between the æsthetic and the practical. The one is to the other as feathers to the bird; we cannot say, " Here are feathers, counting for beauty; that which remains is bird." It is quite in accord with modern thought and practice to assume that a practical man may attend to the practical side of a problem, leaving an artist to ornament or decorate it. We even look upon the terms *ornament, decoration* and *design* as synonymous; applied design as something that is applied to something. We put "designs" upon a thing, hoping thereby to make it beautiful, or to cover up shabby workmanship, as the case may be.

As an illustration of the organic relation of the æsthetic and practical, note the chair in Plate 6. It is clear that beauty has been achieved through the constructive use of wood, leather, and tacks; the designer has merely given æsthetic arrangement to practical features. There is no "ornament," in the usual acceptance of that term; or, if we choose to call the tacks ornament, we shall find, like the feathers on the bird, that they are performing a very commonplace, functional purpose. The legs might be called enrich-

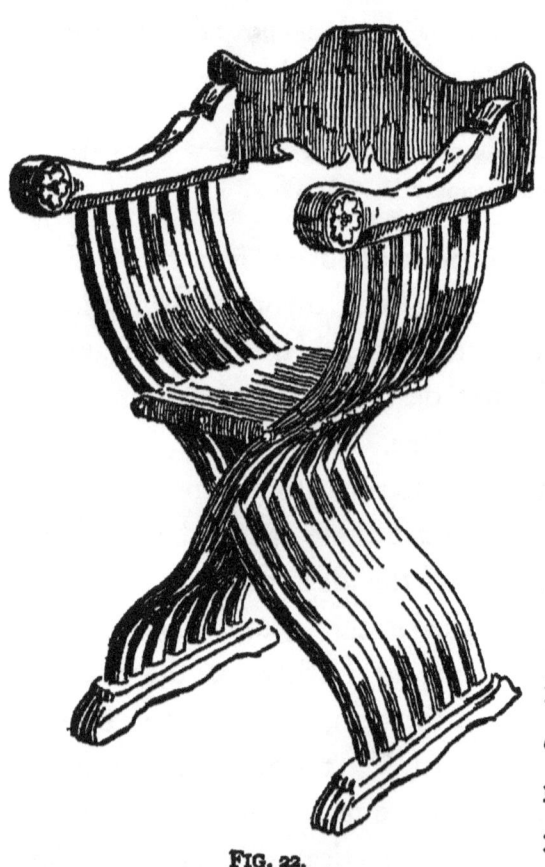

FIG. 22.

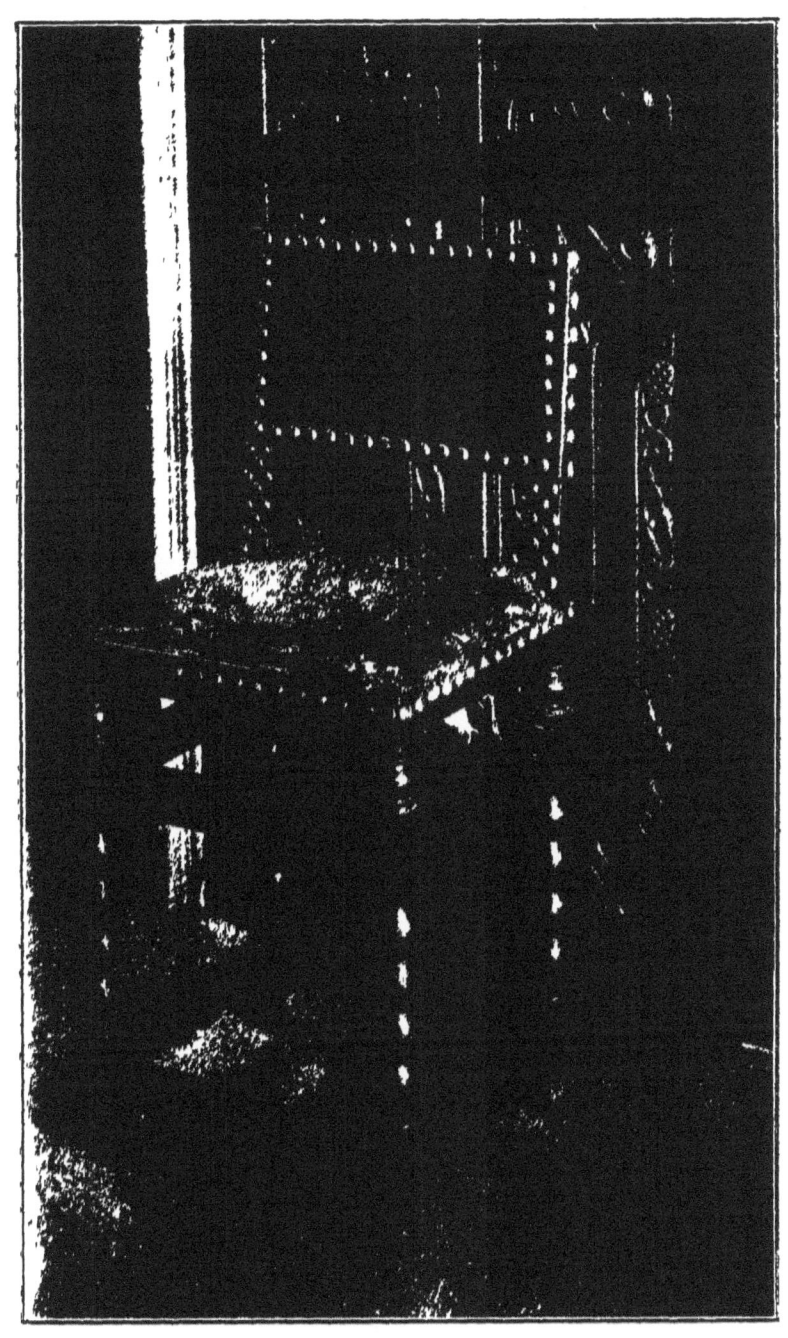

PLATE 6.

CHAIR. (BOSTON MUSEUM OF FINE ARTS)

ment, refinement, or construction, æsthetic or practical, for they are entitled equally to all these terms. In other words, the designer of the chair was concerned as much with his practical questions as with æsthetic problems — and made no conscious effort to distinguish between them. He did not build his chair and then set about the problem of trying to " make it beautiful." The beauty of the chair in Figure 22 is of the same sort. The little carved rosettes on the arms are not " applied

designs " ; they are merely de- tails of *a design,* a touch of en- richment as in- evitable as the leaves that come forth on the trees in the spring.

Of similar na- ture is the work in Figure 23, the joinery of a shop- trained man

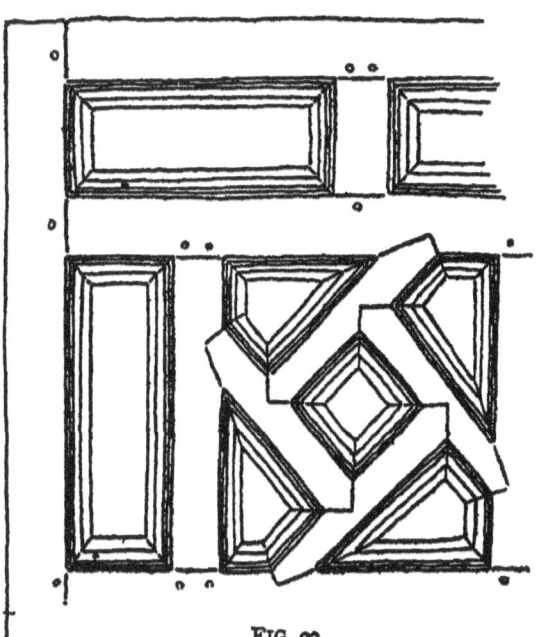

FIG. 23.

turned to an æsthetic purpose. In fitting his rails and panels together he has been economical of labor and materials, has adopted methods suggested by his inti- mate acquaintance with the practical phases of his prob-

lem, — but always with the æsthetic end in view. In
Plate 7, the carved doors of the Duomo at Verona, the
refinement and enrichment have been carried further,
the logical conclusion of such an idea as that in Figure
23.   Here, surely, is something that may be identified
as "ornament" or "applied design."   But it should
be noted that the carving does little more than continue
the thought set forth in the construction; — it counts
for beauty neither more nor less than the purely structural bronze bolt heads.   It is built in, — not built on;
and between the two there is a vast distinction.   This,
then, is the best thought of ornament, — the enrichment
of refined construction; not design, but *part* of a design.

Figure 24 furnishes good illustrations of the functional development of ornament.   Note the way in
which the carving is tucked in at the end of the plane
where it may bump into rough usages, while it attains
its boldness on the handle where it is protected from
damage.   In the Roman ladle the head seems to grow
from the refined lines of the handle as if there were no
other conclusion possible.   Study the position and
nature of the ornament in the lamp.   Here again it is
difficult to say where construction ends and ornament
begins; how much of the distinction is attributable to
the practical, how much to the æsthetic.   In each example it was a process of turning practical principles
to æsthetic account.

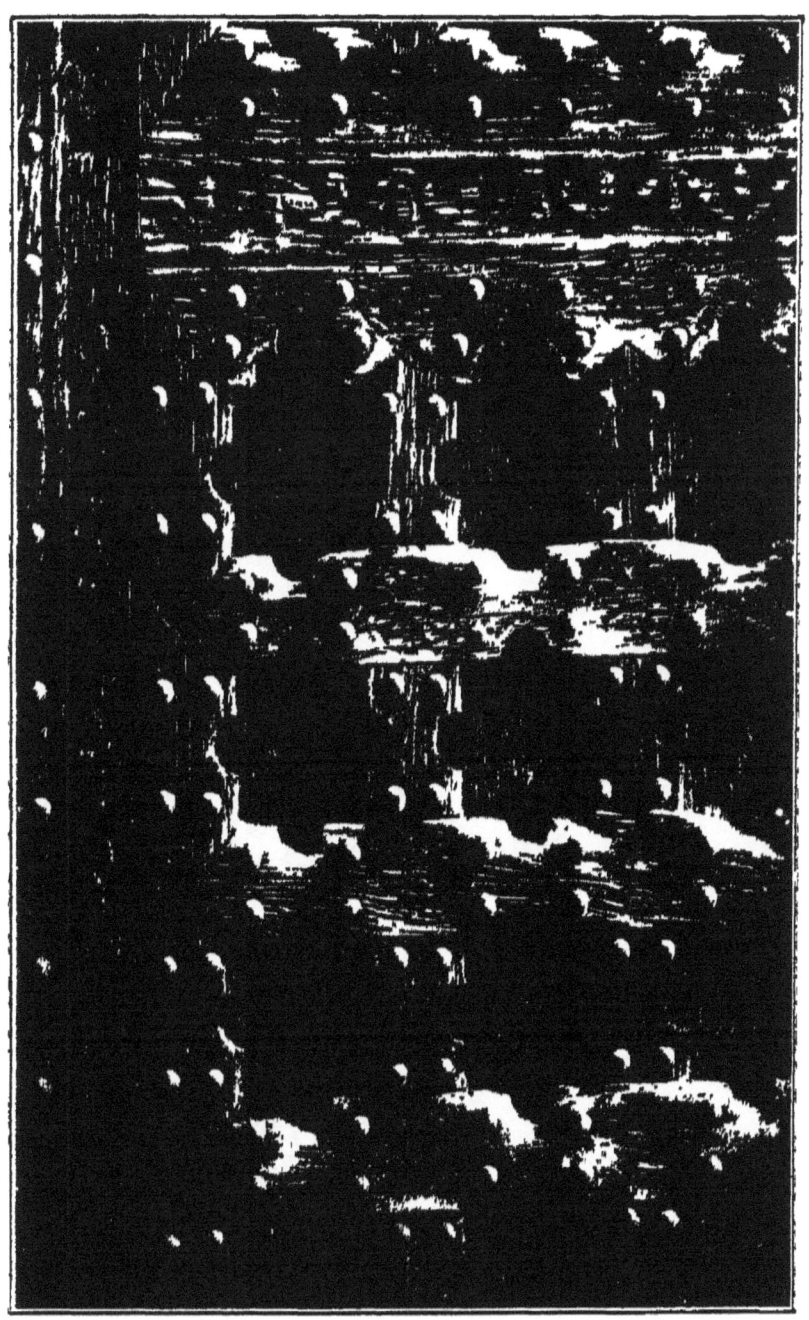

PLATE 7.

DETAIL — OUTER DOORS OF DUOMO VERONA.

The simplest type of designing, in the concrete, must be that in which the worker has achieved the utmost beauty possible through refinement of construction, with a sympathetic use of materials employed.

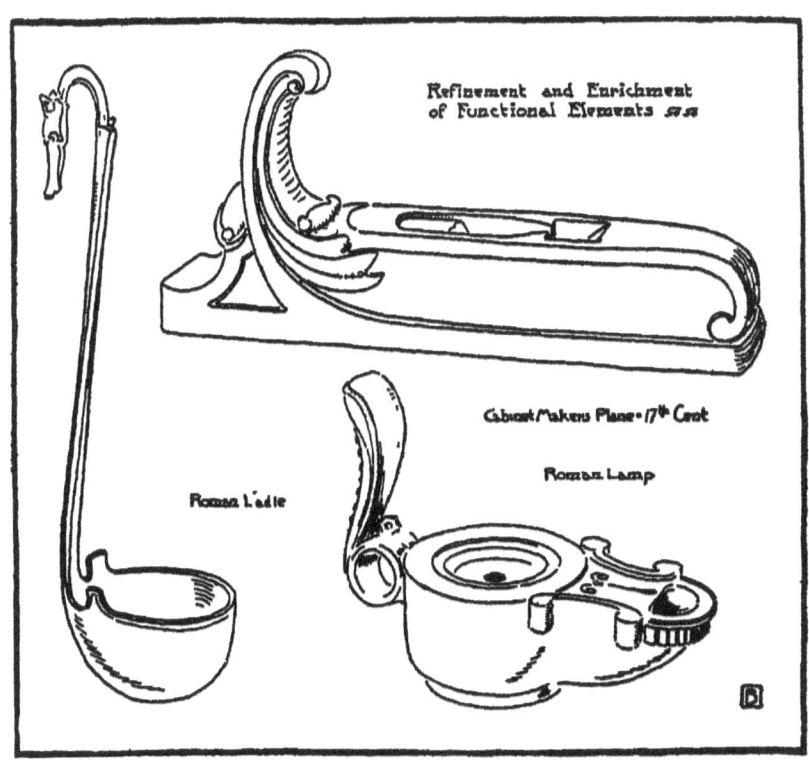

Refinement and Enrichment
of Functional Elements

Cabinet Makers Plane · 17ᵗʰ Cent

Roman Lamp

Roman Ladle

FIG. 24.

He need not go beyond this to produce beauty of the highest order. And the term *ornament*, if properly understood, implies an enrichment of this construction, not as an afterthought but as an integral part of the whole. The design begins with the first tentative blocking out of the idea, continues through

an immediate interplay between the practical and æsthetic principles to the final touch.   Ornament cannot
be thought out before the construction, nor should it
be applied after constructive problems have been
solved.   Working from a constructive-design point of
view there seems no reason why one should strive to
"adapt" this or that style or period of ornament to
his work.   To build a "Greek style" house is to put
the cart before the horse, — to make practical questions
subordinate to a borrowed æsthestic idea.   It was not
thus that the Greek style was developed.   That architecture which was peculiar to Greece was of gradual
formation and represented the æsthetic expression of
practical principles; it grew out of the thought, feeling,
and environment of the people, a combination of peculiar circumstances which has long since passed away.
Quite as distinctive in its time and place was a Japanese temple.   To adapt either of these styles, in part or
in whole, to our needs is, to say the least, a confession
of incompetence.

Much of the characterless work of to-day comes
from lack of knowledge of materials.   Add to this
a lack of practical constructive skill on the part of designers and we have another count in the indictment.
Let the student of design build things with his hands,
or enter into active coöperation with men whose
business it is to build things.   Probably it is not pos-

sible for the student of architecture to work in the quarry, the brickyard, and the lumber camp, or serve apprenticeship to the stone mason, the bricklayer, and the carpenter as a preliminary to the practice of his profession ; but it is certain that he might employ to better advantage " on the job " some of the time now spent in assimilating styles, orders, traditions of the past, and thereby make architecture more vital as an æsthetic expression of practical, twentieth-century problems.   The designer of to-day often actually deplores the very things from which he may hope to realize true style and character.

We may assume this proposition then : The form of an object, together with its structural or functional elements, should suggest the general character and position of any enrichment that may be developed.

In Figure 25 are some examples of pottery from the work of the past, selected almost at random because the conditions counting for effective design during the various periods when these designs were produced were of the right sort.   Study each example in this plate and note how the æsthetic and practical have developed together in the minds of the designers.   It is unnecessary to consider each in detail ; it may be seen that there is a *reason* for each line, form, and tone employed ; its position, measure, and shape is determined by struc-

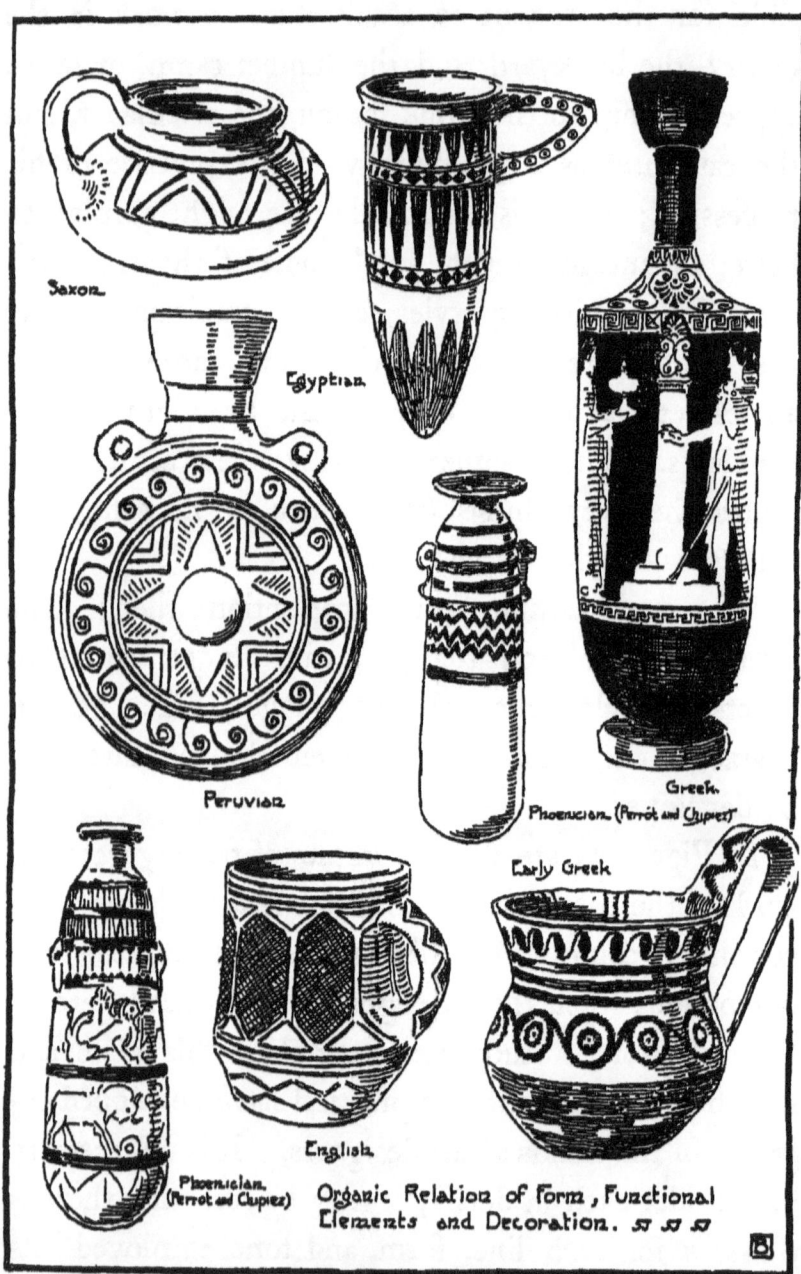

Saxon.

Egyptian.

Peruvian.

Greek.

Phoenician. (Perrot and Chipiez)

Early Greek

Phoenician.
(Perrot and Chipiez)   Organic Relation of Form, Functional
Elements and Decoration.

English.

FIG. 25.

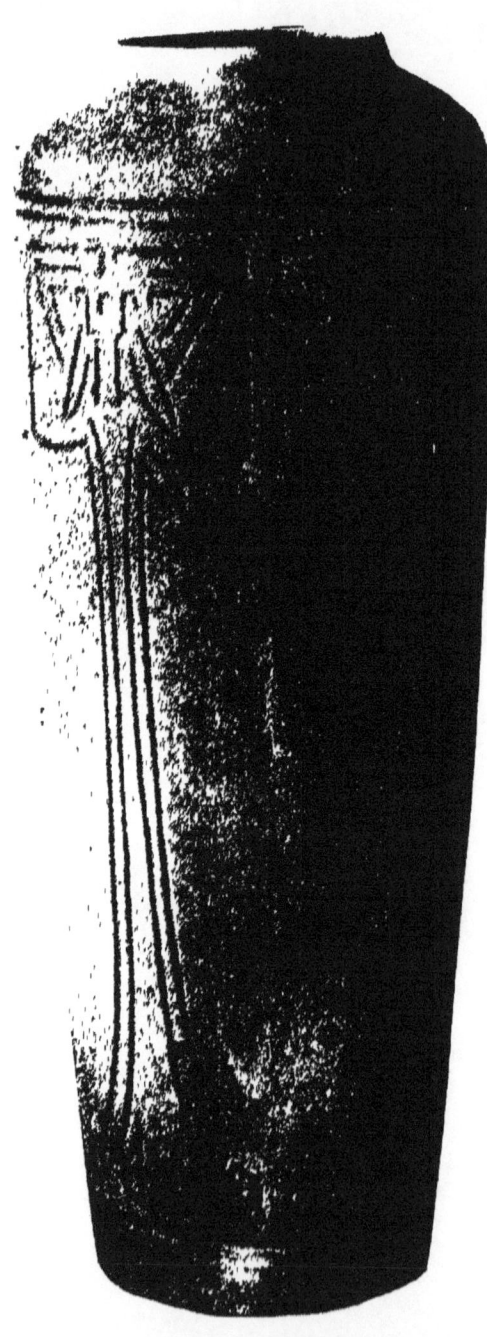

PLATE 8

INCISED DESIGN FOR POTTERY.

tural features. In Figure 26 is brush-made ornament; every stroke of the brush emphasizes the functional elements of the vase and is directly related to the general form.

In the development of our abstract problems two methods will be followed, — that which proceeds from a given whole to a consideration of details, as in the first problem; that which proceeds from an adjustment of details to a definition of the whole. The end

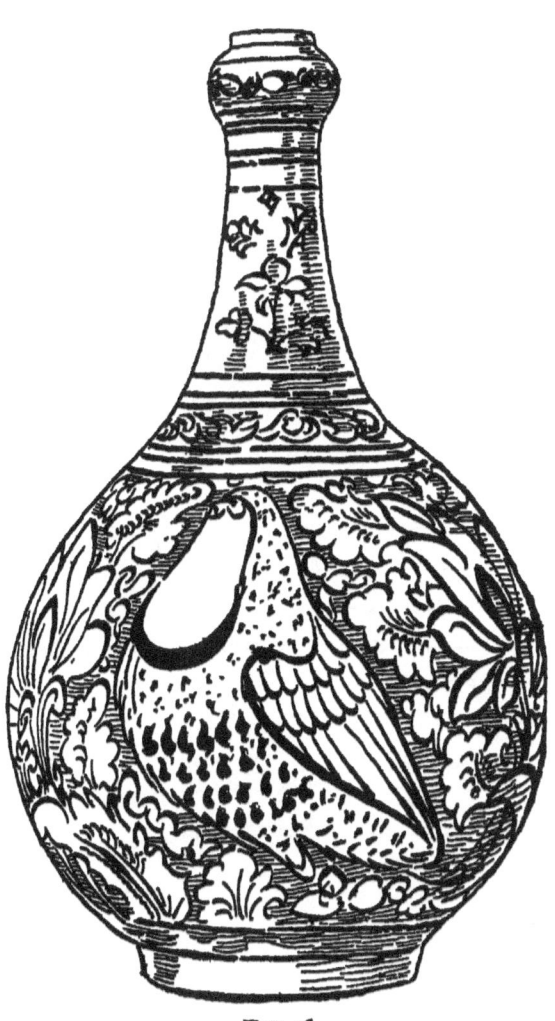

FIG. 26.

sought, the unity of all elements involved, is the same in both cases. In the evolution of a constructive problem the first method would naturally be followed, though it will probably appear that one unconsciously follows both methods before the design is completed. The position, shape, and measure of a detail would be determined by the first method; but the building up of the lines and forms within that detail might lead one to the second method or continue the process of the first method according to the nature of the detail. Plates 8, 9 and Figures 27, 28 illustrate the idea with motifs that occur in two of our problems.   In Plate 8, incised pottery, the subdivision of the big form came first with a dominant interest at the top and a subor-

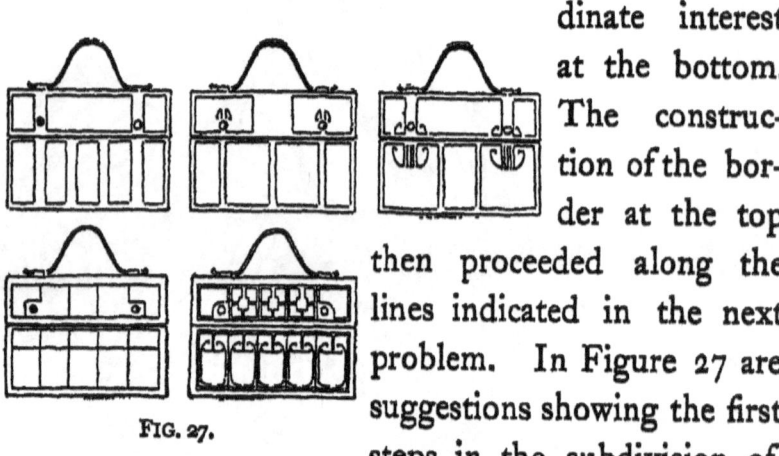

dinate interest at the bottom. The construction of the border at the top then proceeded along the lines indicated in the next problem.   In Figure 27 are suggestions showing the first steps in the subdivision of

FIG. 27.

the main form on a basis of the functional elements. The form, of leather, has two elements, cover and bag. These must be designed in such way that they count for unity when seen as one, with the cover buttoned into position; they should also be so planned that each will be complete in itself, when the cover is opened.

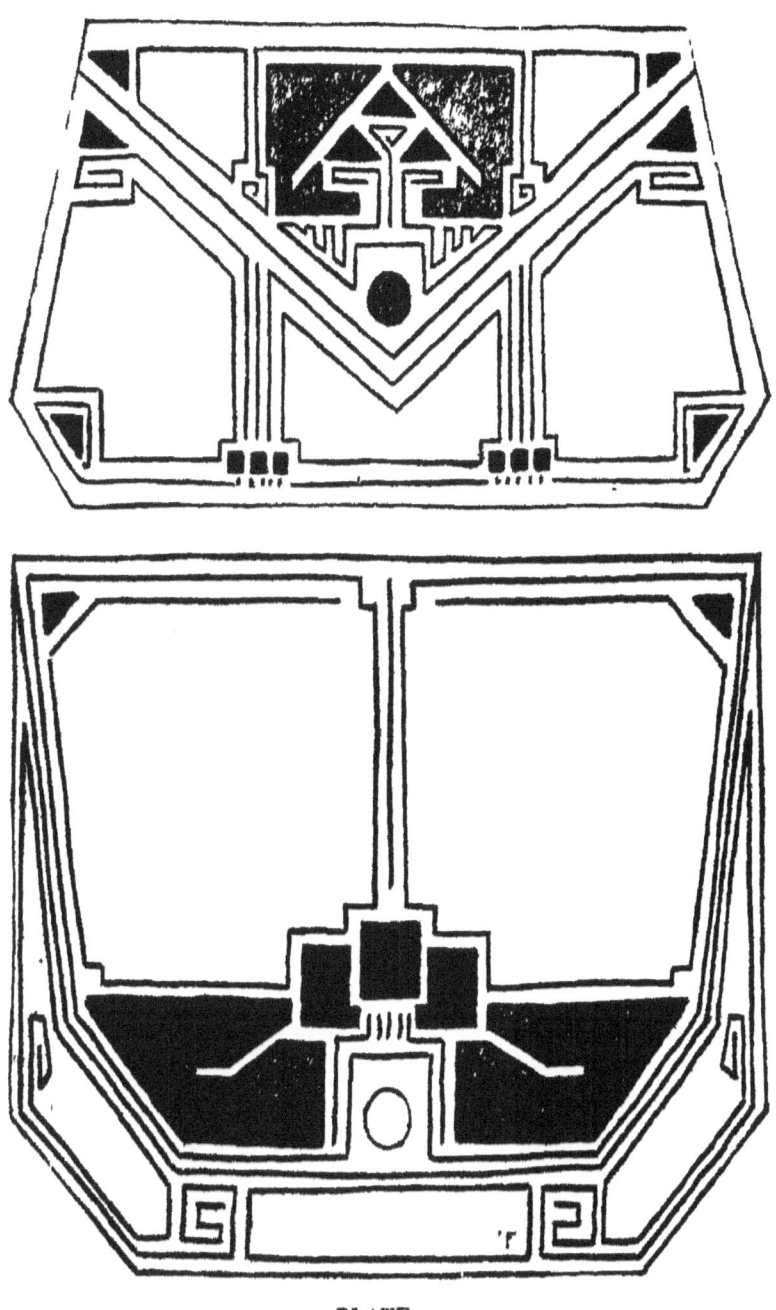

PLATE 9

CONSTRUCTIVE ARRANGEMENTS OF LINE AND FORM FOR LEATHER.

The handle and buttons are structural features that must be accepted, not ignored; they furnish at once the clews for the main subdivisions of form. In Plate 9 and Figure 28 are other constructive designs built up in a similar way. They should, of course, be seen in the leather with tooling, texture, and color, to form

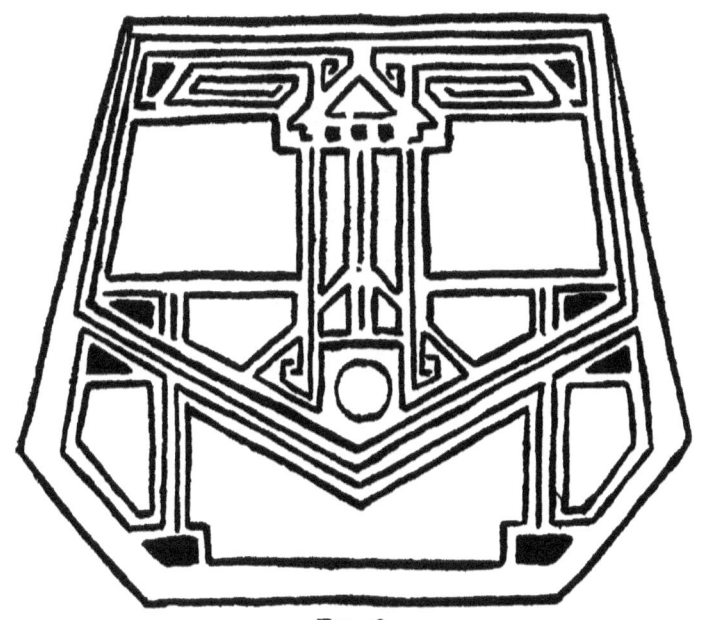

FIG. 28.

an adequate judgment of the results. On paper they are merely organic, *constructive arrangements of lines and forms in space and mass*, planned for a technique peculiar to simple processes of leather tooling. They are not "applied designs" in the usual acceptance of that term; each is a "built in" design on a basis of structural elements. Note in each the *dominant and subordinate interests* and the *concentration* of the terms employed.

In the completion of the details another thought occurs that takes us back to the reasons why abstract design may be studied with profit. While the general form and structural elements may suggest a clew for the position and character of the enrichment, the strength and interest of that enrichment will be no greater than the measure of artistic invention possessed by the designer. We are often told to " ornament construction ; do not construct ornament." The *intent* of the phrase is doubtless right and accords with the content of this chapter ; but it is only a half truth after all. We must have wit, imagination, invention to devise ornament worthy of the position it occupies. The design as a whole will clearly guage the personality of the designer. Confronted by the question of enrichment he may be at complete loss for a motif, a thought, that will give that enrichment distinction. Or, having a motif, his invention may be of a dull sort that fails to make the best use of his motif. It is one of the purposes of the problems in this book to strengthen the inventive faculty, to give it exercise, to demonstrate the fact that the beauty of abstract design is dependent on constructive principles quite as much as concrete design. In the application of these æsthetic principles to practical problems we may

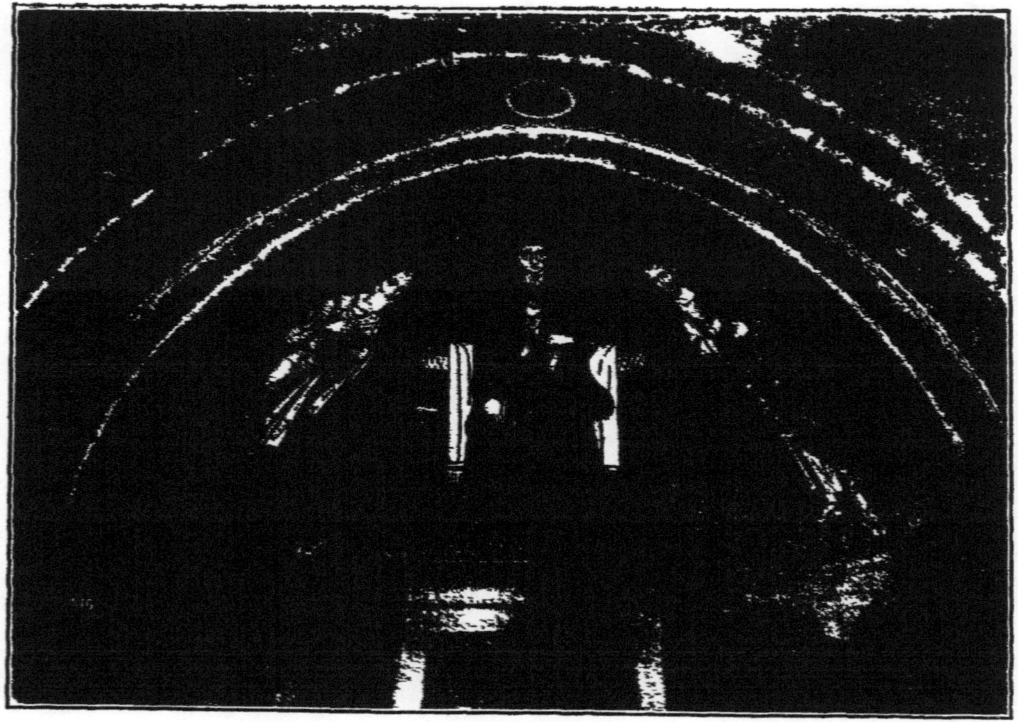

PLATE 10.

BYZANTINE MOSAIC, SAN MARCO.

hope to *ornament construction with thoughtfully constructed ornament.*

The mosaics in the church of San Marco, Venice, furnish an interesting study of the rise and decline of constructive designing. This old church offers a rare opportunity for the comparative study of mosaic work from the ninth century to the present day. Plate 10 shows one of the early Byzantine mosaics. Plate 11 is the work of the brothers Zucato from the sixteenth century. The first illustrates the beauty of construction; its design in line, form, and tone is in structural unity with its architectural environment; it is organically related to the constructive lines and forms about it. The second represents the construction of beauty; it is the work of men who accepted their commission as an opportunity to display their ability as painters; it is a picture within a half circle; its beauty is of a character quite independent from the structural features of the church. To understand the first it must be seen in the space which it occupies; the second can be quite as well understood when it is isolated from its surroundings. The ingenious brothers Zucato even ignored the limitations of their material and employed the brush to acquire gradations of tone in their picture which a legitimate use of mosaic did not allow.

Illustrations might be multiplied from every line of

industrial activity.   As shop-trained men ceased to be designers the structural fitness of the work decreased and the peculiar character that came from an intimate knowledge of practical principles gradually disappeared.

In the evolution of a Gothic cathedral from the early chapels is a most impressive object lesson in the coördination of the practical and the æsthetic.   The unique character of these structures would never have been possible if the builders had not frankly accepted the constructive clews that appeared and turned them all to æsthetic account.   They were not conscious of any distinction between building and architecture; the one merged into the other as naturally as a root sends forth and provides nourishment for the flower. In the final expression of the Gothic idea we find a structure in which every feature, one might say every stone, performs, or did perform at some stage in the development of the style, a functional purpose.   The cathedral is a living organism, vital in every line and form, a nice adjustment of thrusts, counter thrusts, and weights, in which each detail, from the carved pinnacles to the traceried windows, may be followed back to a constructive origin.   Those flying buttresses (Figure 29) which give unique character to the exterior started as strengthening pilasters, were, through gradual evolution, pushed above the roof of the aisles to those

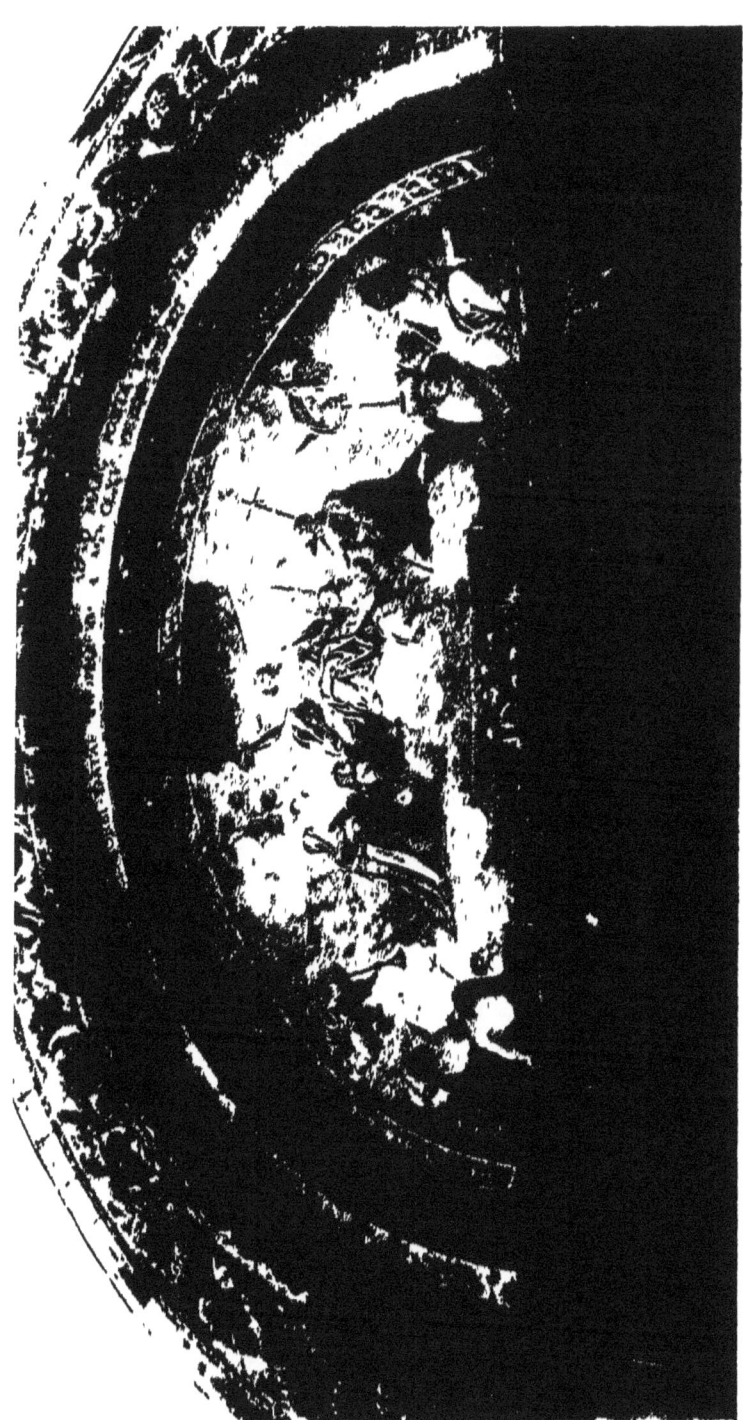

PLATE 11.

SIXTEENTH-CENTURY MOSAIC, SAN MARCO.

remarkable systems found in such churches as Amiens, Rheims, etc. The window openings, starting from a need for subdivision, gradually extended into the wonderful tracery of the later years; and with the builders came the glass workers, growing in strength and power as designers with their growth of opportunities. In the cathedral as it finally appeared we find those factors so essential to vital creative work: a real need, a thought to express, a consummate

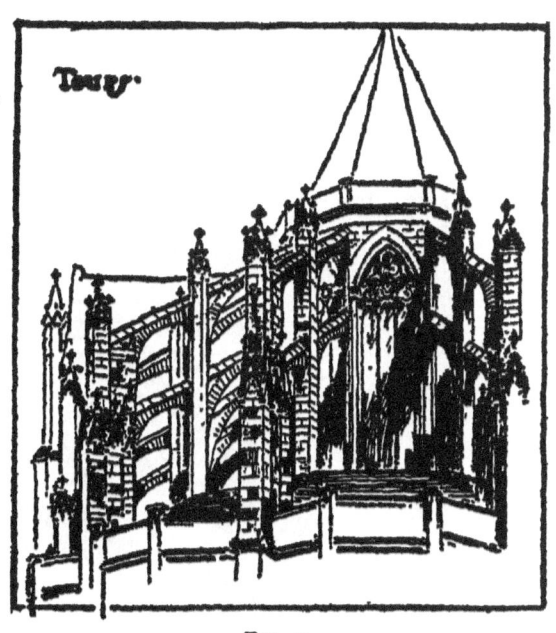

FIG. 29.

command of the practical principles of construction, and an æsthetic sense which enabled the builders to make the most of every clew that was offered.

A similar spirit may be followed like a golden thread woven into the product of all the mediæval craftsmen. It is true that throughout Gothic craftswork may be found forms devised by the builders but freely employed by other workers more for sake of enrichment

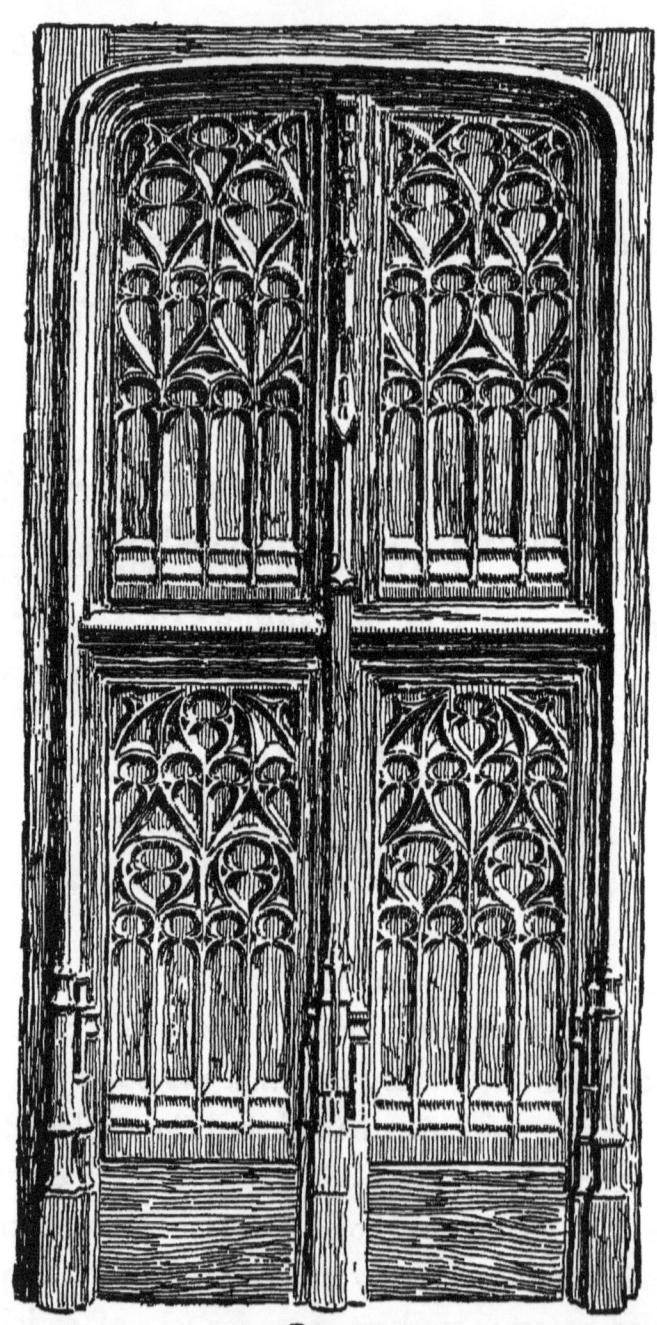

FIG. 30.

than function. In Figure 30 the carver has borrowed
an idea from the stone masons of the cathedral in his
traceried forms. A detail of
this work (Figure 31) shows
the grouping of pier bases
such as may be found at
Rouen. The locksmith in
Figure 32 has chiseled in iron
similar forms of architectural
derivation.

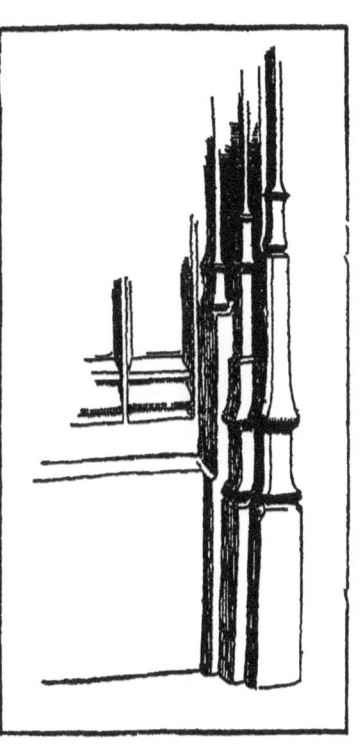

FIG. 31.

Back of these traceries bits
of bright silk or velvet were
generally placed, suggested no
doubt by the glass of the
church windows. Other va-
riations of tracery occur in
the keys of Figure 33. In
one key two tiny windows
have been pierced. But if this man borrowed, he also
gave something in return. They worked hand in hand,
those old craftsmen, always to something better and
finer. In Figure 34 is another instance in which forms
peculiarly functional have been employed for enrichment. It is this which gives to that period of work
the unique distinction which we designate a " style," —
varied interpretations of a similar thought. Under the
conditions which led to that work coöperation was the

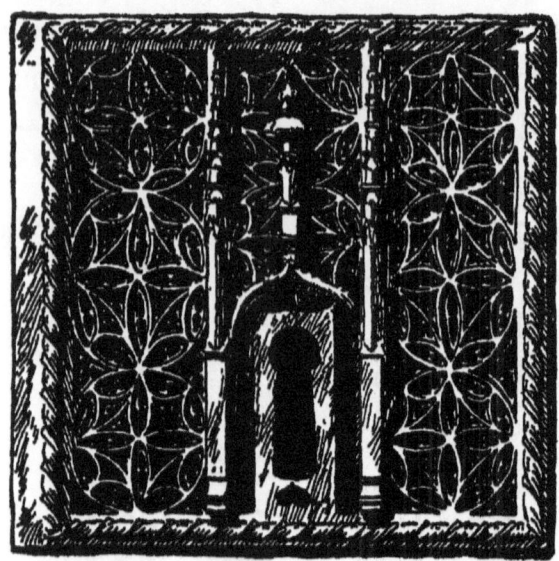

FIG. 32.

keynote rather than individuality; the persistence of forms in construction and ornament was a logical sequence. But the thought which led to those forms has long since passed away; the principles alone remain vital. It is not in imitation of those forms, however skillfully achieved, that we may hope to give character to twentieth-century work.

The message of the past is of principles, not of "periods." In following its principles we, too, may create something expressive of our lives, our needs, our environments. But in a superficial

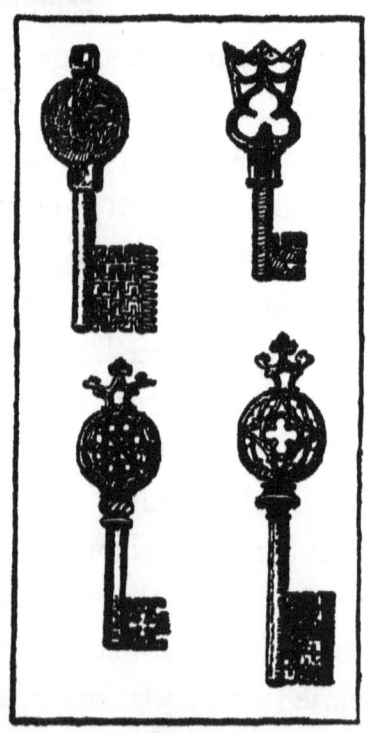

FIG. 33.

adaptation of its outward forms we have a crust, but no pie. To-day we are continually haunted by the characterless semblance of things which we have loved in the original, because in our study of the originals we found ourselves living again in the past with those old craftsmen who lingered over the last details of their work with a sincerity of purpose that imparted real worth and human interest to the product.

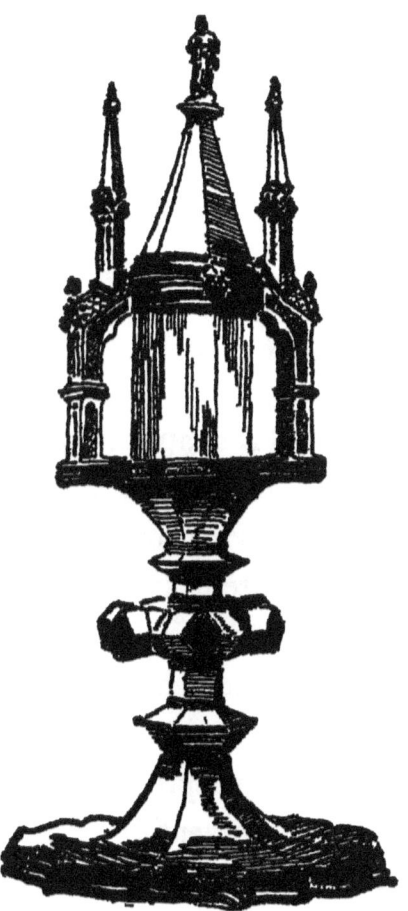

FIG. 34

CHAPTER V

MATERIALS

"Primitive art offers the best possible facilities for the study of the fundamental principles of æsthetic development." — WILLIAM H. HOLMES.

THE simplest type of designing is that in which the worker is concerned with assembling and giving orderly disposition to materials inherently interesting or beautiful. Of such type are the two necklaces in Figure 35. In the first example a cachelot tooth has been chosen; possibly it possesses some fancied charm to the wearer; but it is material ready at hand, provided by Nature, with a minimum of skill or invention in the way of preparation. Assembled with this central piece are shell disks, black, white, and red in color, all strung on braided strands of light and dark brown vegetable fiber.

The second necklace is composed of shell sections, light in color, graded in size. Into the crevices of each shell section some dark substance has been rubbed of a tone similar to the brown fiber to which the shells are bound; and on the inner circle is a row of teeth, with holes drilled in them, one tooth overlapping another.

Both of these are very beautiful indeed, — in the pearly white of the shells, the rare, creamy tone of the teeth, the rich browns of the fiber, and, in the first,

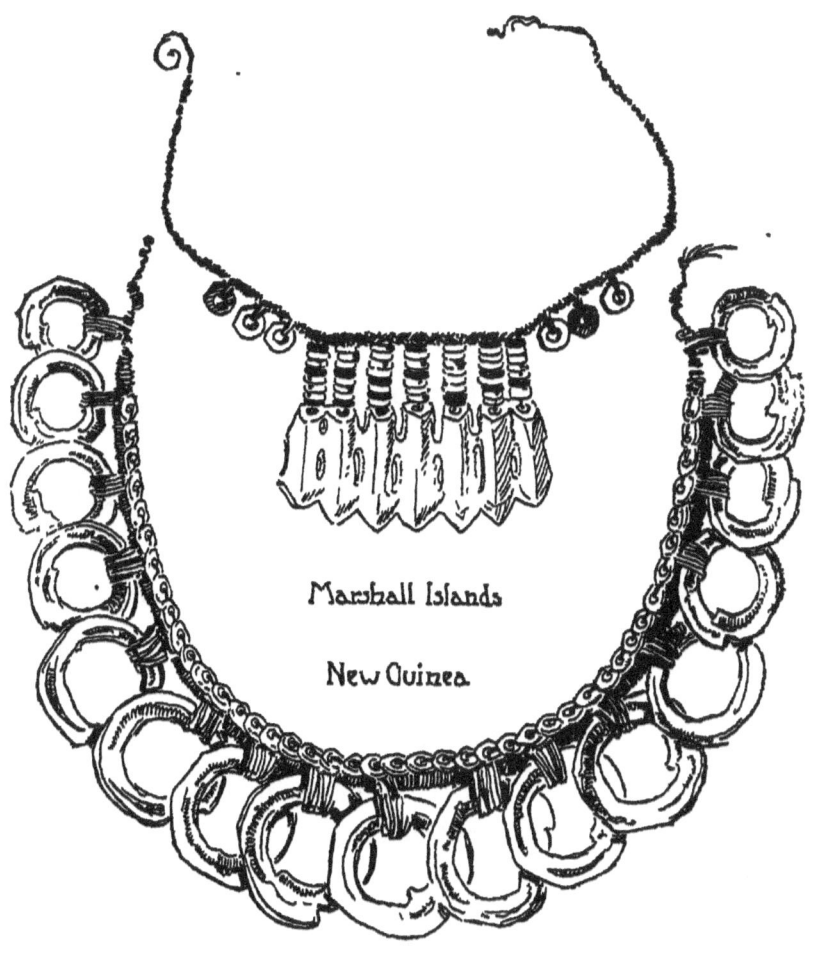

Marshall Islands

New Guinea.

FIG. 35.

the contrasting touches of black and the coral-like red. To Nature the beauty of materials; to the designer a discriminating selection, and a composition of the materials to the utmost advantage. The results are infinitely more beautiful than many of the modern, mechanically spaced strings of pearls or diamonds having little claim for distinction beyond the intrinsic value of the materials employed. There is a vast difference between intrinsic value and inherent beauty. The commercial jeweler of to-day seeks materials of the greatest intrinsic value, brings mechanical skill to bear upon them, and may generally be counted upon to rob the materials of any inherent beauty which they may have possessed. A man with less skill but more taste may seize upon a beach pebble and a scrap of copper and so utilize their inherent beauty as to produce a design of true artistic excellence, though of little intrinsic value.

But it is plain that the two necklaces here shown involve a narrow margin of artistic invention. The instinctive feeling that chose and arranged this material is often quickly shaken at the sight of a few tawdry glass beads or a yard or two of cheap calico. Primitive man, left to his own devices, produces work of artistic merit; his materials and appliances are few and simple and his instinct leads him to an appropriate use of them.

In Figure 36 are five unique hairpins of primitive workmanship. The first, like the two necklaces, represents a happy choice of material. A bone, nicely

adapted to its purpose, has been shaped into serviceable form, carefully rubbed and polished to display
the material to the best advantage. The second and

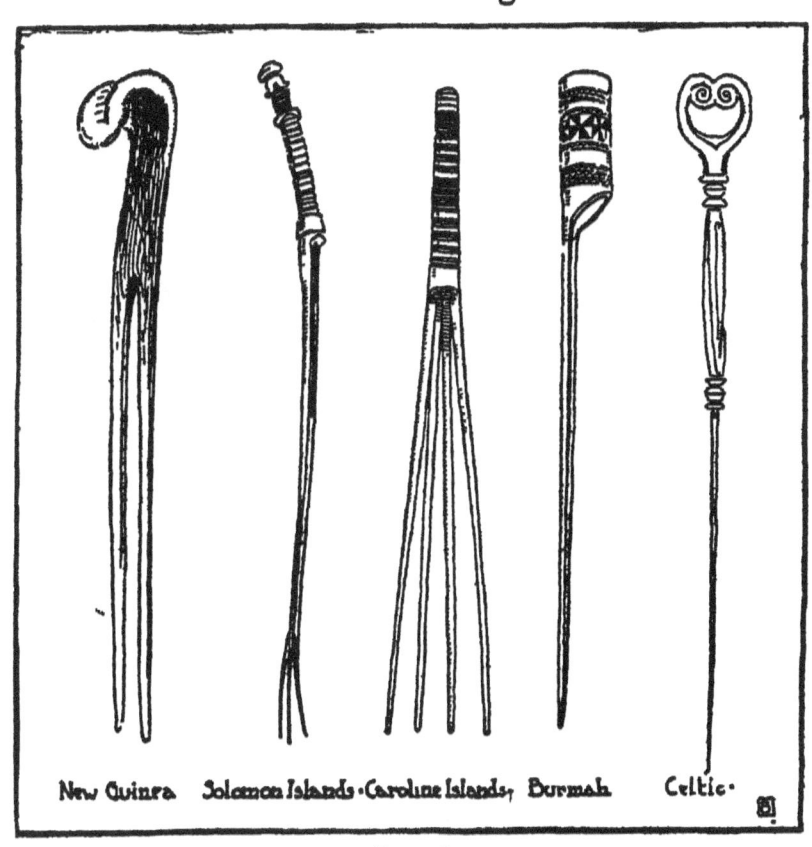

New Guinea   Solomon Islands ·Caroline Islands,   Burmah.   Celtic·

FIG. 36.

third represent combinations of simple materials, fine
feeling, and excellent workmanship. The second is
as charming a piece of craft work as one might hope
to find, exquisite, refined in every part. One may see
how a slightly bent bamboo sprout has been cut to the
center and then split to the bottom, the top whittled

to the shape of a square with a little knob, and with slightly cut ornament at the end. The lower part of the top is neatly wound with yellow straw, the upper part with red straw. In the third, shell disks of two colors have been pushed over a spindle left on the end of the hairpin, the whole being carefully polished. The fourth pin is perhaps no more interesting or important than the others, but it involves designing of a somewhat different character. It is a single pin of bamboo; but the pattern scratched about the top is a bit of pure invention; there is nothing in the material to suggest it, as in the other three. The cylindrical form of the bamboo would naturally suggest a banded treatment; but there is no clew here in the material to the pattern itself. In the fifth pin we advance beyond any of the others to a point where all the credit belongs to the worker. The material was in the form of an unsuggestive and unlovely chunk of bronze, furnishing not the slightest clew to the product as we see it. Here then, assuredly, is designing of the highest order, in which the worker fashions materials to conform to his own needs and ideas, the beauty dependent upon thoughtful design, fine craftsmanship, and an intimate sympathy with and understanding of the materials that will give to the result a character peculiar to bronze. Following the same thought of these pins, study the combs in Figure 37, a development through all the

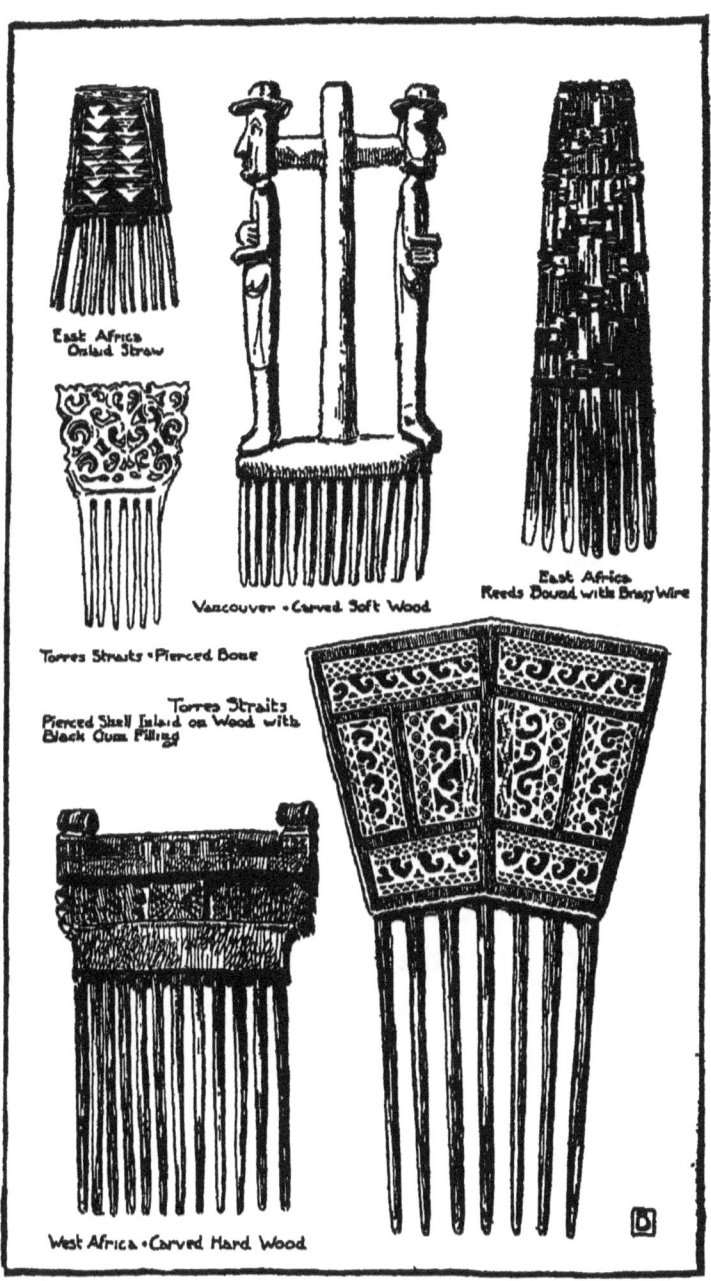

East Africa
Oxlaid Straw

Vancouver - Carved Soft Wood

East Africa
Reeds Bound with Brass Wire

Torres Straits - Pierced Bone

Torres Straits
Pierced Shell Inlaid on Wood with
Black Gum Filling

West Africa - Carved Hard Wood

FIG. 37.

stages from simple, æsthetic use of materials ready-made to the skillful expression of an idea in the materials selected.

It is unfortunate that a serious study of primitive art is left very generally to the archæologist. To many students of design this vast, intensely interesting field is unexplored. Racinet, in his laborious " Grammar of Ornament," defines primitive work as " anterior to rules of art," and devotes a single page of ill-chosen and mechanically rendered fragments to its elucidation. One should be thankful that there still remains open for study a field that is anterior to " rules of art." In the study of Historic Ornament it is usual to take a first deep plunge into Egypt, and emerge with the idea that the beginnings of art are somewhere away back in distant ages and of minor interest.

On the contrary, the story of primitive art is one of absorbing interest and much profit for the beginner. And why go so far afield? Here close beside us and within reach of all is the remarkable art of a people who have just left the stone age behind them ; an art almost contemporary with our own times, indigenous to a soil and climate which we know. Through our own National Museum and its invaluable publications, to be found in any library, the student has access to a most important period of work. Here may be found the art of people who were unhampered by conflicting traditions, whose natures demanded beauty in all objects of daily use; and if this is not "fine art" in the best sense of the term, how indeed may it be defined? The work of more advanced civilizations may offer a wider range of invention, finer distinctions in line, form, and tone than the work of primitive man; but certainly no more evidence of the spontaneous development necessary to the very life of art.

We know too much to be true, and simple, and spontaneous in our own work. We are burdened with too many conflicting traditions and precedents. In this day of inexpensive casts, pictures, and photographs we find the world's work spread out before us. We select for purposes of study those things that are far beyond us in the terms of our own experience. We are induced to imitate and copy those things because of their manifest superiority over our own immature efforts. We are impatient of time, and study, and experiment. If we are workers in wood, or metal, or what not, we find it easy to achieve a logical solution of the constructive demands of a problem, but difficult to complete it with appropriate refinement and enrichment; we have no ideas to express, so bring forth a formidable array of arguments to prove that there never was such a thing as originality in design; and in the meantime complacently appropriate the work of others to our own ends.

G

Primitive art comes as a refreshing breeze. Here were people with real needs to meet with such beauty as they could devise. They gathered, perforce, their own materials from the mountain slopes and the river bottoms, made with their own hands all the tools, and wrought a product simple and honest in construction, strong and insistent in its grasp of fundamentals. The work of primitive man comes from his heart; from his nature rather than from his knowledge. He designed beautifully because he could not help it, and the step from his idea to its vigorous execution is so simple that it can be readily studied. In all justice the feminine pronoun should be used in a description of Figure 38; but to simplify matters let us allow man to shine with reflected glory!

The questions of tools, materials, and processes are reduced to their simplest elements; we may trace the experiments and influences from one material or process to another. In our Southwest, gourds were common in many sections, and were used as utensils for various purposes. For convenience in carrying the gourd, and possibly for protection, a coarse weave of wickerwork was made about it. There is good reason to believe that this suggested the weaving of baskets, merely by increasing the strands of the wicker covering. A wicker basket lined with pitch or clay was more durable than a gourd; it also demanded

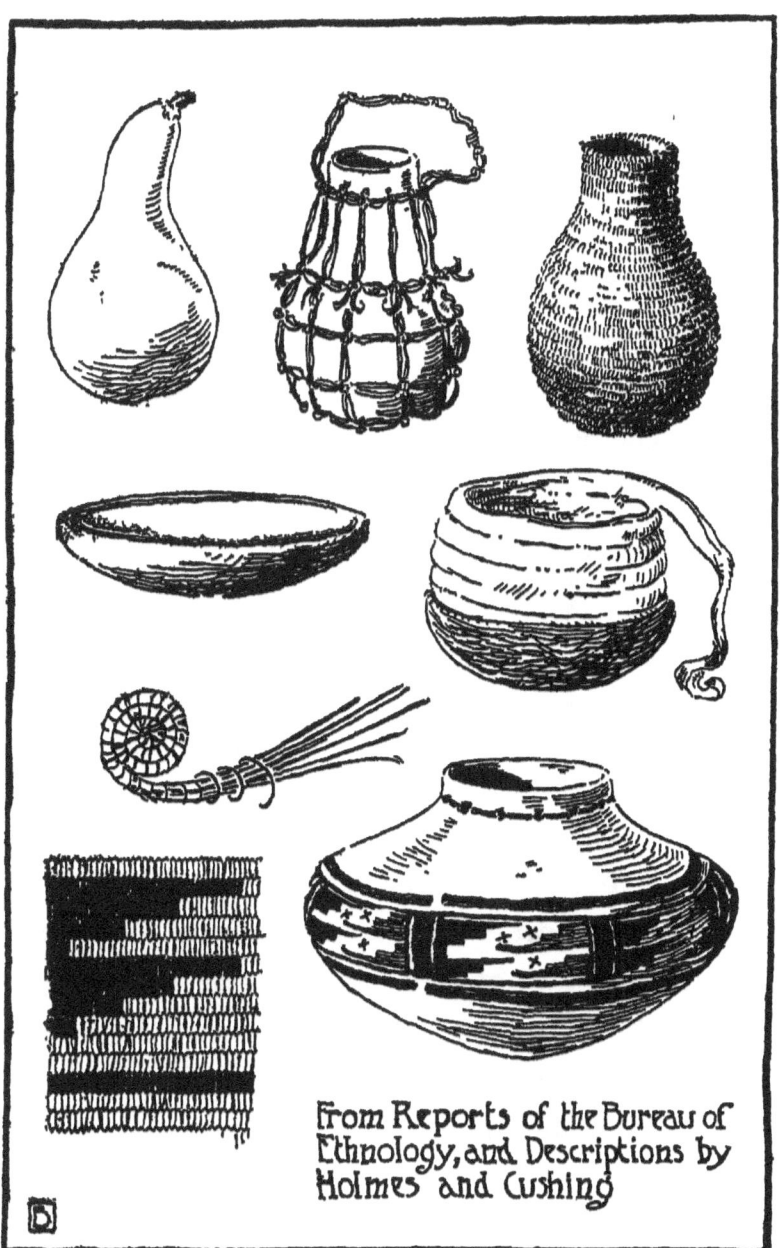

From Reports of the Bureau of
Ethnology, and Descriptions by
Holmes and Cushing

FIG. 38.

greater strength than is possible with the loose weaving of a wicker framework.   As basketry came into wider practice other utensils were made, and the materials and processes involved in the craft underwent a development on their own merits.   Strands were bound together in coils to give greater strength; baskets were made for boiling water, after the primitive method; for parching pans, and for other domestic uses.   Now the parching pan was lined with clay, as were also the cooking and boiling baskets, to protect the basket from the charcoal.   Naturally the heat baked the clay, shrinking it into a form similar to the basket.   A clay pan was an obvious suggestion.   Here was a new material with new possibilities to be studied.   But while clay may be pressed into the shallow parching pan and then fired, it is apparent that forms for boiling or carrying water cannot be made in the same way without destroying a good basket for each piece of pottery made.   Knowing no better way, the primitive worker employed the same process of coiling developed through basketry, even using a basket at the start for shaping the bottom of the clay vessel.   He is ever slow to abandon old materials and methods.   The first pottery was rough and partook, not only in form but in texture, of the antecedent baskets.   In the course of time a slip was devised which gave a smoother texture to the pottery; and with this new texture the basket character decreased. Here was a different kind of surface to be treated. In the meantime there was developing through basketry a variety of weaves and a highly organized system of geometric ornament. With the dyes employed in basket making, the first of the smooth vessels were painted; and for motifs the artist naturally turned to the geometric ornament of weaving, for there, through hard-earned experience, he felt on safe ground. One of the dyes stood the test of the fire and thus became the standard. Gradually the severe geometric ornament of weaving underwent modifications during the translation with new tools, materials, and processes; angles were softened, curves appeared; yet throughout the periods of the best pottery the lessons so well learned in weaving were never quite lost from sight. And so the story continues, always interesting, always instructive, proceeding along the lines of least resistance, clear and spontaneous at all times. Space does not permit us to follow it to a conclusion; but it is hoped that enough has been said to induce the reader to seek at first hand, from those who are able to speak with authority, the story of primitive art.[1]

The technique of weaving and basketry inevitably gave rise to a geometric ornament. The growth of pattern was slow, because primitive man, as we have already seen, was a conservative designer in spite of

[1] Reports of the Bureau of Ethnology.

the vigor of his utterance. From one generation to another the simple patterns were passed, with gradual changes tending toward a more complete expression. We cannot appreciate the completeness of the result until we sit down to a careful examination of an Indian basket; count out the strands of the pattern and note how difficult the task becomes.

Into these patterns there entered at an early stage a fresh element of interest. The primitive man looked out upon the world through the eyes of a child. Science had not robbed him of his fairyland; the forces of Nature, from the forked lightning to the blade of grass pushing upward with the new rains, were explained only in the lore of his mythology. His gods of the wind, the rain, and the sun were real deities to propitiate. He lived close to the heart of Nature. And, as the hand serves the mind, there inevitably appeared in his work earnest efforts to interpret the natural phenomena about him, developing in time a rich symbolism which we can only in part understand or translate.

His pictorial art, like his designs, strikes out boldly for essentials, for lines expressing movement, action, life. He was more intent on recording impressions than in nice distinctions of texture, color, light, and shade. He was the first of the "impressionists." He even recorded his ideas through pictographs in lieu of a written language.

There entered, then, into the technique of his weaving certain nature-derived elements, often arbitrary and unreal. Sometimes we recognize the motif as nature-derived; again it requires the ingenious logic of an archæologist to assure us. The interplay between the two is so intimate that it cannot be said positively:

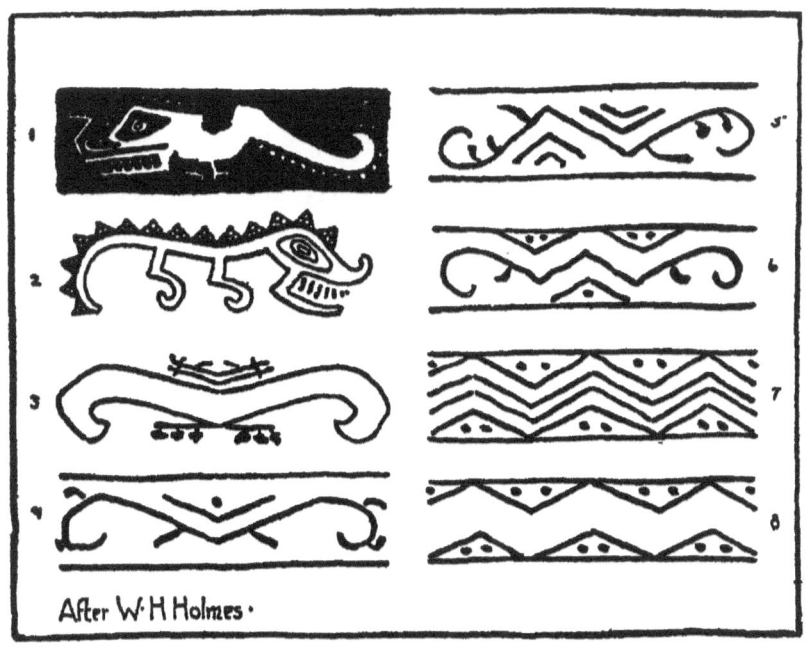

After W. H Holmes.

FIG. 39.

This started in technique; this in Nature. A whimsical twist in a line may have furnished a suggestion sufficient to send a given pattern toward Nature; or again the designer may have done the best he could for Nature under the circumstances. The point is illustrated in Figure 39. Is the development from

1 to 8 ; or from 8 to 1 ; or from the extremes to the center ?

There is a remarkable similarity of development in the arts of primitive peoples, separated though they may be by thousands of years in point of time. Primitive needs were much the same and were met with similar materials and processes, flint clipping, weaving, pottery, etc., each developing in due season. From one art to another we may trace a similar overlapping of materials and forms, whether in ancient Greece or in Arizona. The early clay vessels of the Iroquois Indians show the influence of birch bark forms. If the Alaskan Indians had chanced upon the making of clay vessels, we may be sure their first efforts would have been influenced by the wooden forms in ordinary use among them.

The persistence of forms from one material to another may be traced throughout the history of art as well as among primitive workers. We know that conch shells were in use for lamps in early Babylon, — because the first stone lamps were cut in that form. The Lyceans, in their tombs, laboriously cut from the solid rock a form of timber construction in common use; and the influence of timber construction undoubtedly survives in many of the forms and some of the ornament of the Parthenon. Gothic work, as we have seen, is full of translations of form from one material to another. The first silk weavers of Florence imitated the designs of the tiled floor in the Baptistry until they found assurance in their material and its processes. Many other illustrations might be cited; but one point must not be overlooked,—all of these instances came at times when art was a growing organism, and were the results of an intimate coöperation among many workers. It was what may be called a process of unconscious imitation. It offers no excuse for the deliberate, thoughtless imitation of cut stone with cast cement so prevalent in building construction to-day, or the molding of plaster forms grained to imitate wood carving. These indicate a thoughtless disregard of material, or a sham and pretense for sake of cheapness.

The designer should learn to think in terms of the materials he wishes to use. Lack of knowledge of the limitations and possibilities of materials, of the peculiar charms inherent in wood or stone, iron or glass, accounts for much of the characterless work of to-day. In such jewelry as that shown in Figure 40 there is the rare beauty that ever distinguishes the work of men who have learned to play with their materials, who have an intimate acquaintance with metal, shell, coral, ivory, etc., and a sense of beauty that seeks to preserve the unique qualities of each and display them to the best advantage. Such things can never be thought out by the paper-trained designer who has, at

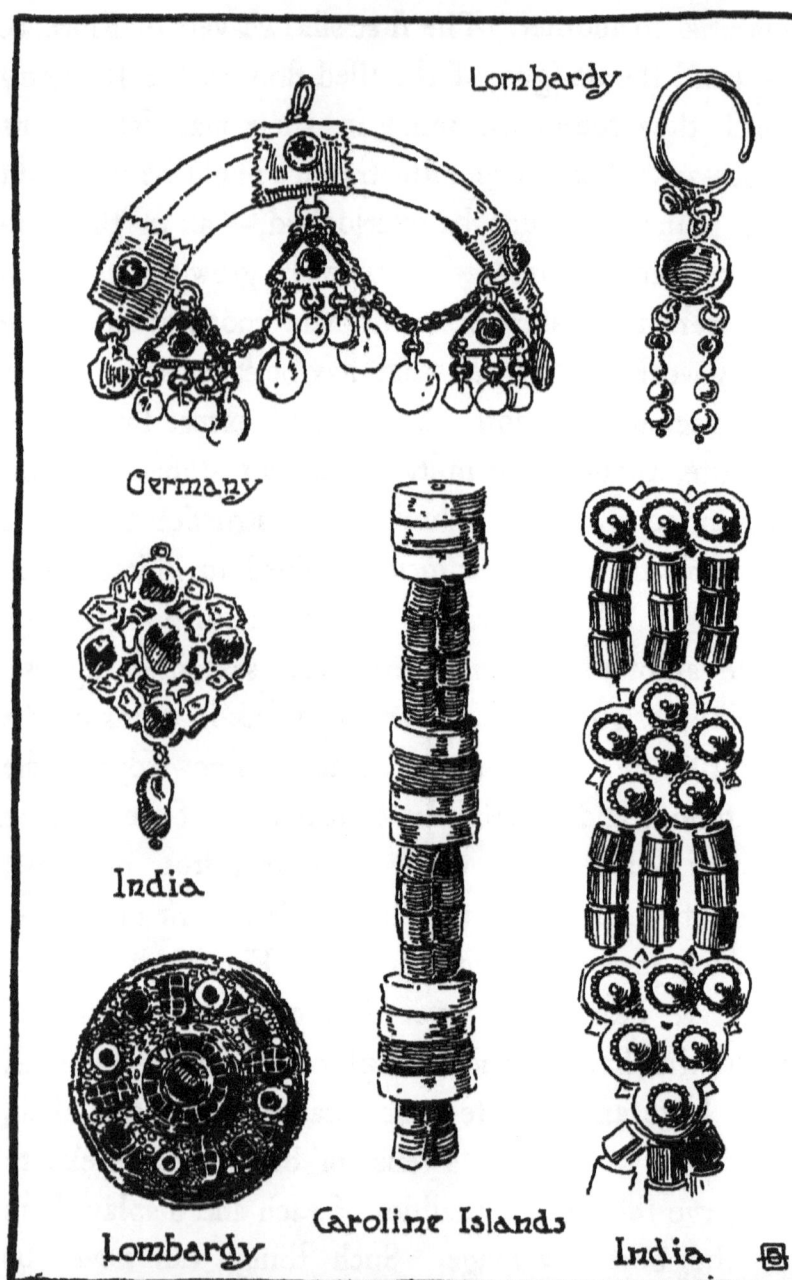

FIG. 40.

the best, a theoretic knowledge of materials, tools, and processes. A man who has carved in wood will find a broad field of suggestion in the twist and turn of the

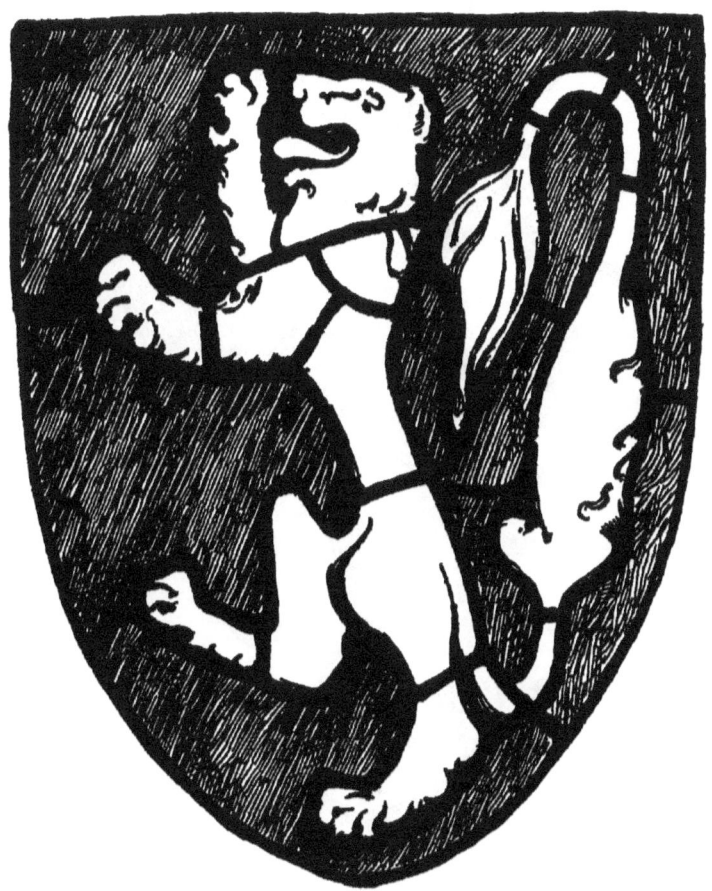

FIG. 41.

grain, the texture, the finish, the handling of the tools, —in fact the very things that distinguish wood carving from stone carving. In the two scraps of leaded glass in Figures 41, 42 we may note how the frank acceptance of materials gives character to the first; while in the second the designer ignored, or sought to

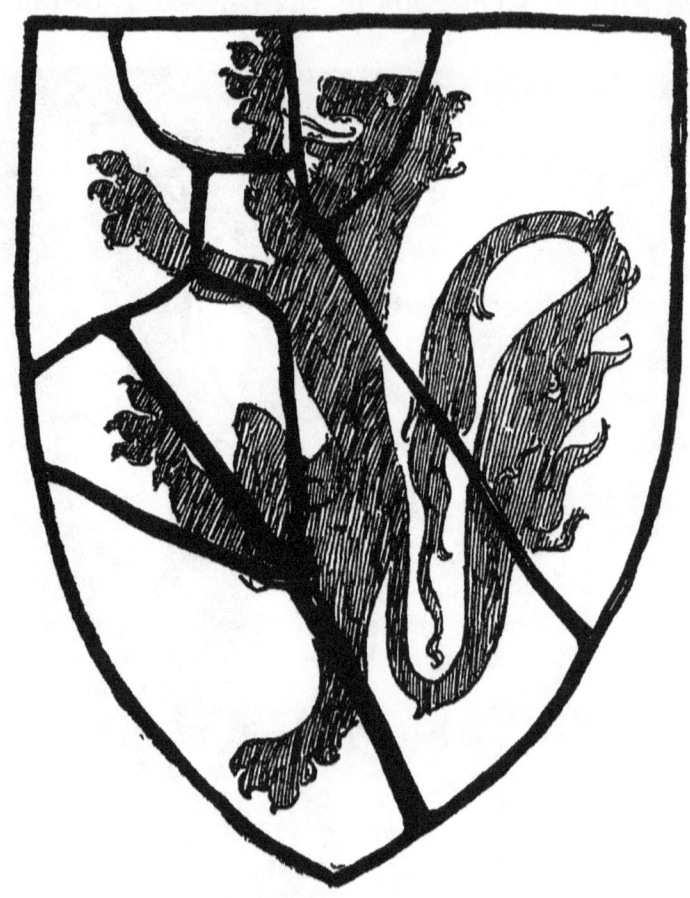

FIG. 42.

avoid, the limitations of lead and glass, with a consequent loss of force and strength.

There can be no doubt that much of the work of the past was thought out directly in the materials themselves. But there is no reason why a man should

not do much of his thinking on paper. The term
paper-made design is a reproach only to the man who
possesses no intimate knowledge of his materials and
necessarily loses thereby the very quality which counts
so much for character and style. There are possibilities
in the materials which find no response in his work.

PROBLEM. From Figure 39 there is this to be
gained of immediate application to the present problem: however much of interest there may be in
primitive man's pictographs, the value of his design
increases as it approaches the geometric. Whatever
the motif employed may be, it is the relation of lines
and forms that furnishes bones, giving character,
strength, vigor to the work.

You were asked, "What do you expect Nature to
do for you?" Just this: she may clothe your
work with fresh life and interest, for the mind may
well tire of abstract lines and forms, however thoughtfully composed; but you must furnish the bones;
and if the bony structure is weak or poorly jointed,
Nature cannot hide the fault. Nature may stir one's
ideas and suggest motifs and forms; indeed, geometry
supplies poor nourishment as a long-continued diet for
the imagination to work upon. But Nature insists
that the organic structure of the design shall come
from the designer; failing there, from lack of skill or
understanding, the result fails as a design.

Let us now bring to the "bones" of the previous problems a fresh element of interest, working toward rather than from Nature. Insect life offers a suggestive and, at this stage, a comparatively safe motif. For our purpose the insect is a mere symbol characterized by lines and areas combined. It is not the intention to "conventionalize" any particular insect; the suggestion of Nature is merely a bit of fancy woven into the fabric of the design. Hence we may treat the insect with considerable liberty in the construction of the design. The closer Nature is brought to the abstract the less essential it is to keep to any particular, recognized form; as the abstract character of a design decreases consistency demands a correspondingly closer study of and adherence to Nature's laws of growth, and a recognition of the distinctive characteristics of special forms. Nothing could be more stupid than the mere repetition at regular intervals of a naturalistic insect.

Think of the designs in Figure 43, as well as in the following plates, from a broad view point first. Study them as wholes, as compositions of space and mass; then descend gradually to details in order to find what it is that binds the results together into unity. Analyze the structural arrangement of the lines and forms; if an attempt is made to change a line or a form, it is soon found that it bears some relation to other lines

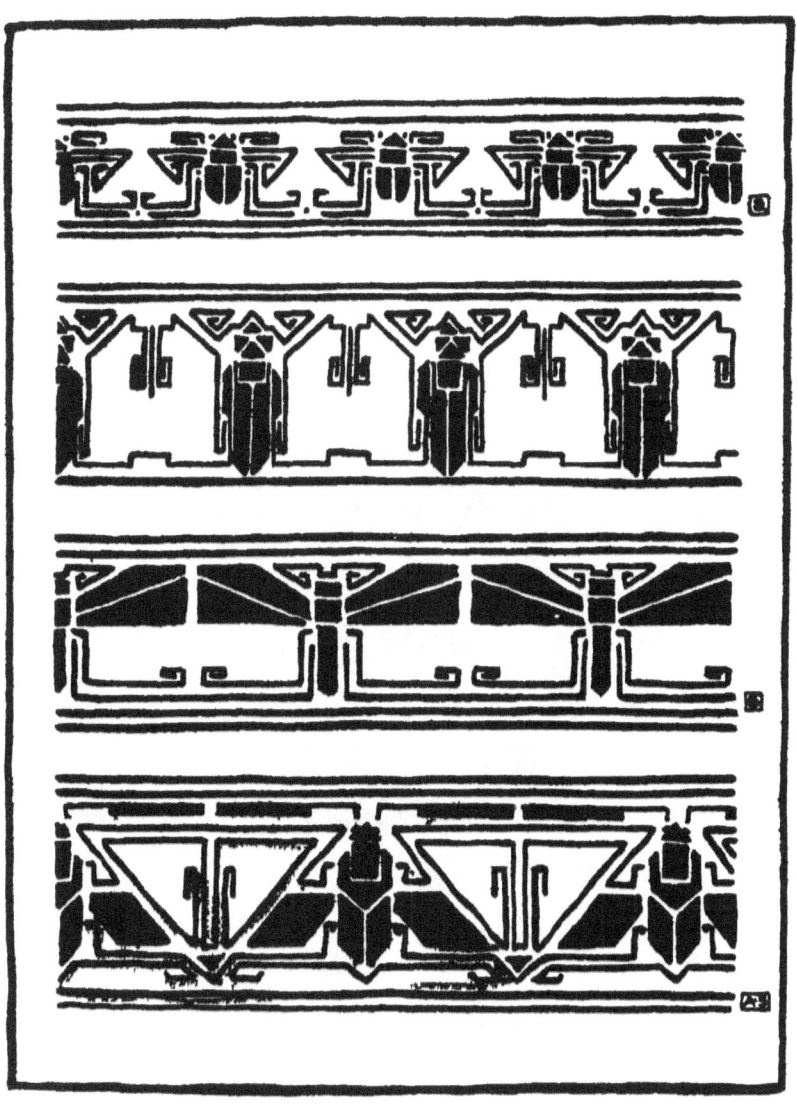

FIG. 43.

and forms; they all work together like a good team of horses. It is this how and why of each element in a design that should interest us as students.

This interrelation of the elements of a pattern has been defined as Rhythm,—that reciprocal relation of the different parts of a design which enables the eye to find a way through all of its details, binding them together into a unity.

In Figure 44, 1 the regular repetition of an unique shape carries the eye through the pattern like the beat

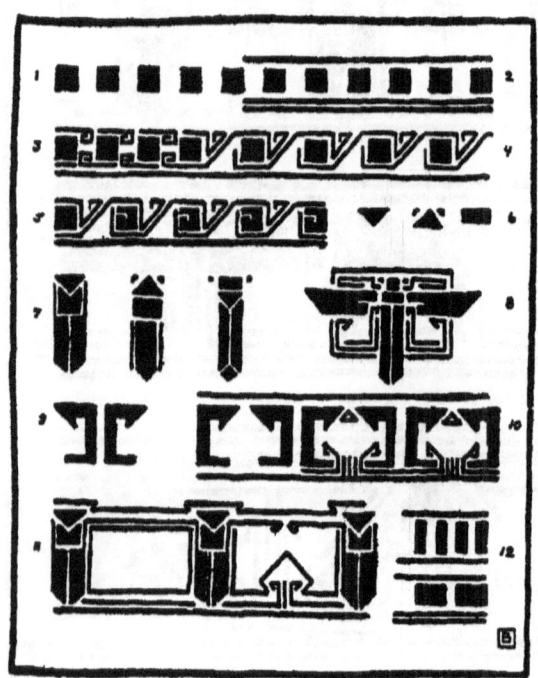

FIG. 44.

of a drum in a march. The parallel lines in 2 strengthen and support the movement; there is nothing in the result to give direction to the movement, though the eye, presumably from force of habit in reading, seems naturally to move from left to right. In 3 a slight element of variety is introduced without breaking the essential regularity of repeat. In 4 the element of variety is increased, in space and mass and in the directions of lines; but not at the expense of unity,—it is still bound together as an organic whole. As an illustration of a still closer binding together of the elements 5 is added. Here the white, or space, hooks into the black, or mass, if it may be explained through such a picturesque phrase. Now to this simple demonstration it is the purpose to add such interest as the statement of our problem has already indicated. In 6 are suggestions for a start; carried further in 7. In 8 the structural relations of line and form, space and mass are readily seen; note the value in this result of the two little white spaces; note also the importance of *concentration*. It is practically a design in three tones, — black, white, gray.

It has been said that there is no special virtue attached to the mere repetition of a unit at regular intervals, however interesting and complete the unit may be in itself. In 9 is a symmetry of shapes; in a regular repetition of this symmetry, as in 10, it is found that another symmetry appears in the design and must be accepted as a playmate whether we wish it or not. In the present case this second symmetry has the greater attractive force, and we find our interest immediately transferred from the mass to the space. It is now the playmate that sets the pace, and furnishes a clew to the completion of the design in such way that all the elements may take part in the game. Having some such motif as is shown in 7, the interval of repeat would be sought and the space between studied, as

H

in 11.   This space may be given more interest; but it would be well to subordinate one or the other of the two symmetries involved.   In constructive problems the interval of the repeat is governed largely by the part the border might play in the design as a whole or the position it occupies.   In the row of sculptured kings on the façade of Notre Dame in Paris, a distinctly vertical character is given to the repeats of a long horizontal border, as in 12; but every line and form on the façade demands that those repeats shall fall into vertical lines.   On the other hand, if a border in which the lines fall into similar relations were to be placed upon the floor of a room about a rug, we might feel that a movement in the other direction in harmony with the long lines of the border would be pleasanter and more restful.   As an abstract question a comparison may be made between the second and third examples in Figure 43.   It would be unwise to shorten the interval of repeat in the second; quite as unwise to lengthen it in the third.   But to say that it is unwise to do thus and so is quite different from saying, "Thou shalt not."   Ah! how simple this would all be if one might formulate a rule-o'-thumb to be applied upon all occasions when in doubt!   It would save a deal of worry and work!

In Plates 12, 13, 14, 15 are other constructive arrangements of lines and forms built up in a way similar to the examples we have just been discussing.   Each

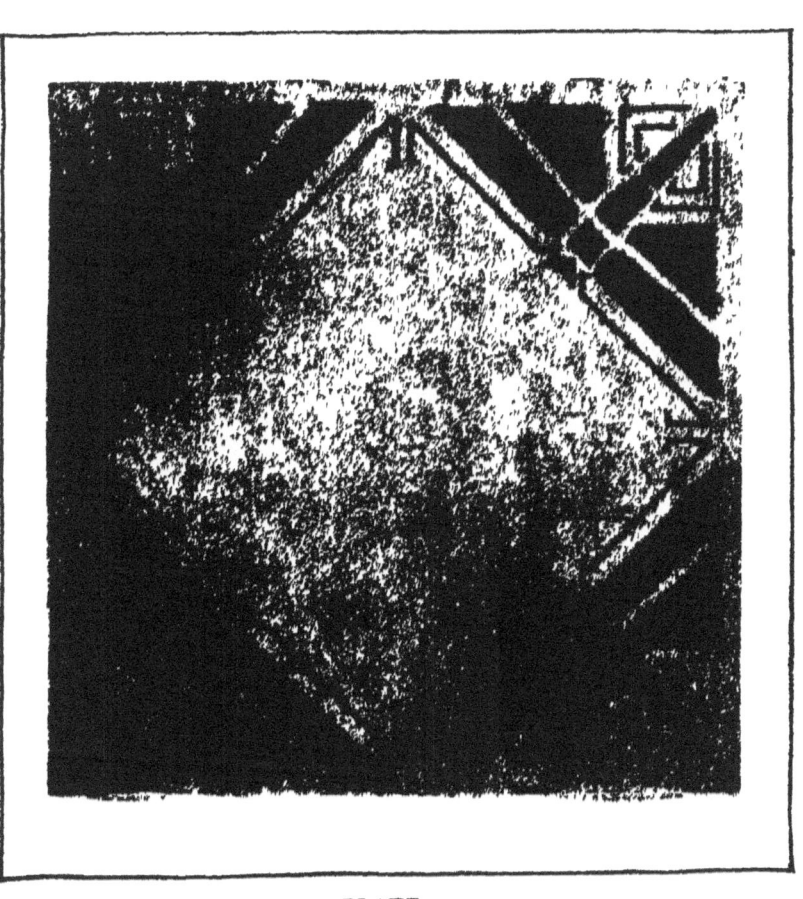

PLATE 12.

NATURE SYMBOLS.

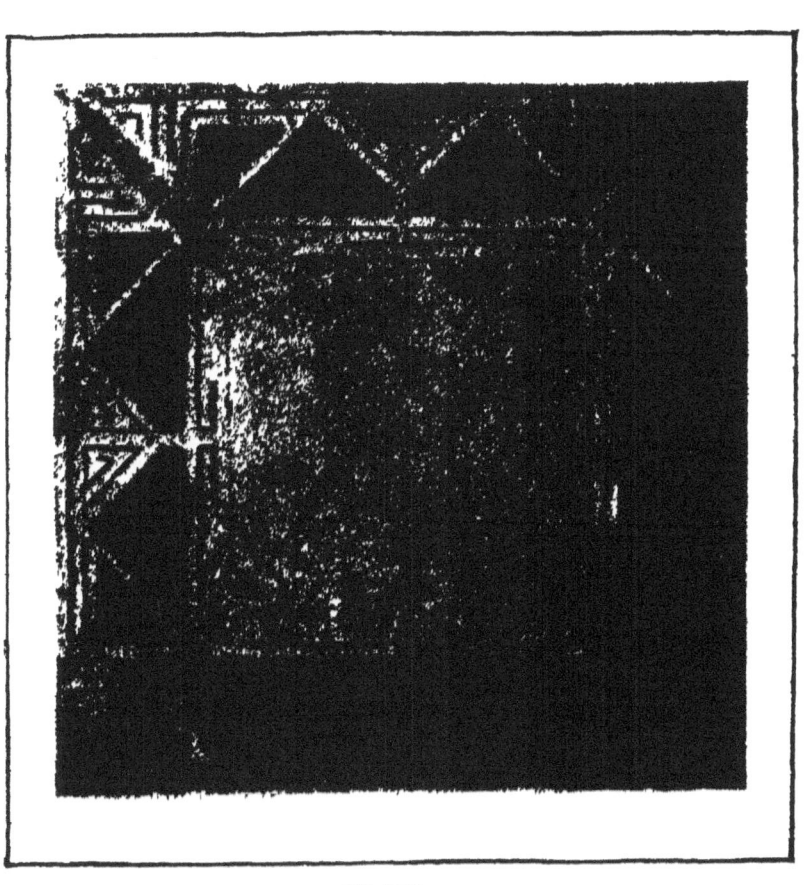

PLATE 13.

NATURE SYMBOLS.

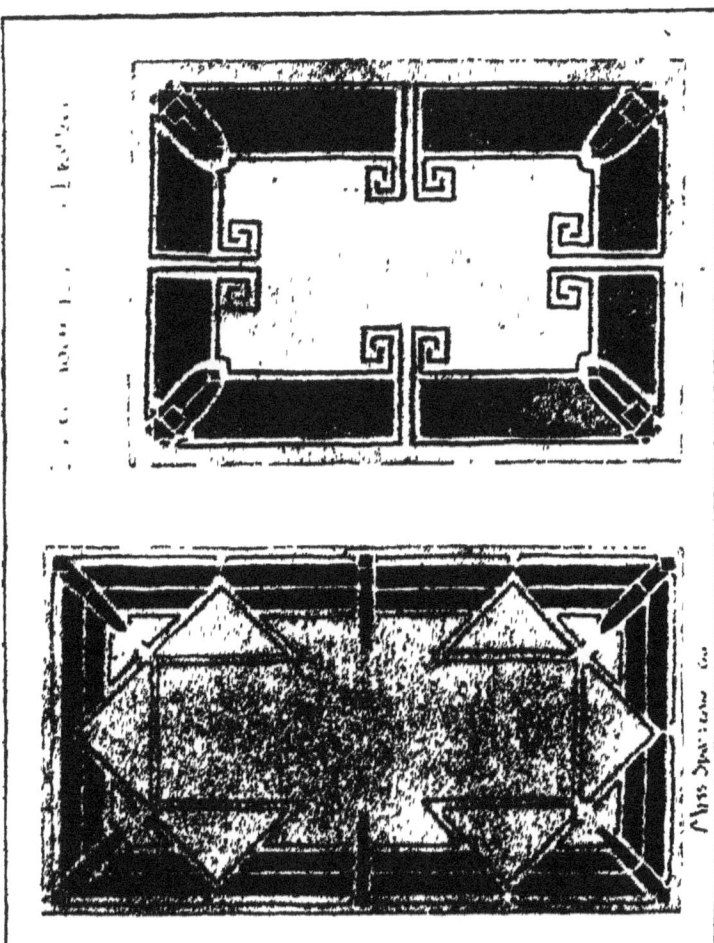

PLATE 14.

NATURE SYMBOLS.

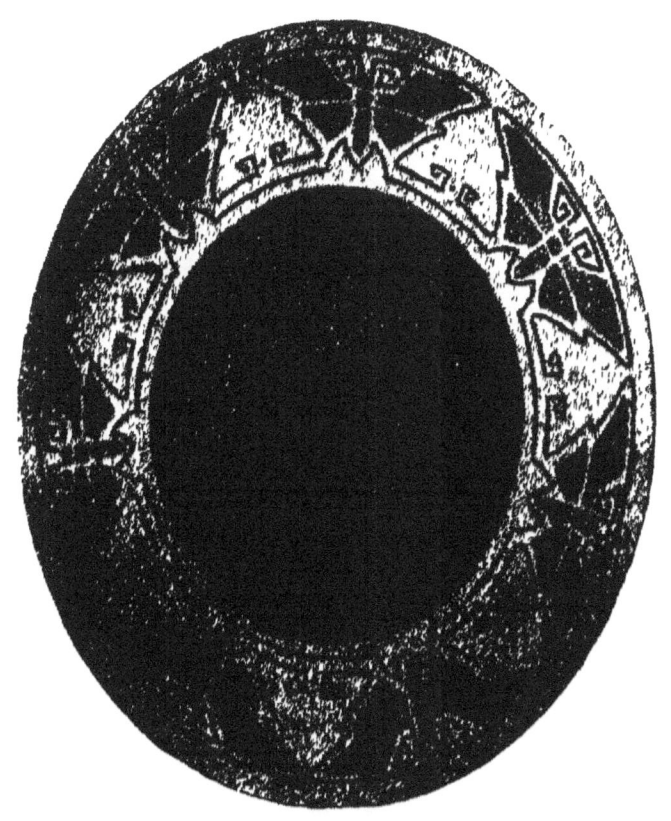

PLATE 15.

NATURE SYMBOLS.

element in these designs has a *reason* to justify its position, shape, and measure, a function to perform as
part of an organic whole. Note in each design the
way in which the details are bound together into oneness by the interrelation of lines.

.

CHAPTER VI

TOOLS AND PROCESSES

"Yet, notwithstanding its remarkable expression of life based on Nature, the work of the Gothic carver is, as a rule, appropriately conventionalized. Only those abstract qualities of form which are capable of effective monumental treatment are taken from nature." — C. H. MOORE.

A GREAT many of the interesting patterns devised by the workers of the past for the purpose of enrichment are traceable directly to the tools and processes employed in execution. A given tool suggests to the tool-trained man a character of treatment in design that could never possibly enter into the work of a paper-trained designer unfamiliar with technique. The old worker knew that certain lines and forms were readily produced by certain tools; and through the combination of different tools many of his patterns were evolved. These patterns in turn were modified through other influences or suggested clews leading to other forms; the immediate effect of the tool became less apparent as technical skill increased; but throughout the periods when shop-trained men were designers, the tool influence remains as a potent factor in the unique character of the work.

It is difficult to estimate the loss that modern work has suffered from the designer's lack of tool training alone. The design of the old worker moved along a path through which his experience in execution had previously cleared a way; he unconsciously recognized the limitations of his tools, materials, and processes, and knowing their limitations he was in position to' realize their possibilities to the utmost. His thought in design was in terms of technique; his ideas often, one may say generally, received direct expression without the intermediate step of paper and pencil. If paper and pencil preceded actual execution, it was merely as a convenient shorthand note, a blocking out of big forms in which details were left to clews furnished by the tools.

In Figure 45 is a simple example of what may be termed tool-wrought ornament; the worker turned to

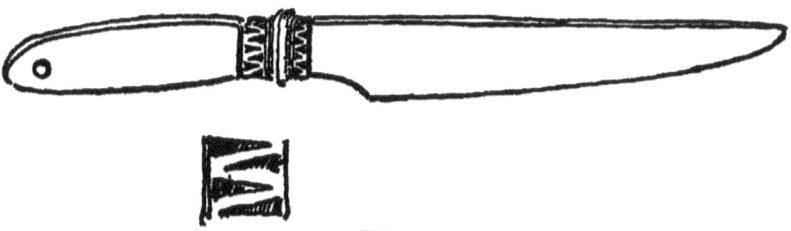

FIG. 45.

his tools for the clew to the pattern. Similar in character is the carved enrichment of Plate 7, or the first spoon in Figure 11. These are all patterns suggested by the tools themselves. Chip carving, when properly executed by those sufficiently endowed with invention to make it interesting, might serve as an illustration of similar work. If any preliminary studies were made for such designs, they were doubtless sketched directly upon the material and an immediate execution started with the tools. The cut-glass worker of to-day follows a similar method. The design may consist of a few broad red lines painted on the glass to indicate the spacing, but quite unintelligible to one unfamiliar with the processes of production. To the worker, with his various-shaped wheels of emery, the lines have a real significance. Whether or not we approve of the results is beside the point; the character of the design is due to the tools and processes employed.

The skilled worker — that is to say, one who is skilled in ideas as well as in execution — generally needs fewer tools than the unskilled worker. Or, to put it another way, the skilled worker is able to gain with a few tools a maximum of effect; his artistic, as well as mechanical, invention finds many uses for a single tool. The skilled bookbinder produces a great variety of patterns from a few simple tools. A preliminary pattern, with the aid of a piece of carbon transfer, may be stamped upon paper; but the effect is due to the artistic invention with which the tool patterns are

combined.   The metal workers of India use the simplest
possible tools and processes, often so primitive that

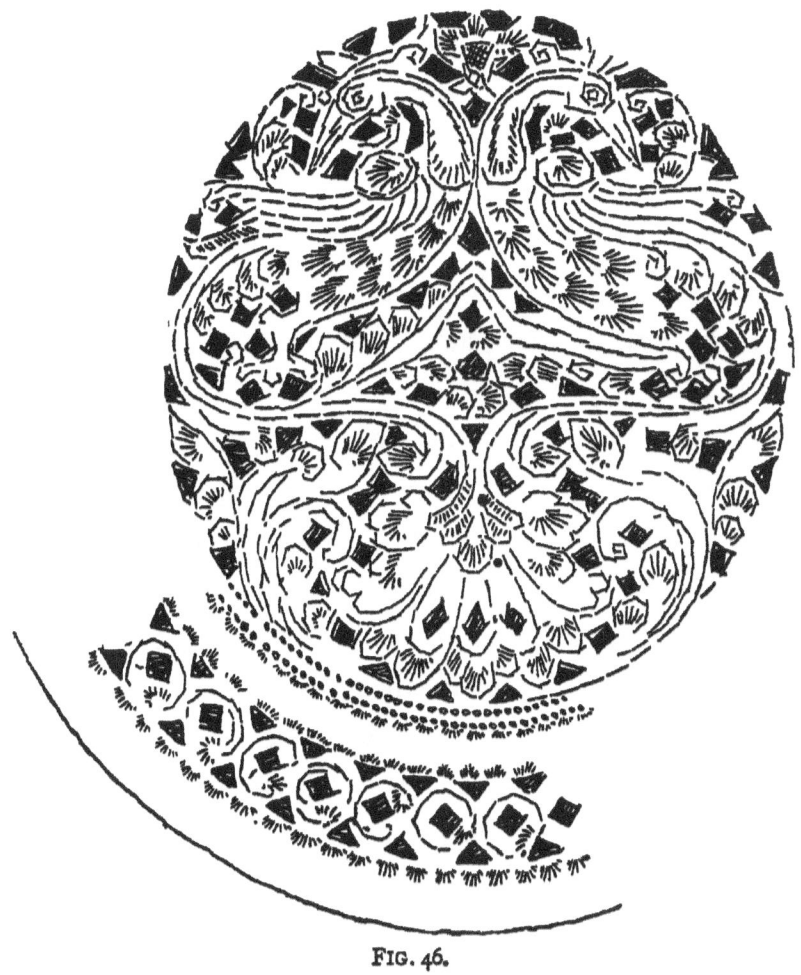

FIG. 46.

the achievements excite wonder.   A fertility of invention enables them to employ their simple appliances to
the greatest possible advantage.   In Figure 46, a portion of a brass plate of modern workmanship, three

tools only were needed for the design: a cutting tool, a circular punch, and a mallet or hammer. The cutting tool used for the holes was apparently used with less force for the lines, the short lines being made by tipping the tool at different angles with the surface. The punch was employed for the double row of circles about the inside of the rim. The result has remarkable interest, rare harmony of treatment, and the unique character which gives distinction to the work of a tool-trained designer. Such designs cannot be foreseen on paper.

There are two points of view from which the influence of tools and processes in design may be profitably studied: first, that work which may be termed *adventitious*, in which the patterns were directly suggested by the tools, as in the double row of circular punch marks in the plate already referred to; second, that work in which the tool has exerted a notable influence in the development of the designer's idea and in which the tool is responsible for the character of treatment, — as in the center and outer border of this plate.

Just where the tool ceases to influence the character of treatment it is often difficult to say. In the hands of a consummate craftsman, such as an artisan of old Japan, the last trace of the tool may be removed. It must not, of course, be assumed that tool tracks are always desirable, or are in any sense essential to a beautiful product. But there is a vast difference between artistic finish and mechanical finish. Where to stop and when to stop are questions that remain with the worker. A plank squared, planed, and laboriously sandpapered has less beauty than the hewn planks of mediæval houses. But to take a plank from the mill and cover it with adze marks, with the idea of making it beautiful, would be an affectation inconsistent with its surroundings, a superficial imitation of primitive methods and results to be avoided. Machine carving is deplorable because it seeks to imitate results peculiar to hand processes. A maker of scientific instruments might turn his hand to leather tooling with accurate precision, yet produce results hopelessly uninteresting; mechanical exactness generally drives the last trace of beauty from a product. A person less skilled of hand but more artistic of mind might gain with the tools a more interesting piece of work.

Mediæval iron work furnishes material that is particularly interesting in a study of tool-wrought ornament. The use of iron as a strong factor in art properly begins with the period of mediæval history. The ancients used iron; but the material occupied a subordinate place in their work. With the beginning of mediæval history the blacksmith enters upon the scene as an artisan of the first importance; in no other craft can one trace more clearly the significant influence of the tool in shaping forms and patterns, — a beauty that was achieved upon a background of generation after generation of tool-trained men.

Iron would seem to be the last material to which a man would turn for beauty's sake alone. Its associations have generally been with stern necessity; its forms have almost invariably been those that utility has demanded for strength and resistance. To other materials more easily worked, or of greater intrinsic value and inherent beauty, such as ivory, gold, silver, enamel, or wood, the craftsman has turned for forms of convenience and luxury. But iron, the least promising material of all in its crude state, has generally come to the hands of the man who must build as utility points the way. More credit to the blacksmith that, through the distinction which comes from fine craftsmanship alone, he should rise head and shoulders above the purely useful trades and place his work beside that of the goldsmiths and silversmiths as a product possessing the highest order of beauty.

Consider for a moment the form in which the iron was delivered at the forge of the mediæval smithy. The ore was smelted by simple processes at the mines back in the forests or on the mountain sides, rudely formed into ingots of such size that they might be easily transported, and brought to the towns to be bartered in trade. To-day the iron may be purchased in a great variety of forms, rolled into sheets of any desired thickness or into bars and rods, round, square, octagonal, of such lengths or dimensions as the worker may specify. But the early smith started, perforce, with the rough ingot, beating it out with the most arduous kind of manual labor into forms adapted to his purpose. Nothing could be more unsuggestive than the raw material left beside his forge. To win from it a straight, flat bar suitable for a hinge was in itself a difficult task. Persistently stubborn and resistant, it could be overcome only during the brief interval after it was pulled sputtering hot from the fire. Then back to the fire it must go again to bring it to a workable condition. There was no coaxing with light taps, no "correction to righteousness"; each blow must needs be forceful, direct.

The worker started with a forge, an anvil, two or three hammers and chisels, a punch, and similar tools of the simplest contrivance. The material, as we have seen, must be shaped while hot; and while in this state separate pieces may be welded together. As work typical of these conditions the early hinge from St. Albans, Figure 47, is a good example. Constructively, the hinge had to spread out over the surface of the door to bind the planks together and secure a firm clutch for the service it had to perform. It was bolted through the door to plates or straps of iron on the inside. In this hinge one may readily note the character that came from the processes employed, and in all of the details the tracks of the tools are plainly indicated. The rudely formed head in the enlarged details is nicked and scarred with chisels; the welding points of

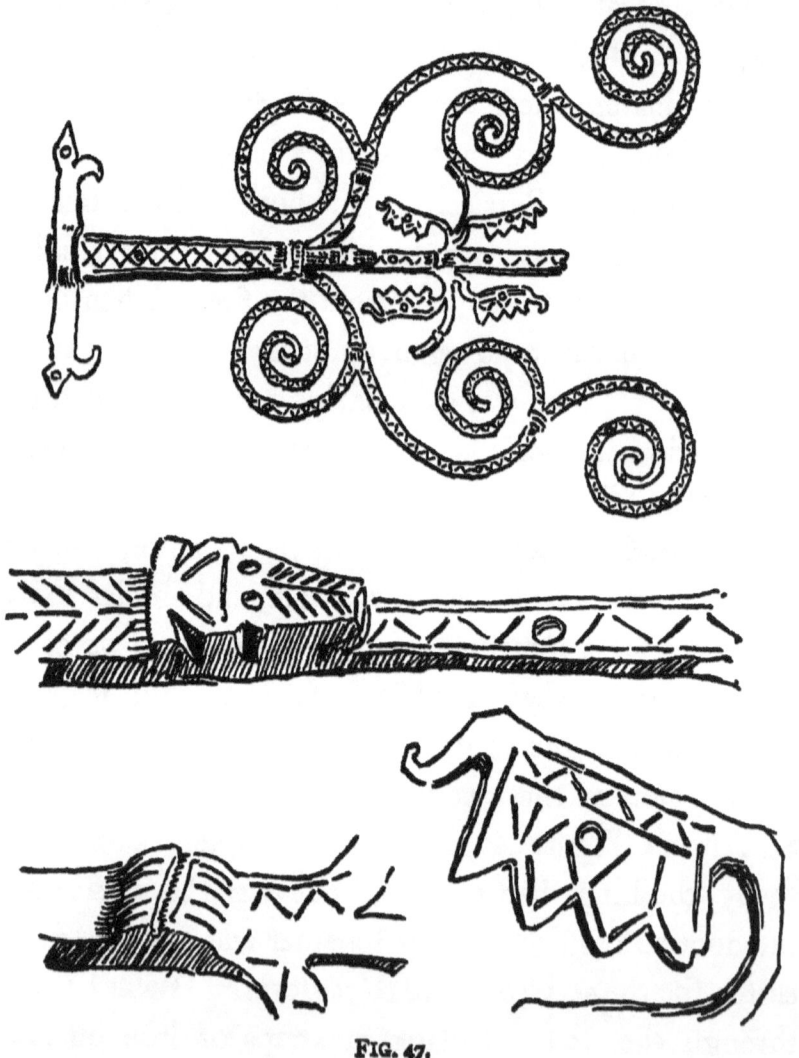

FIG. 47.

FIG. 48.

the various pieces are enriched in a similar way; the surface of the hinge is cut with a simple zigzag pattern. It possesses that organic, intimate, personal quality which none but a tool-trained man could achieve. It is iron, — and looks like iron. In Figure 48 are other typical bits of tool-made ornament, literally split off with the chisel and hammer.

During a period of about two centuries simple, forged ornament of this type continued to be made. In France some ingenious smith devised a method of working that brought a note of variety to the flat treatment generally followed, as may be seen in Figure 49 and Plate 16. The terminating ends were gained by beating the hot metal into swage blocks or

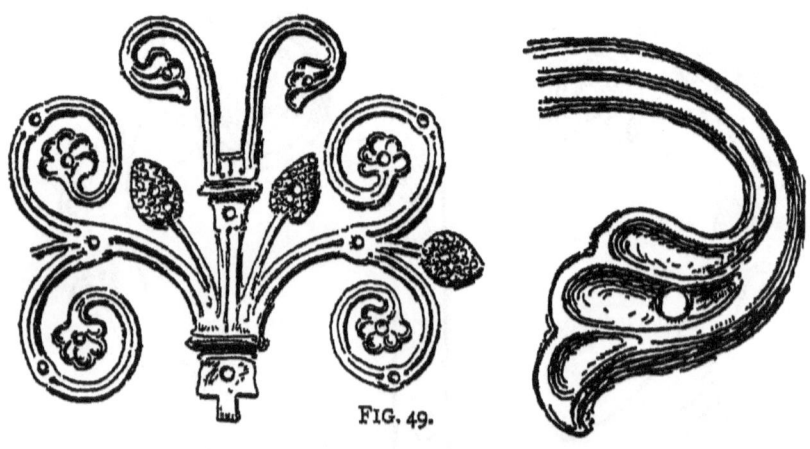

FIG. 49.

dies. It is interesting to trace the wanderings of some craftsman familiar with this method of working into other lands, and the efforts to imitate the work by others unfamiliar with the process. The term *journeyman worker* had a real meaning in those days. Through his handiwork a man established a reputation, and he was often sent for from distant points, followed in the wake of conquest or journeyed on peaceful mission bent, from one town to another. This peculiar type of work offered additional possibilities, culminat-

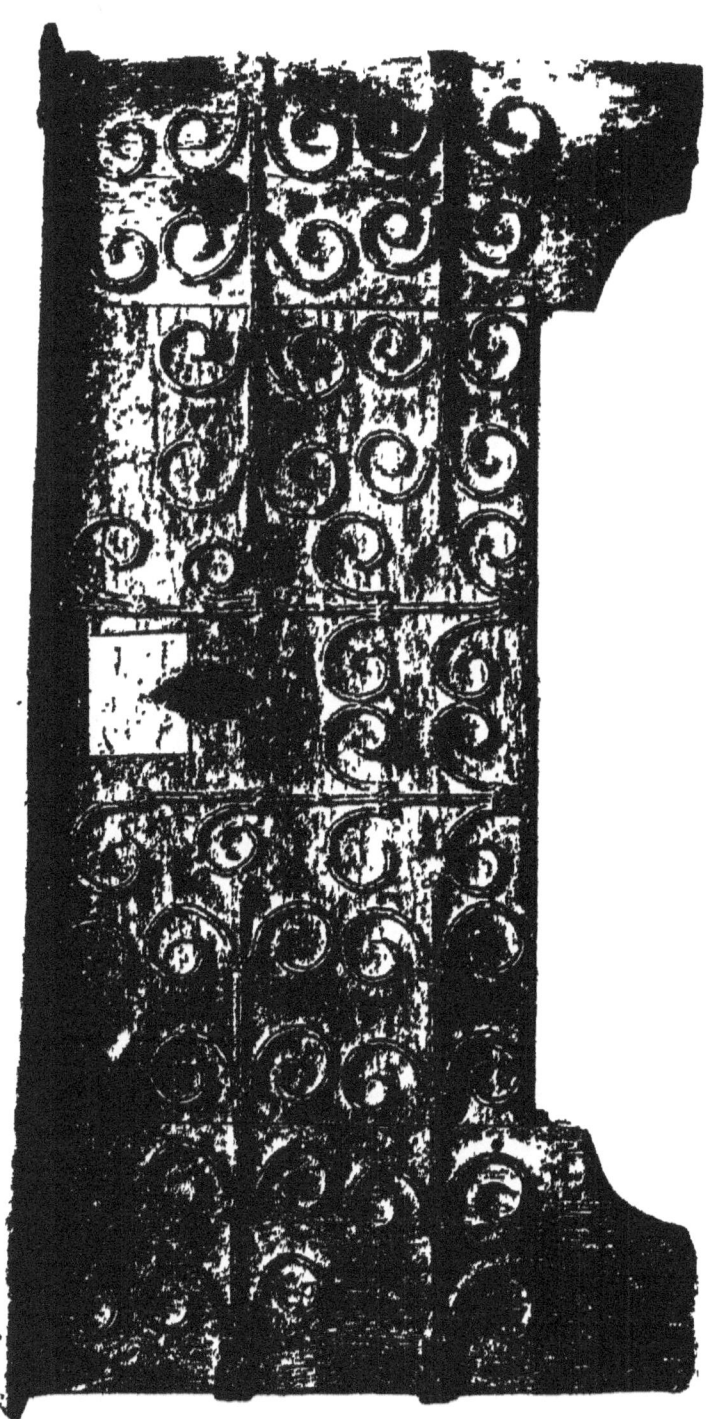

PLATE 16.

THIRTEENTH-CENTURY CHEST — FRENCH. (SOUTH KENSINGTON MUSEUM.)

ing in the wonderful hinges of Notre Dame of Paris, beyond which there seemed no skill to venture. Nothing could serve as a better illustration of the fact that beauty entered into daily work than that these masterly hinges were generally credited to the devil for lack of definite knowledge as to who made them. It was a time when workmen in every craft were capable of rising to the finest achievements in the most unassuming way whenever the opportunity occurred.

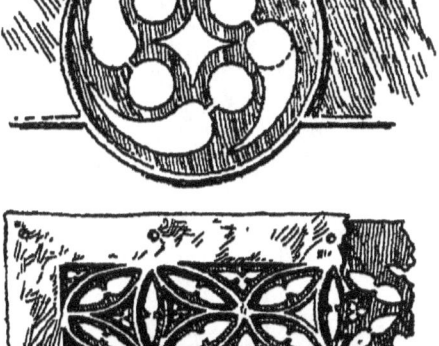

Into the worker's kit there came in due season other tools, such as the drill and file ; and here again we may follow the trail left by these tools through innumerable examples of openwork

FIG. 50.

ornament leading to forms of leafage and intricate traceried patterns. Working on the cold metal was more generally practiced, and the character of the enrichment accordingly underwent a change. The traceried patterns, suggested presumably by the masons, were of rare beauty, often complicated in appearance and of ingenious workmanship (Figure 50).

Plant forms first appear in an abstract way, gradually developing into more specific forms. The worker, with increasing skill and better appliances, turned, as

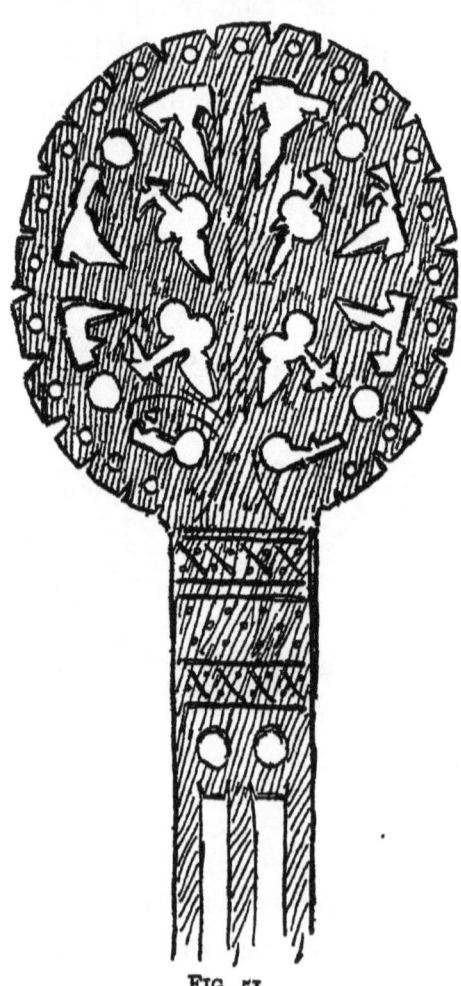

FIG. 51.

does every designer sooner or later, to Nature for assistance. In Figure 51 is a very abstract sort of leafage, just the thing that a workman with punch and cold chisel would shape from a flat piece of metal; it is tool-made Nature. In Figures 52, 53 the tool influence is notable throughout. We may feel sure that the forms of leafage in the early work were first suggested by the iron as it took shape under the hammer rather than from any conscious effort to conventionalize some specific natural form. Abstract leaves, as in Figure 54, would inevitably lead to leaves of a more imitative sort. The

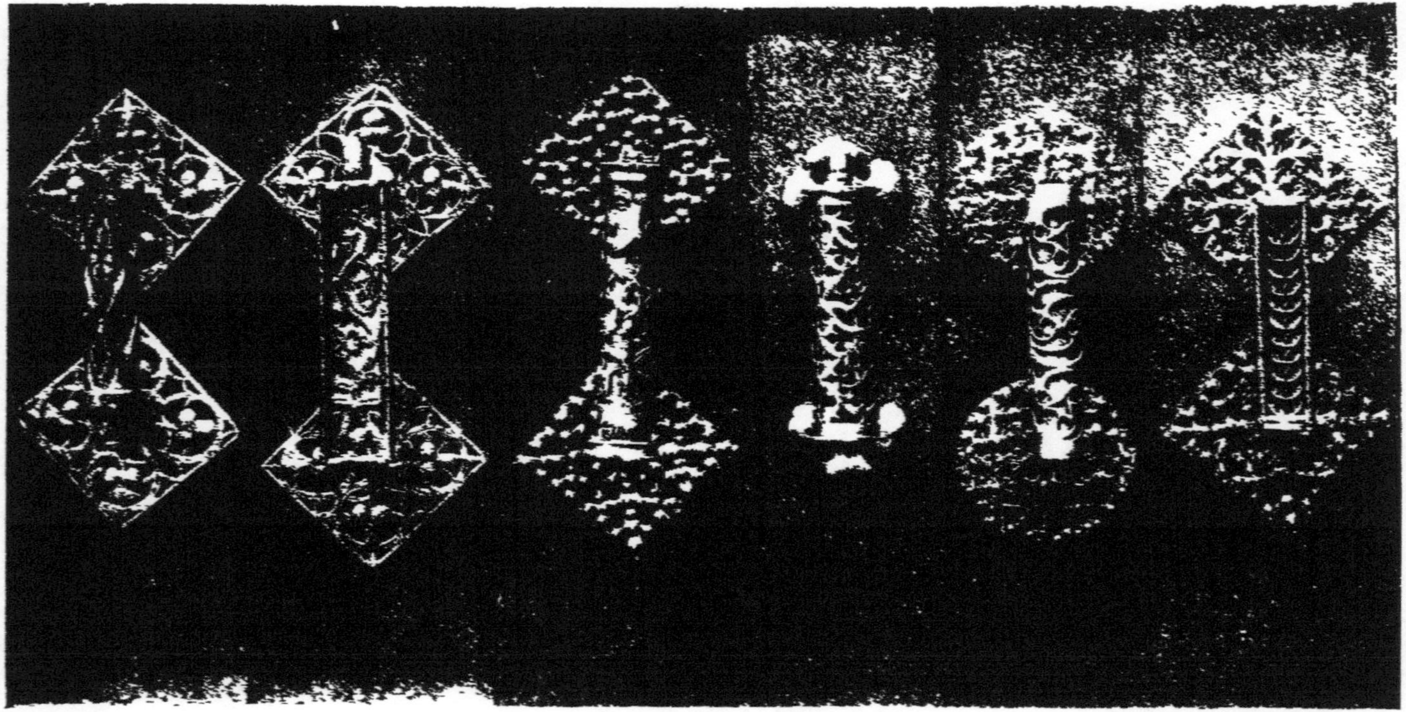

PLATE 17.

GERMAN IRON WORK. (NUREMBERG MUSEUM.)

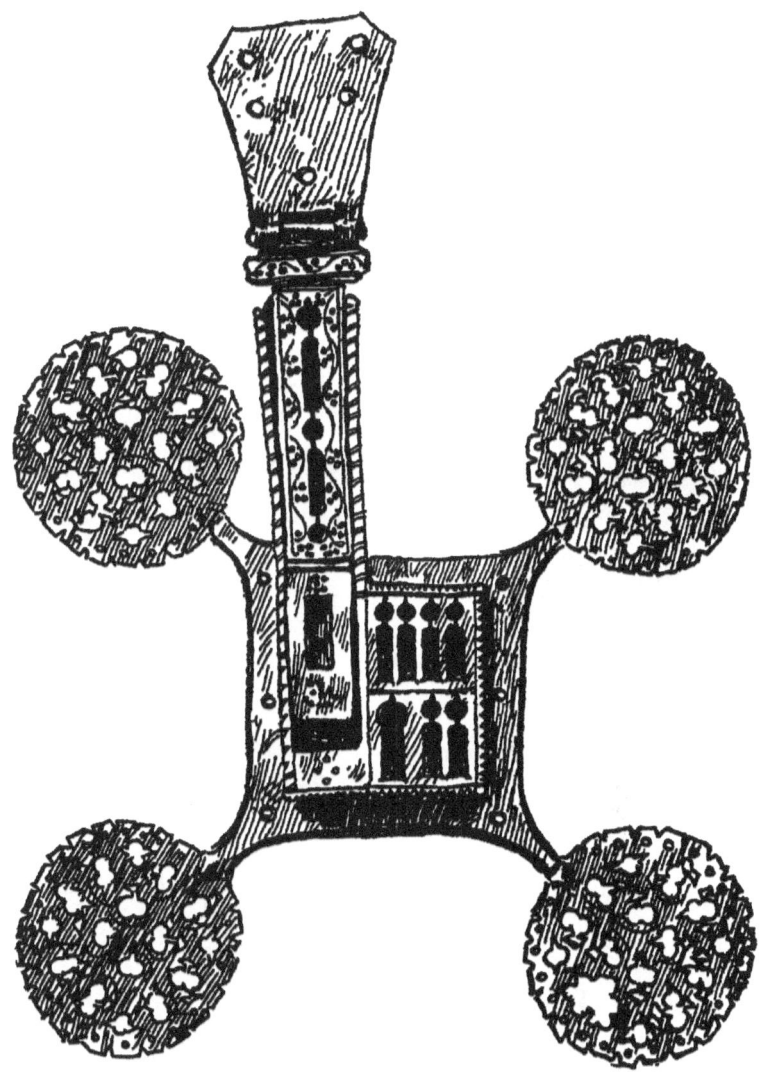

FIG. 52.

hinge ends in Figure 55 illustrate the close relation between tool work of a purely abstract character and tool
work influenced by observation of Nature. In Figure
56 and in the German door pulls of Plate 17 the

I

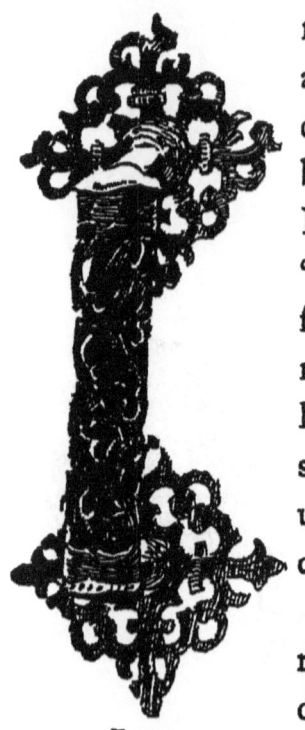

FIG. 53.

refining influence of Nature again appears. For a long time the craftsmen stood at the fascinating borderland between technique and Nature, when it is difficult to say : " This started from the tool ; this from Nature." But even in the most delicately forged and chiseled leaf work we may see how the designer's thought followed closely upon his tools, materials, and processes.

In all these things there is a refreshing vigor, a simplicity, a direct relation between the idea and its execution lost in the work of later years. The rugged quality peculiar to iron gives way to finer finish, to elegance of line and form, and to a close imitation of Nature. The turning point is reached when the iron worker subordinates the technique of his craft to imitative

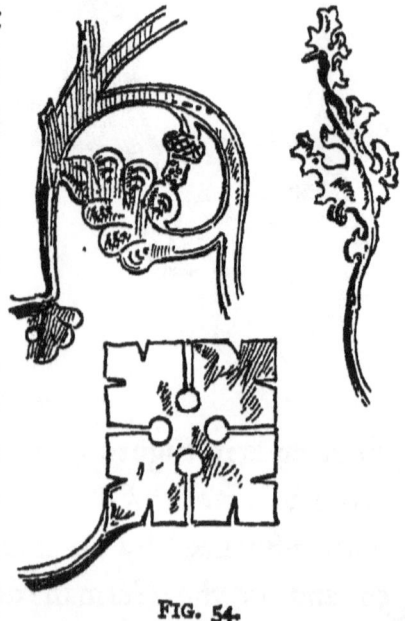

FIG. 54.

work; when he essays the production of such things as may be seen in Figure 57, festooned

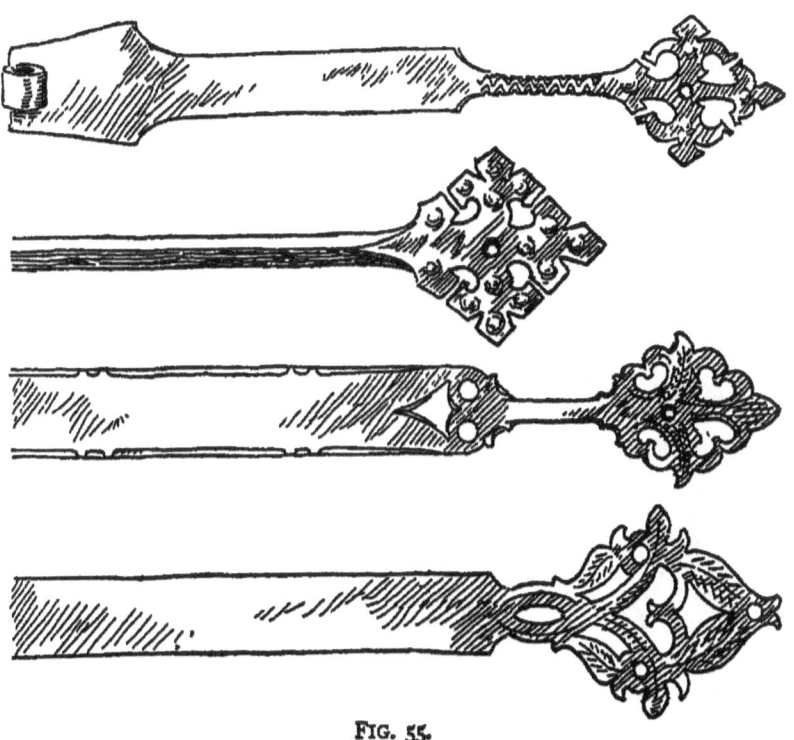

FIG. 55.

garlands of roses with flying ribbons. Whatever there may be of grace and elegance in the result, however consummate the skill of the worker, wind-blown iron ribbons and strings. of naturalistic iron flowers are illogical and inconsistent with the material in which they are executed. Then, when we find that touches of paint were added to enhance the naturalistic appearance of the work, we have arrived at the other extreme of the transition. The iron worker began by drawing upon Nature for suggestions that would add beauty to the structural lines of his design, and ended by subordinating his material to a minor plane of illogical imitation.

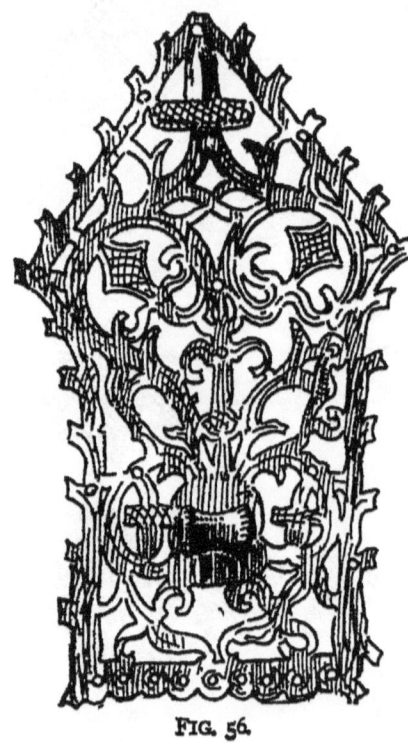

FIG. 56.

PROBLEM. In the definition of principles through abstract work it may be noted that three types of problems are available: A figure inclosed on all sides, such as the square; a figure inclosed on two sides, like the border, but possible of indefinite extension on the two other sides; a pattern which may be indefinitely extended on all sides, like the surface repeats of this problem. As a constructive arrangement of the elements of design the surface pattern demands persistent effort, close attention to space and mass relations, and the rhythmic connection of details to secure unity. Here, as in the previous problem, nothing could be more stupid than the mere repetition of a "unit," leaving to chance the organic relation of the repeats.

The designs in Figure 58, and Plates 18, 19, are not made to meet the technical requirements of print‑ ing or weaving; nor has their construction demanded any knowledge of " drop patterns " or the other

mechanical ques‑ tions which the designer of tex‑ tiles or wall papers must ac‑ cept as limita‑ tions. It is not even contended that these designs are beautiful or that one would care to live with them day by day. They count for " orderly think‑

Rococo Style After Meyer

FIG. 57.

ing "; for constructive skill, as essential to the designer as to the carpenter, under limitations so simple that common sense may be permitted to take precedence over æsthetic " inspiration." The enthusiasm of the amateur is sometimes dampened on the discovery that the study of design is quite as troublesome and arduous a process as the study of music or medicine; that de‑ signs are not inspired during the pleasant interval fol‑

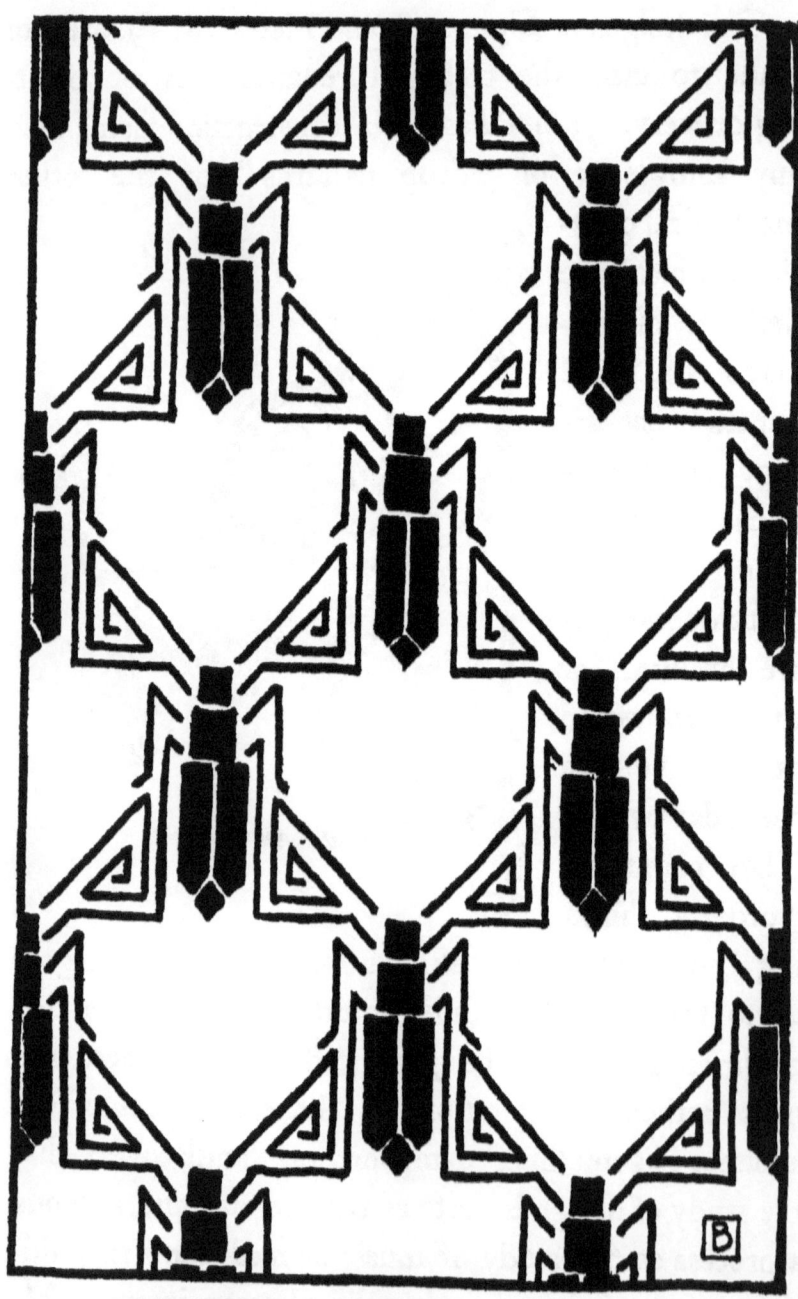

FIG. 58.

lowing lunch, but are built up through the unremitting concentration of every faculty of mind, eye, and hand.

In the development of a surface repeat a " unit " is, of course, necessary ; but of greater necessity is a clearly defined *idea* of what one is trying to achieve with a unit. All that has been said in explanation of previous problems is applicable in principle to the present effort. The motif and limitations are those of the last problem ; the process is the same under slightly different conditions. With a tentative unit in hand draw a vertical line in the center of a sheet of transparent paper and a similar line through the unit itself. A tracing should then be made in the center of the sheet. On two smaller pieces of transparent paper two more tracings of the unit should be made, — four in all. Now, with purpose in mind, try different combinations of these units before committing yourself to the first repeat of the surface pattern. As a problem in design it is now fairly started ; you are in a position to adjust the relations of the pattern as a whole to the end that it

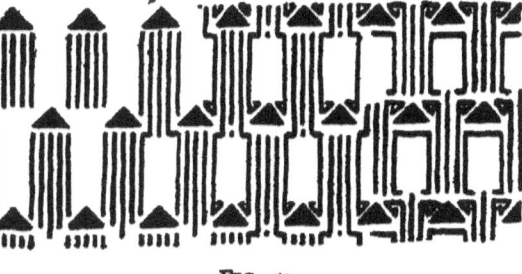

FIG. 59.

may be more than the mere repetition of a unit at regular intervals. Doubtless the unit itself, considered as a detail in a larger whole, will have to be changed. Elasticity of all the details is essential to the building up of the pattern on constructive lines. Figure 59 furnishes a clew to the process. We seek as many rhythmic connections as possible counting for unity with concentration of spaces and masses, each element to contribute a share in the final result.

CHAPTER VII

REFINEMENT OF PROPORTIONS

"But while beauty, in line and mass, may sometimes seem to be curiously confirmed by such tests as these (analysis of proportions), it may be doubtful whether it can be created by them; for elasticity, life and freedom seem to be the essential qualities of true art."

IT is difficult, in the planning, to acquire the habit of thinking of things as a whole; to work from the whole to the parts; and, finally, to consider each part as related to the other parts in a unity of effect. We are prone to adopt the process of the child who drew a button first and then built a man around the button. It takes more than a multiplication of trees and flowers to make a park; more than streets and houses to make a beautiful city. The whole is always more important than any of its parts; or, to put it another way, it takes more than the association of beautiful details to make a beautiful whole. Each detail, like each instrument in an orchestra, has its part to perform. Its proportion, position, character, are relative to other things.

In a constructive problem the first step toward true beauty would be the adjustment of the proportions of the whole. It may be well to note a radical difference between proportions and dimensions. We feel proportions; we measure dimensions. A draughtsman may develop a remarkable facility with the ruler and compass in the laying out of dimensions, yet be without any appreciation or feeling for fine proportions. Proportion is the comparative relations of various dimensions. In any constructive problem our choice of proportions is necessarily limited by the function of the object. In a table or chair, for instance, certain dimensions must be accepted as limitations. Harmonious proportions result when a unity is secured in which all of the measures are intimately related. Says Hegel, "Harmony is a unity, all the terms of which are in interior accord."

Let us illustrate the point: In Figure 60 the first sketch is a square. This, it may be inferred, is more harmonious in its proportions than the other sketches because the terms are identical. The pleasure which we derive from harmony, though, is not in uniformity, but in variations and oppositions bound together by a " manifestation of their reciprocal agreement." Harmony and contrast, unity and variety, — these are not terms of opposite meaning. Contrast is the spice that gives interest to harmony. Unity with variety in-

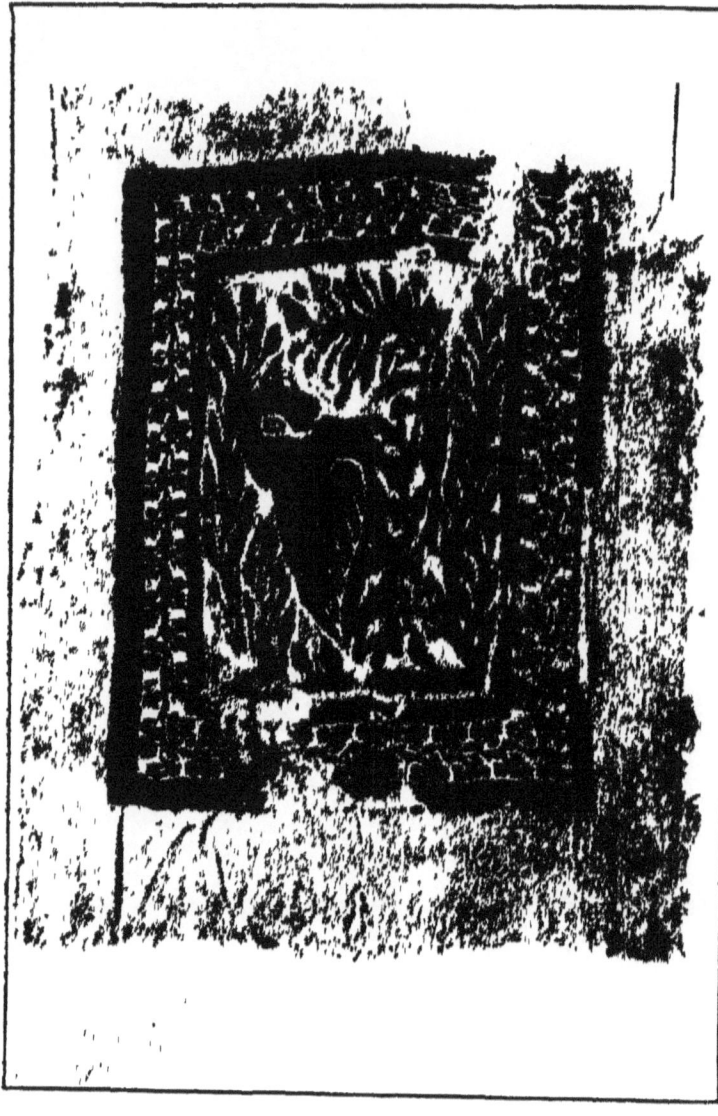

PLATE 20.

COPTIC WEAVING. (METROPOLITAN MUSEUM.)

terests us; but with uniformity our interest ceases.
Even uniformity though, as a relative factor, may be
well justified. In *B* there is variety; but we are
troubled by a lack of clearness. It is almost, though
not quite, a square. It was said that a design must be

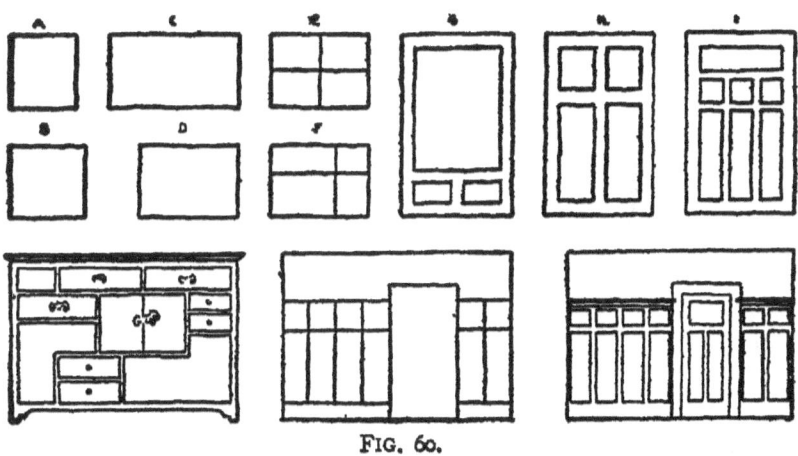

FIG. 60.

clear and coherent in expresssion. In practice this
also may be justified; as, for instance, in Plate 20 one
surely has no desire to attempt an improvement upon
this weaver's idea. In *C* (Figure 60) the square is
doubled, giving an agreement of terms that is obvious.
Continuing to *D* are proportions more subtle, though
bound together by a dominant unit of measure, "the
rhythmic half." One half of the end goes three times
in the side. Considering these four sketches in the
abstract, it may be said that *D* excites our interest
more and holds it longer than the others; it is clear
without being too obvious; it is a harmony of con-

trasts. Suppose we wish to break this rectangle into space divisions. In *E* we approach uniformity again with a consequent loss of interest. In *F* is a more interesting breaking that gives unequal but related areas. With the next step, *G*, the line of safety has been overstepped; the divisions are not only unequal, but are unrelated as well. In *H* there is a return to a sane expression of the idea, continued through further subdivisions in the final sketch.

Note the subtle relations of line and space in the old Korean cabinet shown in the same figure. There is no possible element of chance in it; the designer has achieved beauty through a thoughtful adjustment of proportions. Carry the principle into the setting out of the end of a room; if more thought were given this subject, architects might find more appreciative clients. The question pursues us to the last scrap of ornament that we may choose to employ. Secure variety, but remember that in variety alone there is no merit. There must be coördination of all the parts to make a whole.

It is not the purpose to enter into a prolonged discussion of good proportions, but rather to direct attention to the importance of this point and then develop the significance of the principle as the work progresses. Many ingenious theories and systems have been devised to explain the proportions employed by the Greek and mediæval builders. Any one particularly interested in a scientific demonstration of the subject and the various systems involved should consult such a reference as Gwilt's "Encyclopedia of Architecture." There is no doubt that the builders of the past used various geometric schemes for proportioning a building; it is a logical method. In mediæval times builders were architects, and the elaborate working drawings of to-day were unknown. Cathedrals were built as one might build with blocks. Giotto's Campanile was formed of six cubes, one placed on another. In a similar way we may analyze the proportions of many churches and temples. A unit of measure dominates the whole and the parts. That some dominant unit of measure may be felt, though not necessarily measured, or advertised, as in the Greek fret, seems a logical conclusion from an analysis of many examples of satisfying things.

Let us study some definite instances (Figure 61). A familiar example is found in the Greek fret, so called, though as a matter of fact it was invented sooner or later by nearly all primitive people who practiced the art of weaving. This fret comes perilously near to the obvious; the dominant unit of measure is given advertisement. But it illustrates the statement that it is generally unsatisfactory and unwise to isolate a scrap of ornament from its surroundings.

This fret was often employed in positions where it served as a contrast to other features. The very things that seem monotonous were highly desirable under those conditions. Again, when carved in stone, sunlight and shadow must be taken into account. Below it is the setting out of one type of a Greek

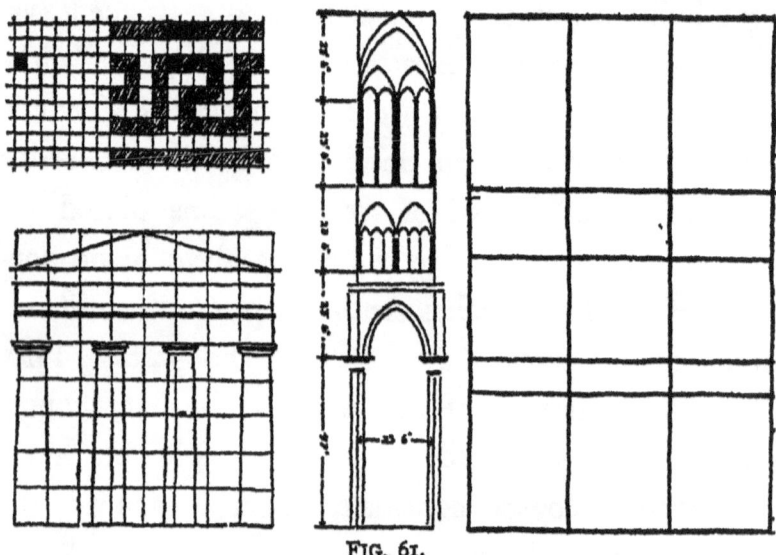

FIG. 61.

temple. Here the unit of measure is less apparent, though quite insistent. In the center is a section from Amiens Cathedral with more spice of variety, yet under the restraint of a dominant measure welding the parts together into unity. At the right is the setting-out scheme of Notre Dame in Paris. The dignity and grandeur of the structure as a whole is dependent on these big relations first established. In this general scheme each detail plays its part.

In Figure 62 is a Greek vase form. We feel that it is right without worrying it with a yardstick. There is no possible desire to change a line, a curve, or a space. That it fulfills its function may be known from paintings and sculptures in which the use of this particular type of vase is portrayed. Then it must be beautiful, else where should we expect to find beauty? In the means employed to gain this singular

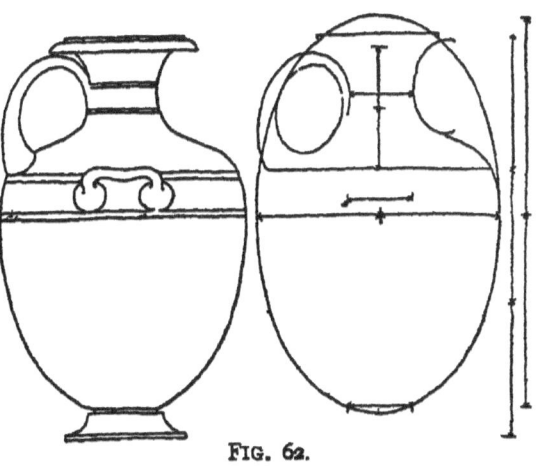

FIG. 62.

charm we have, as students, an interest. The diagram explains itself. Compare some of the measures noted and consider how very important this master designer deemed the question of proportions. Note again the harmony of curves used throughout; the same curve varying in proportions.

In Figure 63 is a Gothic crédence after a sketch by Viollet-le-Duc. A miniature representation of this piece of furniture appears in one of the scenes on the carved choir screen at Amiens. There is no excuse for imitating its superficial details; it would be better to trace its beauty back to the source. The first test is in the elimination of its ornament. Is its beauty gone? Far from it. A tree is still beautiful after its leaves have fallen; when the poppy is gone, the seed pod remains; more, it was for the sake of the seed pod that the poppy was given its transient beauty. The charm of the crédence is not in its ornament, but in the con-

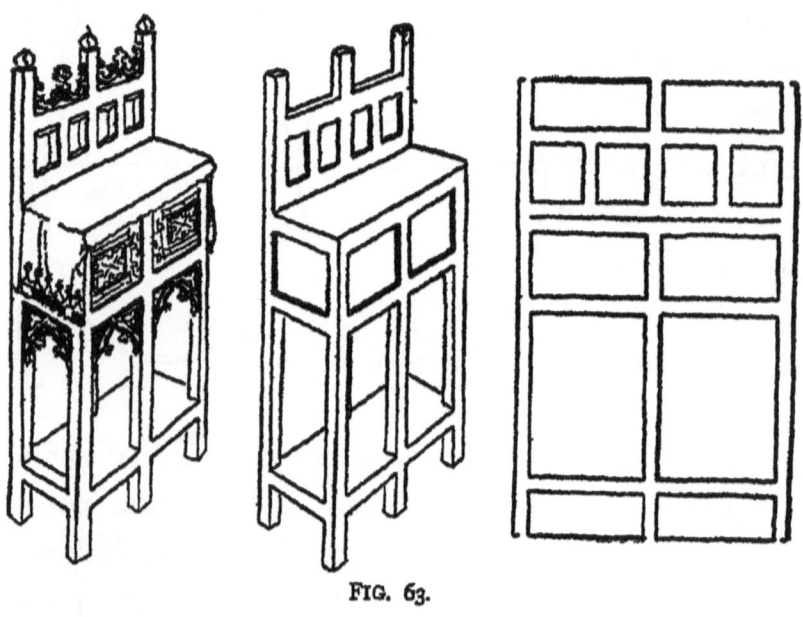

FIG. 63.

structive relations of which the ornament is merely a part. In the adjustment of these constructive elements, in the "reciprocal agreement" of all the parts, is the mainstay of its beauty. Last of all, though first in importance, does it adequately fill the purpose for which it was made? Now reverse the process and follow it up to the last shred of ornament, and we have the logical development of any

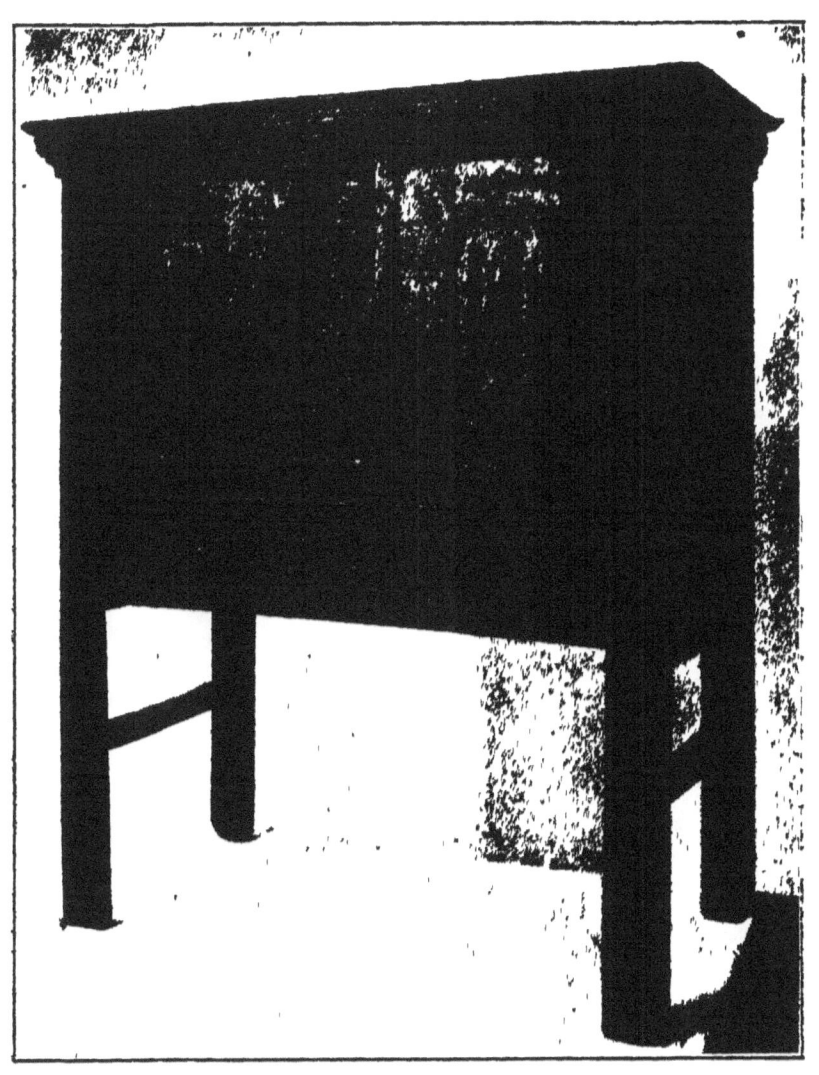

PLATE 21.

MEDIÆVAL CABINET WORK. (METROPOLITAN MUSEUM.)

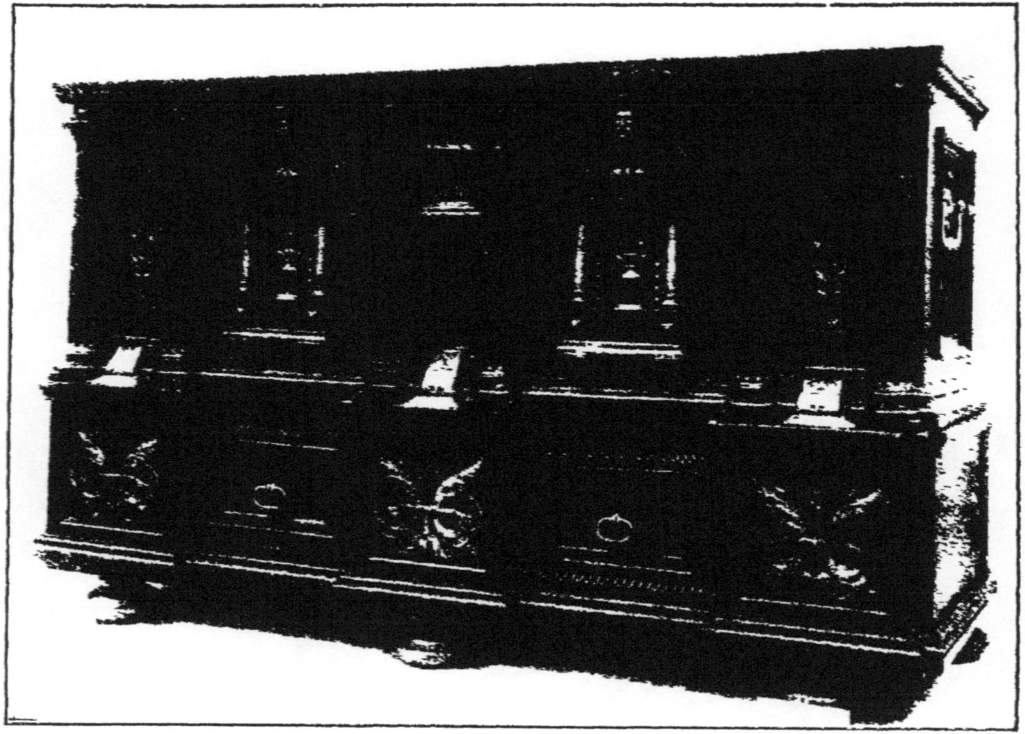

PLATE 22.

CABINET WORK — DECADENT IN DESIGN.

constructive design. Nature teaches us that parts
which differ in function should
differ in appearance. With
this in mind note the way in
which the ornament is used.

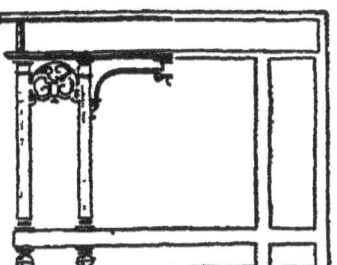

Plate 21 is a conspicuous
example of well-related proportions, the practical and the
æsthetic bound together, as
must ever be the case in a
constructive problem. In
Figure 64 are other schemes
showing the setting out of
proportions and the continued
subdivision of forms into details of ornament. It is this
process that results in "built-
in" ornament. As a startling
comparison with these simple,
organic, restful things examine
the cabinet in Plate 22. Here
a sense of oneness is lost in a
jumble of unrelated details;
too many elements clamor for
attention. Much of the or-

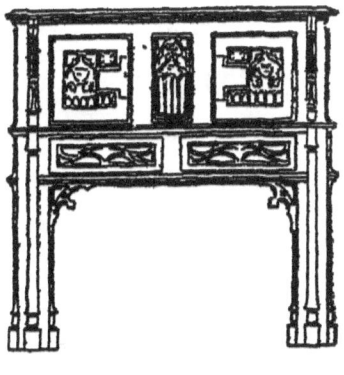

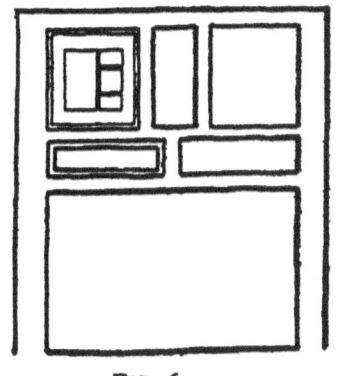

FIG. 64.

nament might be lost or mislaid and one would never
miss it; it is not organic enrichment; it is *built-on*

K

ornament, not *built-in ornament.* Skilled technique has outbalanced fine discrimination.

As a study in the proportion of parts and the distribution of space and mass nothing could be finer than Plate 23. It is a piece of Coptic weaving, a masterpiece of the highest order. Study it as a dark and light composition; it leaves nothing to be desired. Similar in character is Plate 20, a splendid adjustment of proportions and relative interests.

In the planning of proportions we may adopt the logical method of the Greek potter in Figure 62, or we may depend upon intuition, as doubtless did the Coptic weavers. In either case we are led to the same conclusion: proportions in the final test are felt, not measured; and no amount of ingenious juggling with ruler and compass will establish harmonious proportions if the sensitive feeling for them is not within us. Lacking this feeling, there is no theory *par excellence* by which good proportions may be obtained at all times and on all occasions; no system on which we may hobble about as if it were a crutch. We, too, may design a temple and invent some ingenious formula for the purpose, — only to find when it is completed that it is wholly bad and uninteresting. That intuition which *feels* good proportions may be cultivated only through persistent study and practice. Many experiments of an abstract nature may be tried with profit,

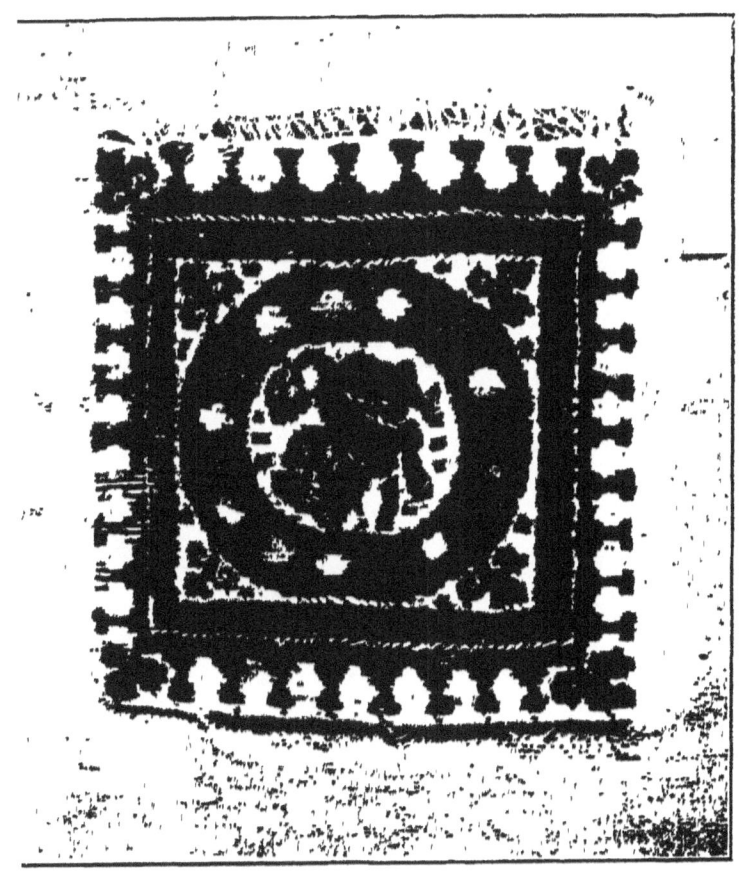

PLATE 23.

COPTIC WEAVING. (METROPOLITAN MUSEUM)

for it is not alone through observation but through experiments and comparisons that one's judgment is strengthened. Such little things as those indicated in Figure 65 may make all the difference in the world between a "carpenter-made" chest and a piece of furniture that challenges one's attention through harmony with contrast, unity with variety, in the scheming of the relative proportions involved.

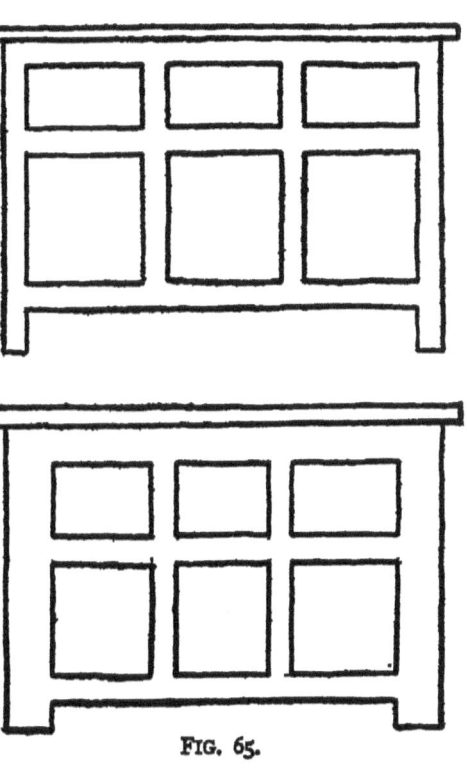

FIG. 65.

Let us note the application of the idea to a definite problem, — a jewelry casket. Its construction involves the use of wood, leather, and metal. In Figures 66, 67 the general form and proportions are assumed and the structural elements indicated. The function of each part is emphasized, body, cover, feet, hinges, handles, and clasp; the relative proportions of these parts of wood, leather, and metal to the proportions of the whole is decided upon. In an acceptance of these elements we have the clews for a consistent design. In such a problem it is, of course, necessary to think in terms of three dimensions. A cover, a side, an end, each good in itself, may not make a good whole. It is the relation of these three that counts.

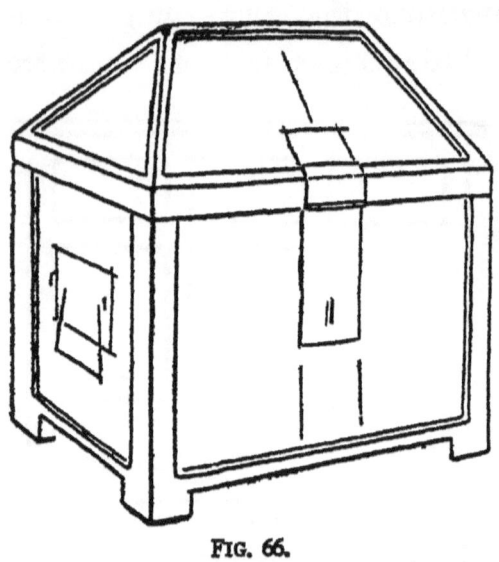

FIG. 66.

In Plate 24, the first example, a very simple refinement of the structural elements is shown. Dominant interest is given to the metal work; to this all else is subordinate. The metal handles, hinges, and clasp furnish the clew for the space divisions of the body and cover. Each func-

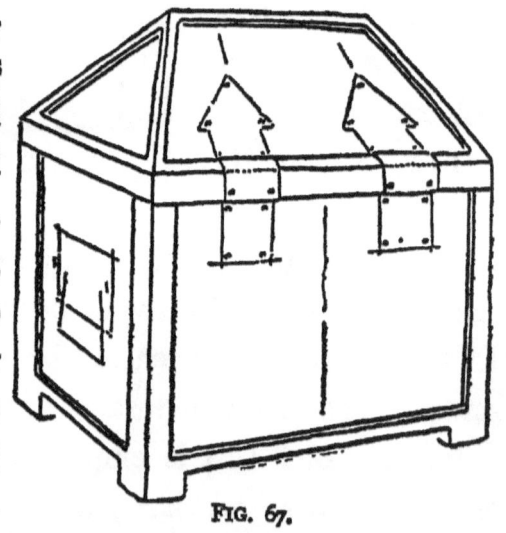

FIG. 67.

tional element is strengthened and emphasized by the parallel lines tooled on the surface of the leather; the

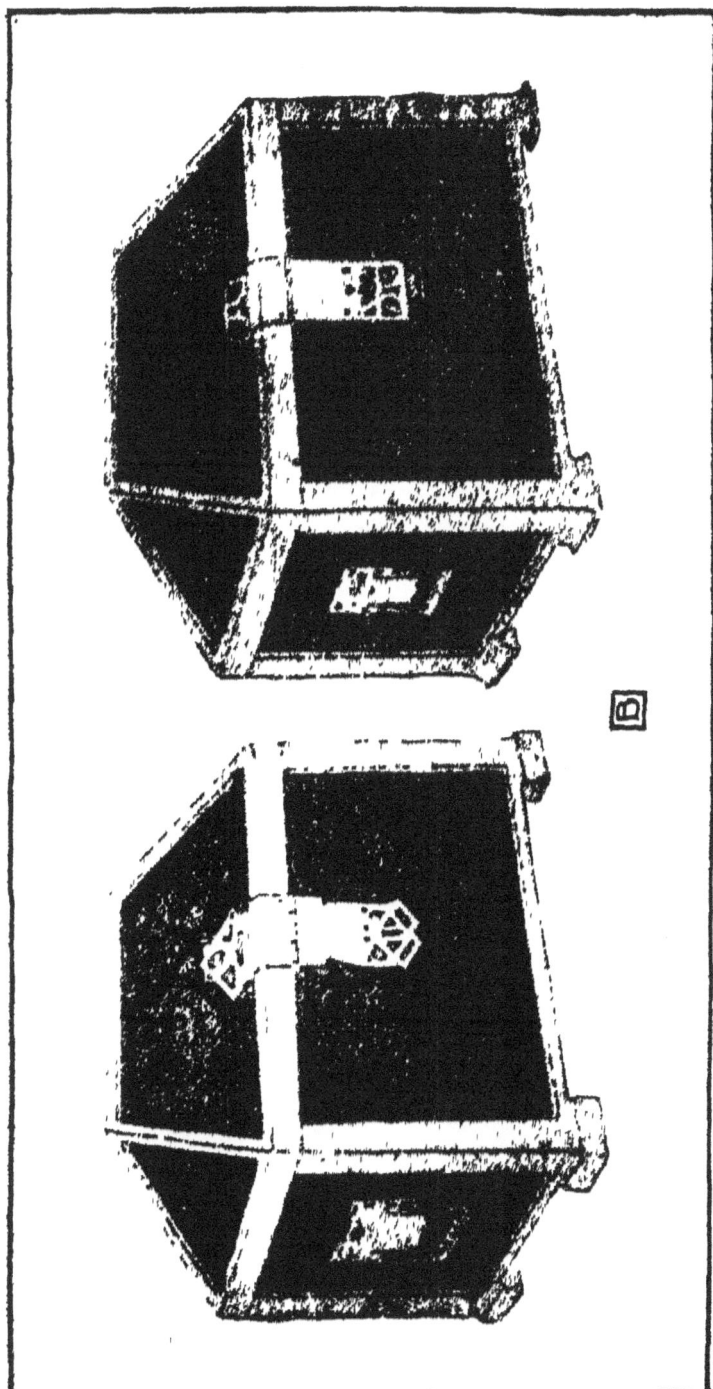

PLATE 24.

CONSTRUCTIVE DESIGNING.

angles are strengthened and a note of variety given to the tooling by a slight opposition of lines.   In the second example of Plate 24 an enrich-ment of a more complex character is suggested; but the development from the whole to the parts (Figure 68) is the same as in the simpler   example. Whatever the char-

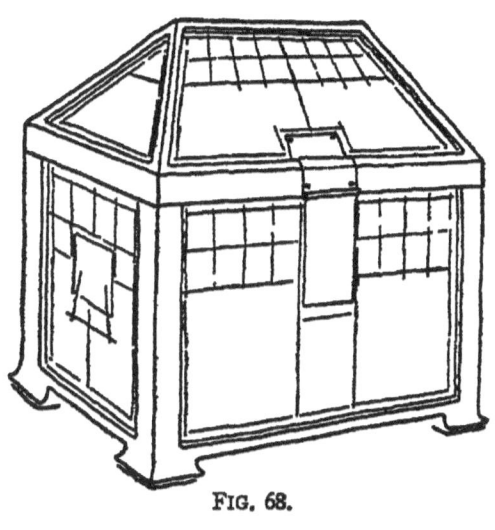

FIG. 68.

acter of the enrichment, it must be organically related

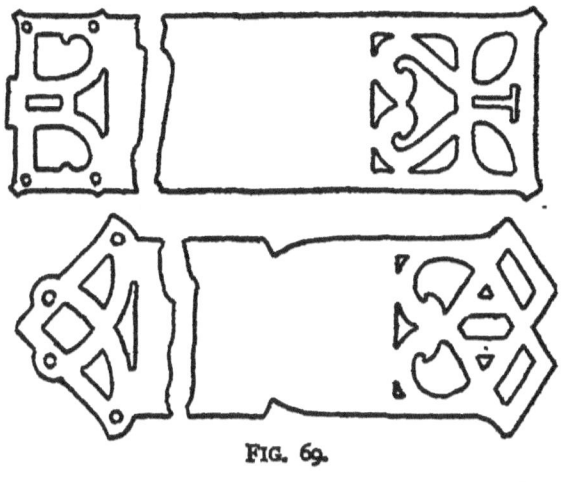

FIG. 69.

to the struc-tural elements, of which it is merely a part.

Now, in or-der to justify the interest which is directed to the metal work, it should,   of course, be given thoughtful attention.   With punch, drill, saw, and file, holes might be cut to define a pattern or framework (Figure 69).   The lines of this pattern should be bound together so that there would be no loose ends or sharp points. The interest may be primarily in the lines of the pattern, though it is necessary to keep in mind that the holes must have variety in shapes and measures, and must not be left to group themselves awkwardly.

To the mediæval craftsman metallic features of any kind were accepted as structural necessities in his design. He seized upon them joyfully, gloried in them, wrought them with all the loving care of an artist. About them he built his panels; to them he made the lines of his carving conform. But now we of a more enlightened age call them " hardware." The door fixtures, handles, lock plates, which were the joy of the old craftsmen, which men once deemed worthy of their best thought and effort, are now a cheap and brassy mockery. The blight of modern commercialism has descended upon them. They are ugly and unlovely because to make them beautiful would demand deep and earnest thought; and the only evidence of thought to be found in our hardware is of a mechanical origin; for the rest we seek diligently to cheapen the material, cheapen the process of manufacture, cheapen and degrade the workman, — and from this array of cheapness beauty flees as from a plague. Beauty has demanded ever that men shall question, " How thoroughly and with what thought and feeling may this piece of work be fashioned?" not "How cheaply may the job be finished and how much of sham and pretense may enter into its execution?" There are bits of metal work on the doors of houses in some of the old German towns with an honest beauty sufficient to stampede all of our pretentious modern hardware back to the melting pots. Those things possess a human interest because they were fashioned to meet the demands of adequate service; but, more than this, because those who made and used them were impelled to rise through and beyond all demands of immediate necessity to the expression of some sentiment or feeling in all that became a part of daily life and work.

Study the hinge as developed by Gothic craftsmen (Figure 70). With a broad, firm hold it clings to the casing for support, and reaches out across the door to grasp it in a strong, secure clutch. It must be actually strong; but it must also convince us of its strength. This is always an important consideration in design. A functional element must be adequate for the service it is expected to perform; but that it is adequate must be made apparent to the eye. We must feel its strength. The leg of a table might be so strengthened that it could be made comparatively small in diameter; but the result would be unsatisfactory because it would not assure us that it possessed the strength necessary to support a burden. The hinge clutches the door by means of screws or bolts. Thus, while the hinge itself is functional, it in turn must conform in line and form to the elements which secure it to the door. In

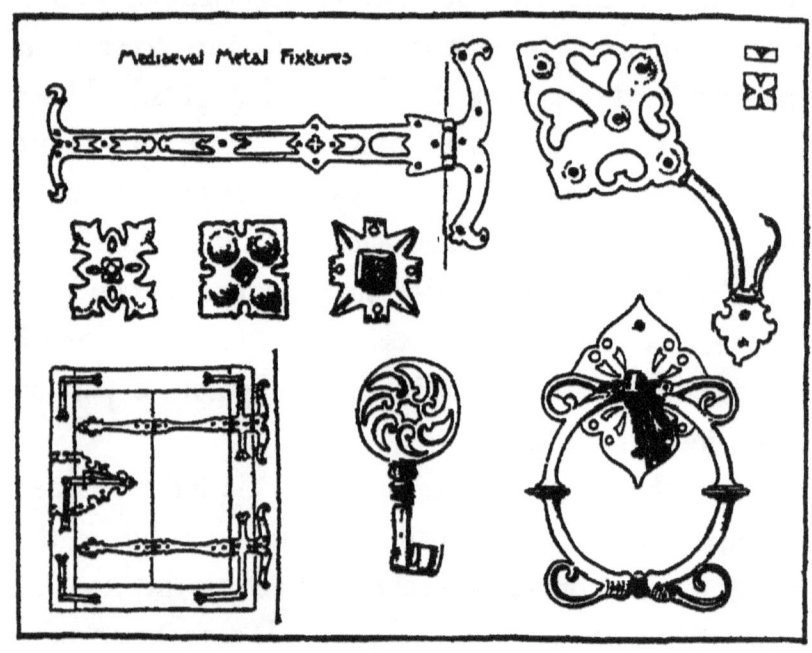

FIG. 70.

other words, the only structural reason for designing the hinge is to give position to a certain number of screws or bolts. Note in Figure 70 that the curve on the casing is so fashioned that the screws will not all enter the same grain of the wood. This would tend to split the casing and destroy the value of the hinge. A piece of work is not finished until the last scrap of detail has been accounted for. If a washer appears in the design, it should be given a distinctive beauty of its own.   Even the head of a bolt may be given interest by the judicious use of a file. Keys, knockers, handles, — to hide them from sight or to ignore the claims which they have, or to shirk the possibilities which they offer is a confession of our inability to design on the basis of adequate service.

PROBLEM. To think of Nature in terms of design is one of the difficult tasks that confronts the student. As the beauty and interest of the design is not in the motif or subject-matter chosen, but in the constructive relations of lines, forms, and tones, it would seem desirable, before approaching Nature for assistance, to acquire through practice the habit of working from a design point of view. The term *conventionalization* unfortunately conveys to many the idea of worrying some natural specimen into an unnatural appearance, of putting Nature into a strait-jacket, as it were, through a process that tends to rob the original motif of its peculiar, often transient, charm without supplying that other subtle charm from which a design derives strength and character. Students frequently seek help from Nature before they have learned to think from a design point of view; and having little to take to Nature, they receive little in return.

It is the thought of the present problem to develop a design from an abstract symbol suggesting plant form,

though not "based on" any particular natural specimen. The symbol may be stated as *three berries —
two leaves*. The limitations are the same as in the
last problem, lines having the directions of the vertical
and horizontal, right and left oblique forty-five degrees.

The possibilities of any design are to be sought in
its limitations, — to shirk or ignore them is to form a
dangerous habit. The wise designer generally seeks
his limitations first. In practice they are from constructive or technical reasons. There are two reasons
for the arbitrary imposition of limitations in these problems; one is to simplify matters in order that a rhythmic
interrelation of details may be assured and a harmony
acquired through the recurrence of certain clearly defined lines; the other is purely a matter of discipline.

The demonstrations to the present point have been
sufficiently detailed to require no further explanation
of the method to be employed in building up such designs as those shown in Figure 71, and Plates 25, 26.
The four inclosed figures in the last plate have been
chosen with purpose. Study them carefully with these
thoughts in mind: (1) Each result is complete in
itself. (2) There are three things to consider in each,
— the center, the sides, the corners. (3) Note the
proportion of space to mass in each. (4) Note the
shape relation of the space to the inclosing form.
(5) Note the different positions of the dominant interest

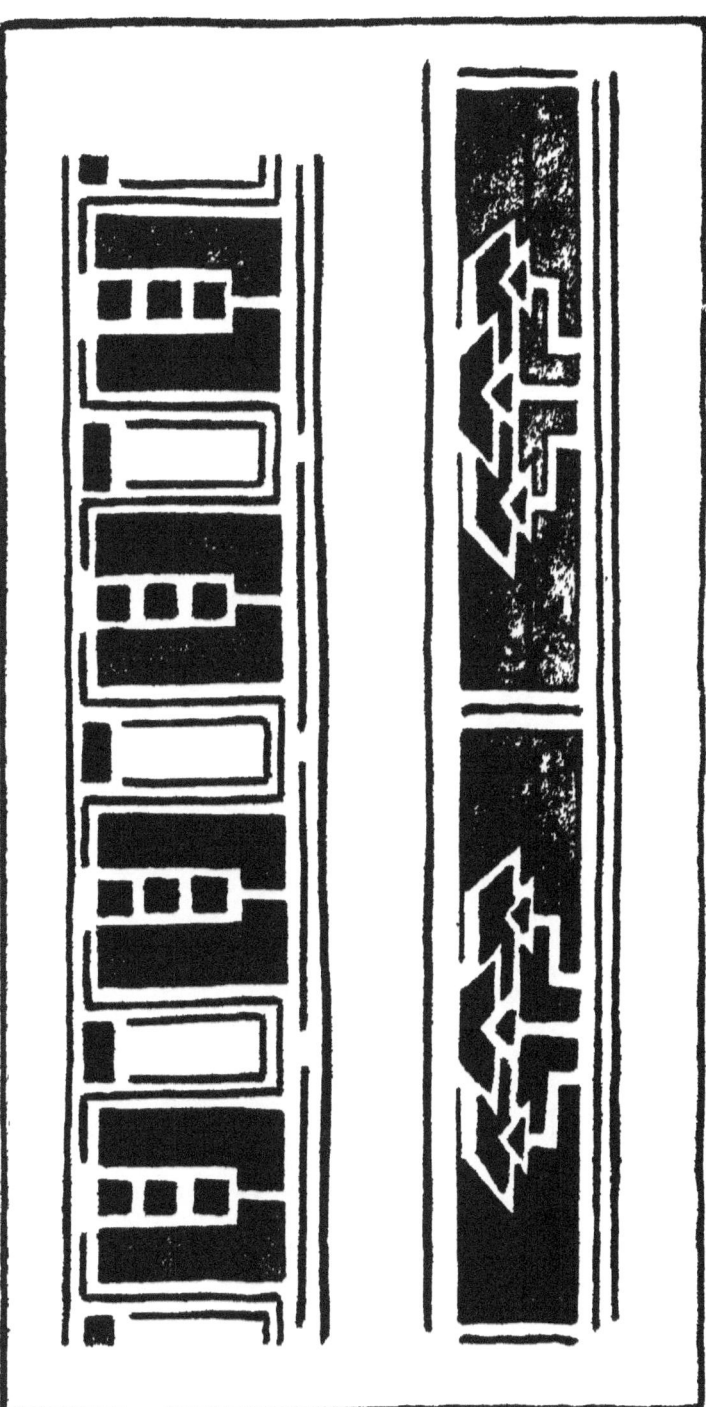

PLATE 25.

NATURE SYMBOLS IN THREE VALUES.

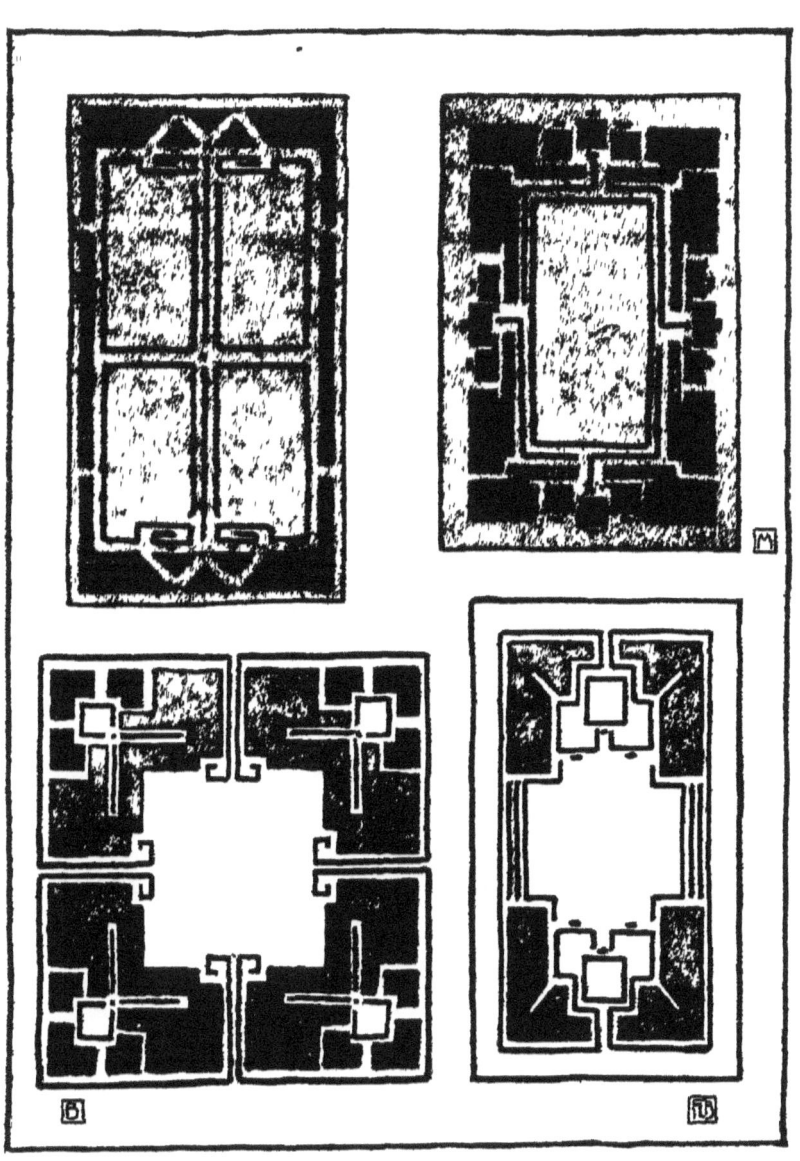

PLATE 26.

NATURE SYMBOLS.

in each secured through the concentration or grouping of unique shapes, or from tone contrast, or both.

Let us utilize another factor that may contribute to the interest of the problems, — the adjustment of tone

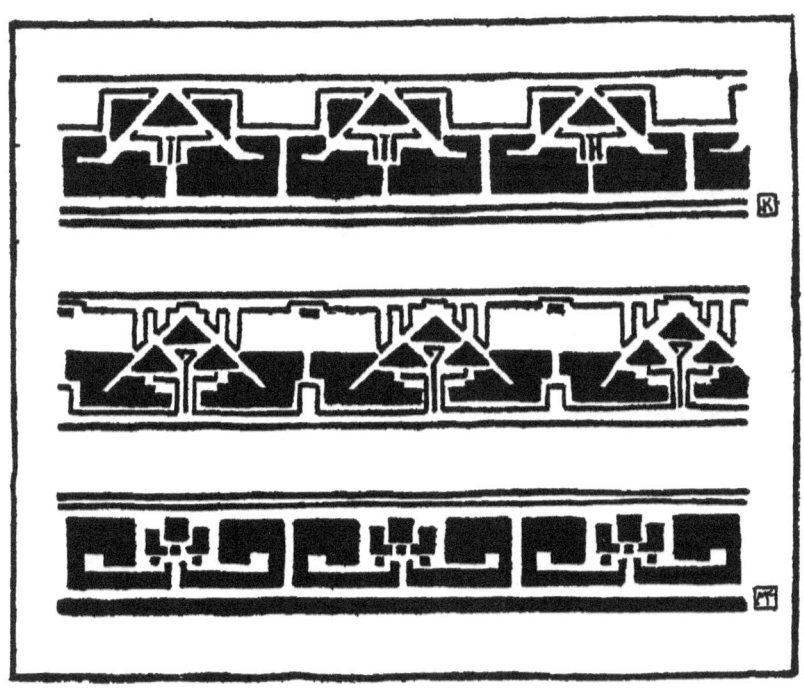

FIG. 71.

relations. The " charcoal gray," as mentioned in the preface, is a neutral pigment. With this pigment and varying amounts of water it will be found that a grada-tion of tone can be made from black to white. It is desirable for purposes of study to render this gradation in a series of definite notes. The number of distinct value notes which the eye can discriminate is surprisingly few, probably not more than twenty-five. It will simplify matters to choose a scale of five notes of gray corresponding to the scale in Figure 3. This may be referred to as the value scale; the value of a tone, whatever its color may be, means the relative position it bears to black or white. Such a scale of values is shown in Plate 2. It seems unnecessary to explain how it is made; its mechanism has been so often explained in other publications that the scale now may be accepted as a fact accomplished. It is enough to emphasize the importance of the half note as the key to the scale, midway in *value*, as well as position, between the extremes. It will be seen that ten different value schemes of three notes each are possible with this simple instrument.

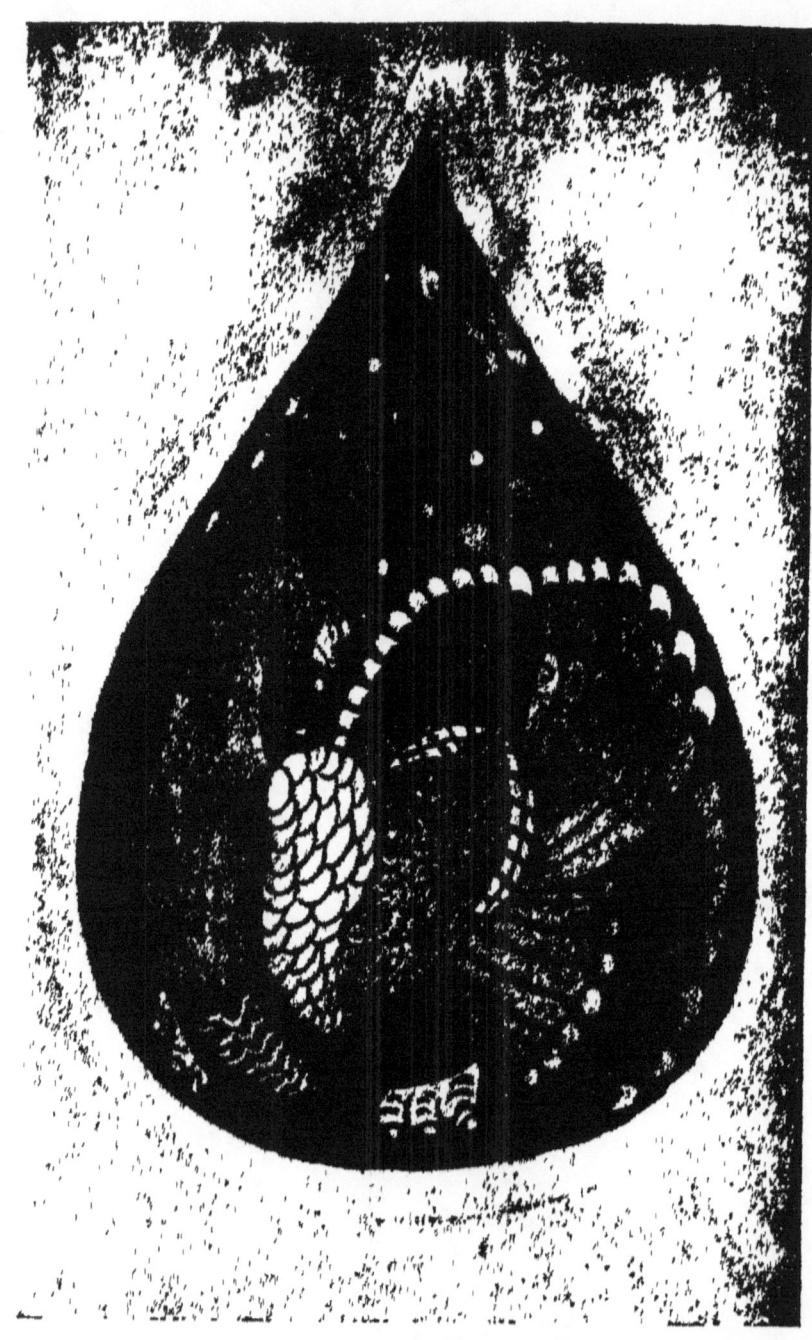

PLATE 65.

PEACOCK DERIVATIVE.

CHAPTER VIII

THE PLAY IMPULSE

"When man no longer finds enjoyment in work, and works merely to attain as quickly as possible to enjoyment, it is a mere accident that he does not become a criminal."
— THEODOR MOMMSEN.

THERE is a peculiar and never failing source of interest in that type of work which has an element of the grotesque in its make-up. If we were to remove from the field of art all that is of a grotesque nature, we would lose much that has appealed to human sympathy, much that has given joy and pleasure to the producers. There are few things indeed that approach the height which a philosophy of art defines as ideal; and if we in a study of art history examine only those things which achieve the ideal, we shall miss, through lack of sympathy and understanding, many things that are real and vital. We generally try to read into art that which we think should be there in the light of our own thought and experience; it is difficult to place one's self in the position of the man who produced a piece of work. We learn much *about* art; but the information acquired often fails to respond to our own environment and needs. Information about art is vastly different from artistic feeling. We pass over much that possesses fresh interest, real significance, because our experience has not been such that we are in a position to appreciate that bubbling over of the play impulse which comes to those engaged in creative work under favorable conditions. We seek those things that have become crystallized into a " period " or " style " which may be conveniently labelled and classified in our minds, but have no formula that enables us to follow the trail of art through humble, unclassified products which are often strong and insistent with personality.

Broadly noted the grotesque is of two sorts: that which is purposeful, intended to incite laughter or fear; that which is unintentional, the result of incomplete observation or unskilled technique.

It is always necessary to draw a distinction between the wholesome grotesque, which arises from a spontaneous and irresistible play impulse, and the unwholesome grotesque, which proceeds from a determination to be bizarre and unique at any cost, descending to ribaldry and insolent jest in the effete and waning days of the Renaissance, and in much that we call Art Nouveau of the present day. The wholesome grotesque comes straight from the heart; its appeal is to that side of human nature which makes all the world akin. There is in it the same quality that is found in the work of children who, at certain ages, express themselves with pencil or brush in a way that is free and genuine. We can find nothing of interest in the child's work unless we have a sympathetic understanding of the spirit in which it was produced. The unwholesome grotesque is of a self-conscious sort; lacking imagination the worker seeks to devise senseless, formless shapes disclaiming law and order, leering figures terminating in floral or vegetable growths, an incongruous association of ideas and motifs.

In primitive art, in the work of the mediæval craftsmen, and in many phases of Oriental art, the wholesome grotesque is found at its best. The pleasure which men derived from their work is reflected in every stroke of the hammer or cut of the chisel. We are entertained, even amused, by playful fancies, by a naïve and spontaneous touch. Figure 72, from Peru, and Figure 73, the work of a mediæval blacksmith, are typical examples of the wholesome grotesque. Those men were not striving after unattainable ideals; nor were they

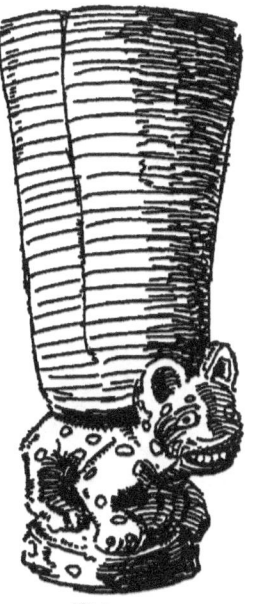

FIG. 72.

hampered in the expression of their thought by the fear of breaking some precedent; they were pleased with their jobs and brought to their daily problems such unaffected invention, wholesome sense, and honest craftsmanship as they could.

Similar in character are the sketches in Figure 74 from an old Byzantine hunting horn, and in Figure 75 of the twelfth century. If there was any humor in a situation, those men might be depended upon to depict it.

It is true that much in primitive and mediæval art that appeals to our sense of humor may not have been intended by the makers to be of a humorous nature. There are many rude designs that had a significant message to people of contemporary times, long since lost to us. It is sometimes difficult to say whether a given design was intended to be quaintly grotesque or was symbolic in character.

FIG. 73.

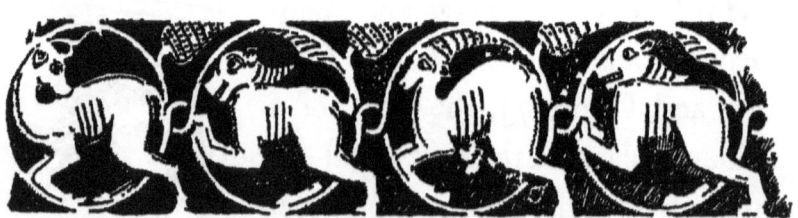

FIG. 74.

But we cannot help feeling that even the chimeras, griffins, and other monsters of the mediæval craftsmen were wrought in much the same spirit in which two

boys carve a jack-o'-lantern out by the back yard fence.
They assure each other that it will frighten all who be-
hold its fearsome countenance, yet they know full well
in their hearts that no one is going to be really fright-

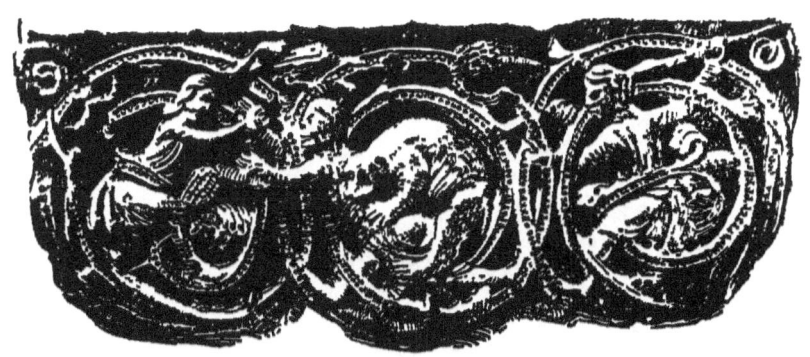

FIG. 75.

ened. It is merely a symbol, and an evidence of fear
on the part of the beholder is his share in the game.

To follow the grotesque back through primitive art
is to pass from comedy to buffoonery. In the effort
to make his image really frightful the primitive worker
displayed unique ingenuity. Yet in his dancing masks
it is still the symbol rather than the actual form that
inspires fear. Instead of putting a "keep out" sign
on his grain storehouse the New Zealand Maori
carves the house with symbols calculated to strike
terror to the heart of evil prowlers. Figure 76 is a
dancing mask from Nigeria and Figure 77 a wooden
image from Nicobar Islands. These latter people
strike close to the extreme limit of the grotesque,

L

with their wooden images smeared with paint. The primitive man carves a grotesque figure on the prow of his canoe or paints one on his shield, not to scare

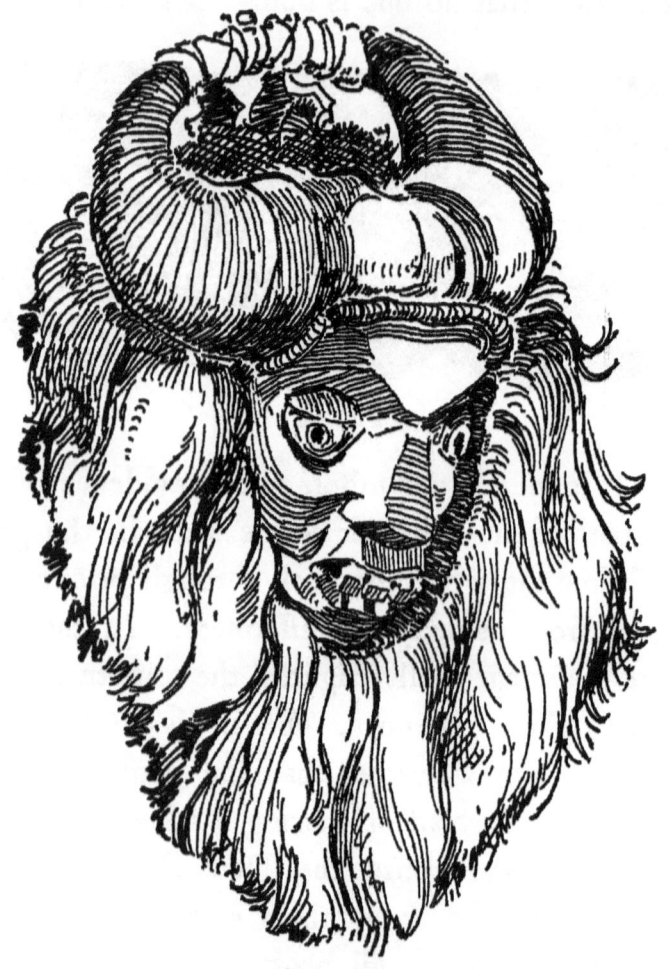

FIG. 76.

his enemy but to taunt him with a symbol proclaiming his fearlessness.

Again, much that we deem as quaint was doubtless

the result of technical limitations and incomplete observation. In Figure 78, for instance, a figure from the front of Saint Andrea in Pistoja, it may be assumed that most of the quaintness is due to incomplete observation and clumsiness of execution. We can easily find in our art schools and studios hundreds of students who can draw or model a figure more truthful in proportions and with more grace of action than did this old carver. But there are comparatively few who will ever speak out with such virile strength, vigor, and enthusiasm. There are many who spend years in the training of observation and in the acquisition of technical skill who have nothing to

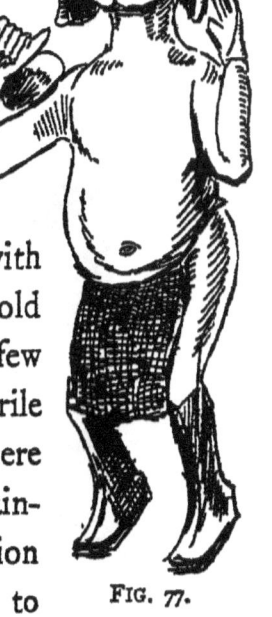

FIG. 77.

say that is worth while, nothing that touches human activity at any point. To this old craftsman technique was merely a means to an end. He had something to say, an idea to express, and struggled with his limitations as best he could. "If you would have the thought of a rude, untaught man, you must have it in a rough and untaught way, — but get the thought, and do not silence the peasant because he cannot speak good grammar or until you have taught him his grammar.

Look for invention first, and for such execution as will help invention."

It is a long way from the rudely carved Christ in

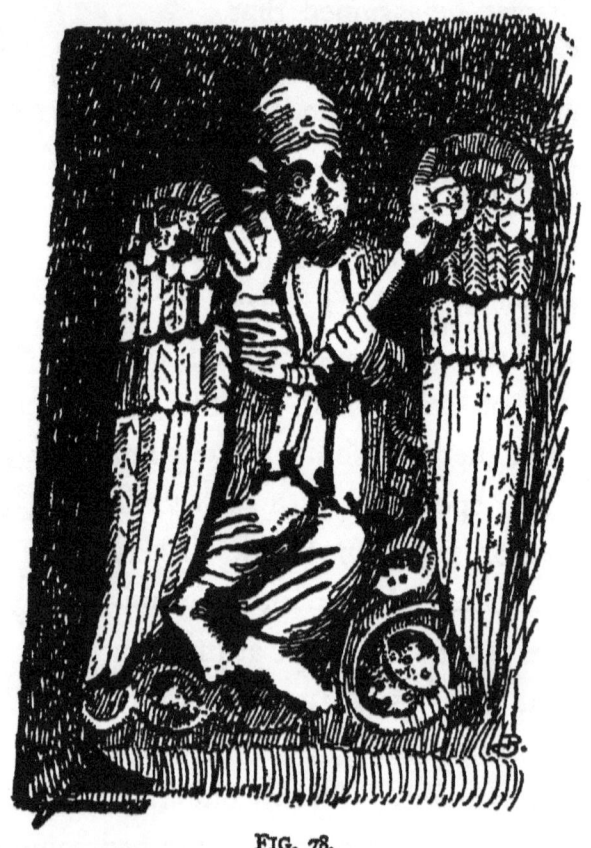

FIG. 78.

Figure 79 to that other Christ that stands at the portal of Amiens. Yet each was sufficient in its time and place, and each represented the best effort of the worker.

In Figure 80 is an old Benin savage's representation of one of his European conquerors. How closely

it resembles that other bronze figure made in Sardinia
many centuries before. Uncouth and barbarous, we
insist. Nothing of the kind! It
is charmingly frank and genuine,
full of character and action. Every
line tells of the honest pride which
the workman found in making it.
Moreover, supposing the average
person of to-day were to attempt
to model in clay his impression of
a man on horseback! Ten to one
it would be incoherent, without half
the interest or character to be found
in this one. Our ideals are so vague
and indefinite that we cannot work
them out at our finger tips. It is
easy to criticize the work of another; but few of us dare try for
ourselves. "The step from knowing to doing is rarely taken."

As art products these things may
be relatively unimportant; but if
we would penetrate below the sur-

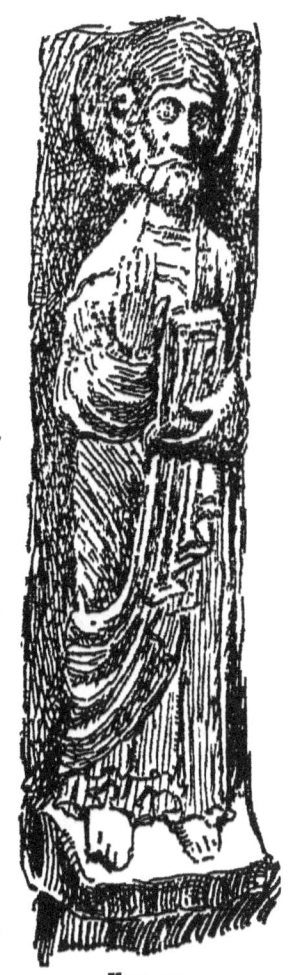

FIG. 79.

face of many things which we pass as rude and uncouth,
and seek the spirit of enthusiasm that prompted men
to speak out with such skill as they possessed, we might
find a deeply interesting story in unimportant things.

It is what men have to say, the strength of their emotions and the clearness of their assertions, that makes art vital, rather than skillful technique and fine finish.

Much that we pass as uncouth has within it a potential force which we fail to grasp,—imagination. If we

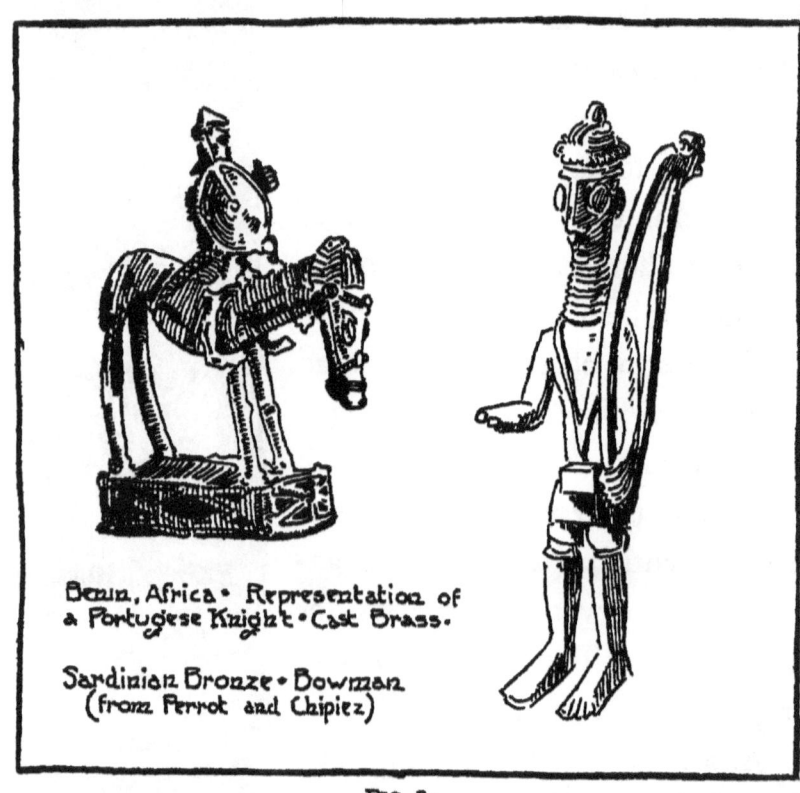

Benin, Africa · Representation of a Portugese Knight · Cast Brass.

Sardinian Bronze · Bowman (from Perrot and Chipiez)

FIG. 80.

scratch the surface of many rude things, we shall find an imaginative force, deep, intense, real. Many of the mediæval workers, who did common things uncommonly well, found a wider range for their imaginative power in later life in the production of important works of art. The master designer has ever been the man to whom many childhood fancies have tenaciously clung. The broadening activities of a later life have never been quite strong enough to drive all of the fairies from the grass, or to dispel the voices that laugh and whisper with the winds in the tree tops. He designs in words and we call him a poet; in tones, a musician; in color, a painter; in form, a sculptor. And to whatever task he turns his hand, there appears in his work a touch that we feel but cannot analyze, that finds a responsive chord within us, that brings light to the eye, and a sense of satisfaction to the mind. We sometimes call it personality; it is in reality the soul of his work, that which remains after all else has been weighed and classified. It is the force of imagination that imparts life and animation to a Gothic cathedral. And, per contra, it is the utter lack of imagination that makes all modern adaptations of Gothic architecture incapable of awakening a spark of enthusiasm. One returns to the old cathedral day after day, and each visit reveals new beauty; even away back in cobwebbed corners one comes upon the "soul stuff" of some humble, workaday fellow who wrought in the same spirit and with the same sincerity of purpose as the master who built the pulpit or frescoed the chapels. But in our modern adaptations there is neither interest nor reason in the arbitrary disposition of details in cement and plaster, in papier-mâché and cast iron. We have a husk without meat; a body into which no soul can be conjured to take its abode.

It is the spirit of enthusiasm, of love, of pleasure in work, that gives to mediæval art the most fascinating aspect of any period in art history. We are brought close to the hearts of a multitude of simple, honest, workaday craftsmen who imparted to their work a significance and vitality that made it a real factor in daily life. The sphere of art was sufficiently broad to encompass any task to which a man might turn his hand; nothing, from a cathedral to a candlestick, was too trivial or unimportant to be given its touch of distinctive beauty. It was an age of what we now term industrial art; but then there was no other kind of art. Our modern phrase of " art for art's sake " was unknown either in theory or in practice. It was a time when "any village mason could build a church and any village carpenter could crown it with a hammer-beam roof." What the work of the early craftsmen lacked in refinement and polish was more than compensated for in its vigorous grasp of essentials, in its truth and unaffected invention, and, above all else, in the fact that its appeal was comprehended by all. We have been too much inclined to look upon art as a cultural asset. The practice of art has been left to a few, professionally trained in complete isolation from the practical, industrial problems of life. It was once the glory of art to be of service. It is difficult for us to fully realize the spirit of an age when art was actually practiced by a great mass of people; when carvers in stone and wood, workers in iron, textile weavers, potters, goldsmiths, found daily opportunity and incentive to bring invention to bear upon their problems, to apply creative thought to the work of their hands. It was a time when builders were architects; when workmen were designers; when contracts called for nothing more than sound materials and honest workmanship,—the art was thrown in as a matter of course. Our modern craft workers expect unreasonable prices for unimportant productions because " the design is original and will not be duplicated." What was once the rule is now the exception.

The training received by the mediæval craftsman was peculiar to the guild system of the time. Many of the masters whose names are familiar to us now in our study of the history of art were duly apprenticed to a craft as soon as they could read, write, and count. Often at an age of ten years they went to the home of the master workman, with whom their apprenticeship was to be served, where, as was the custom of the time, they lived. The years of apprenticeship were years of hard work, often of drudgery; but· in the great variety of commissions undertaken by the shops of the time an opportunity was presented to lend a hand at many interesting tasks. There seems to have been a spirit of coöperation among the various shops and workmen that the keen, relentless competition of modern times does not permit.

After serving his apprenticeship a lad became a companion or journeyman worker, and finally tried for his degree, if it may be so termed, by submitting to examination for the title of master workman. In this examination he was called upon not only to produce his masterpiece, but to fashion such tools of his craft as were necessary for its completion. The standards of the guilds were so high that to become a master meant the production of a piece of work satisfactory to the judges artistically as well as technically. This completed the education of a craftsman of the time, producing a workman who was encouraged at every step of his training to combine beauty with utility, technical skill with honest workmanship. The competition was for excellence as much as for gain, and the greatest masters were simple and frugal of habit, finding more satisfaction in producing work that people were proud to possess than in "the pay envelope."

From stories left by Boccaccio, Vasari, and others, and from documents found in ancient archives, we can penetrate into those old-time workshops, pass

back into the busy workaday life of the times where
art was produced by men with tools in their hands.
The greater number of the master craftsmen are not
known, or at best their names are unfamiliar except
to students of musty records.   Most of those whose
names are familiar to students of art history served
their apprenticeships in the shops of the goldsmiths,
—Orcagna, Ghirlandajo, Botticelli, Lucca della Rob-
bia, Ghiberti, Donatello, Brunelleschi,—and when
they in turn became master workmen, we know not
whether to call them goldsmiths or bronze workers,
carvers or sculptors, painters or architects, for their
training was such that they could turn their hands to
any of these with distinction.   Orcagna could build a
church, cut the stone, lay the mosaics, paint the frescoes, or carve the crucifix, and we know not where most
to admire him.   While Ghiberti was engaged in the
production of the bronze doors for the Florentine baptistry, his journeymen workers were seldom so early at
the foundry but that they found him there in his cap
and apron.   Brunelleschi watched the building of the
cathedral from his bench long before he dreamed that
it would be his part to crown it with its great dome;
and when he and Donatello went to Rome to study
the antique, they replenished their empty purses by
following their craft.   What manner of architects
were these who went to the quarry and picked out

their own stones, who superintended the construction, directed the erection of scaffolds, who could teach others how to lay the mosaics or carve the ornament; and during leisure intervals wrote sonnets, built bridges, planned forts, and invented weapons of defense? When a master received a commission to build a church, a municipal palace, a fountain, or what not, he took with him his own journeymen and apprentices; and when the commission was an important one, he gathered about him to coöperate, in a spirit that knew little of rivalry or jealousy, the best master workers of his day.

PROBLEM. Our problem may seem at first thought to be one of amusement only; but a conscientious effort to solve it will soon indicate that it has other claims of a serious nature, — in fact the mental discipline involved in its solution would sufficiently justify it. It is a fitting test of one's ability to think in terms of line and form, and to turn the limitations imposed to the best possible purpose. Previous to this we have brought a suggestion of Nature to the lines and forms employed under given limitations; Nature has been an incident, a symbol. Now, under the same limitations as regards the directions of lines, working to the same end, it is the intention to go directly to Nature, choose a particular type, translate it into straight lines, adapt it to our purpose without losing its individuality or unique character. It is the purpose to seek a happy middle ground between Nature and the geometric basis on which the work has developed, to retain the distinctive character of a natural form without sacrificing the distinctive character that claims interest from a design point of view. A

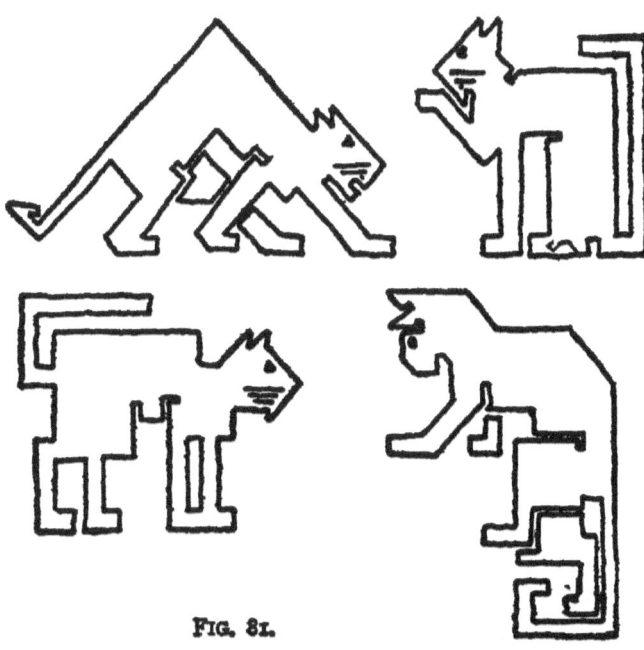

FIG. 81.

reasonable knowledge or observation of animal anatomy is, of course, essential; with such facts of observation at hand, together with a spice of imagination and a sense of humor, the limitations of the squared paper will be found more interesting than if greater liberty were allowed. Figure 81 indicates the general character of the results that might be expected from practice with the pencil, — not from a few moments of playful practice, but from several hours of thoughtful study. Do not try to be archaic or rude; you will fail. Do the best you can under the conditions of the problem. The naïve rudeness of primitive work charms us; but to imitate it is pure affectation, and will generally appear as such. The primitive worker did the best that he could for Nature; his feeling for design dominated his records of observation. He was always sincere; his quaint symbols had a real meaning and purpose, their forms were generally due to the influence of the tools and materials through which his ideas received direct expression.

Figures 82, 83, 84 show the end sought in the problem, a balance of attractive forces in symmetry within an inclosing form. Four points should be kept in mind: the figures must be related organically to the inclosing form, not look as if they were merely fenced in with a line; the two parts of the symmetry should be bound together by as many rhythmic connections of line as possible, — the line analysis in Figure 84 will serve as an illustration; the shapes and measures of the areas of black and

FIG. 82.

white must be given equal attention, — an approximate balance of the two in quantity will be found most effec-

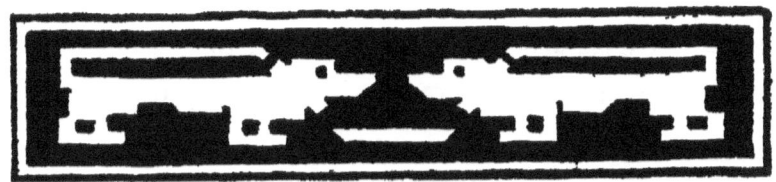

FIG. 83.

tive; it must be remembered that the *space between the two parts of a symmetry forms a strong attractive force in the design whether we wish it or not*, — it should be *studied*, not left to accident. It requires no skill or thought to " fence in " an example of symmetry; but

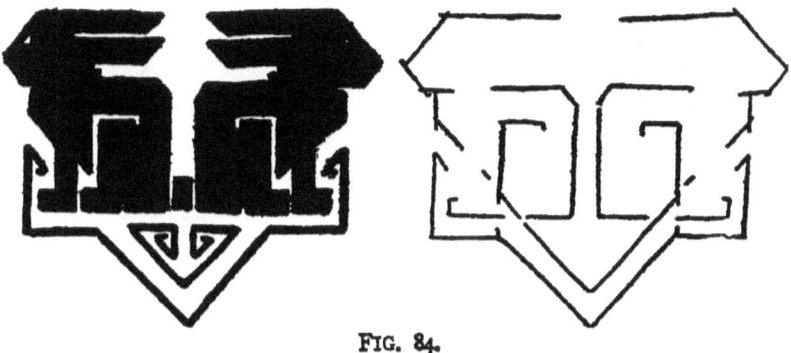

FIG. 84.

there is ample exercise for both skill and thought in the problem as stated. Figure 85 is quite in line with this problem and illustrates the points enumerated above.

Let us now note the constructive application of a motif such as we have been using, — a match safe to hang upon the wall (Plate 27). A match safe is chosen merely because it offers a convenient means of emphasizing the relation between theory and practice, between our abstract problems and constructive designing. It serves to show once more the interplay between æs-

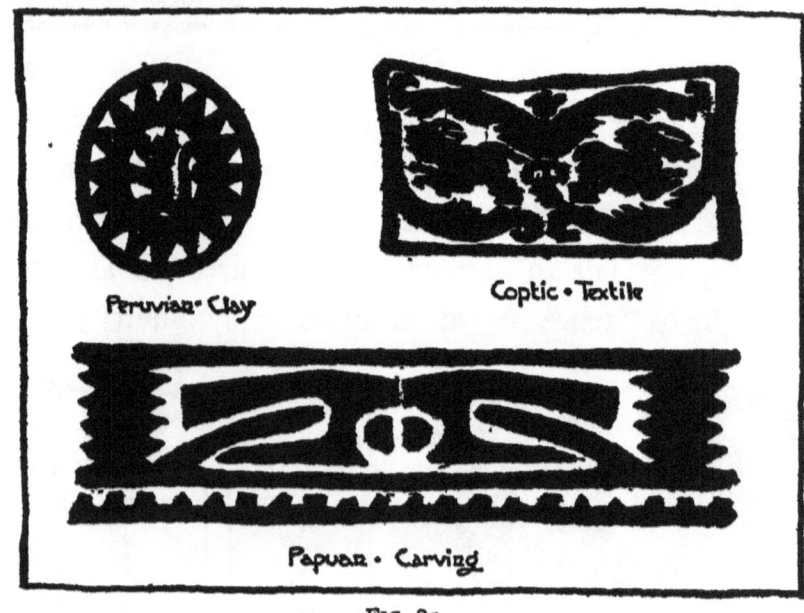

Peruvian Clay

Coptic · Textile

Papuan · Carving

FIG. 85.

thetic and practical principles. The essential elements are of first importance (Figure 86). There must be a receptacle for the matches. It may be vertical (i), or horizontal (ii), its inside dimensions to be determined by the length of a match. If in a vertical position, the dimensions of the box should be so planned that a single match will not fall too far below the top. There must be a piece of sandpaper, a back piece,

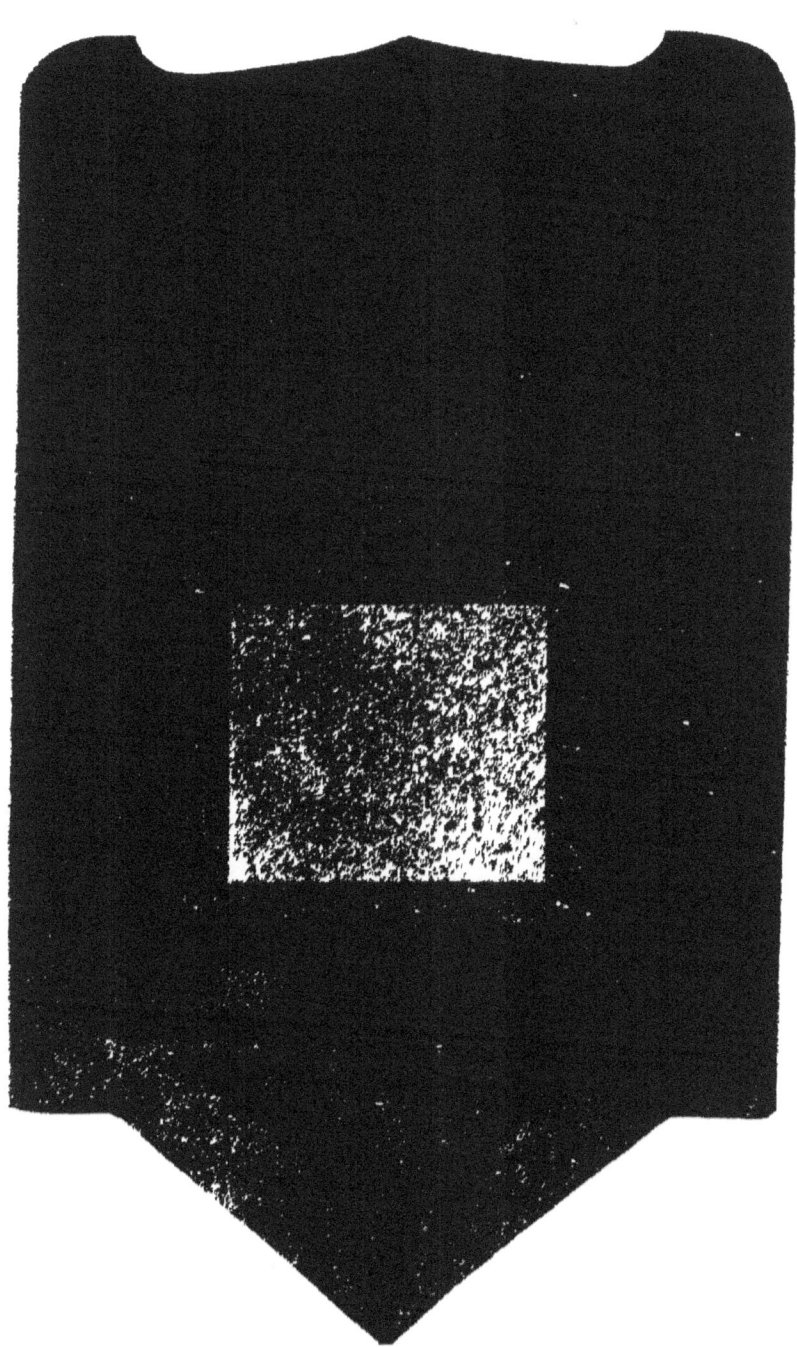

PLATE 27.

CONSTRUCTIVE DESIGNING.

with a hole at the top for the nail or hook on which the match safe is to be hung. These structural elements should form the basis for the design; they are

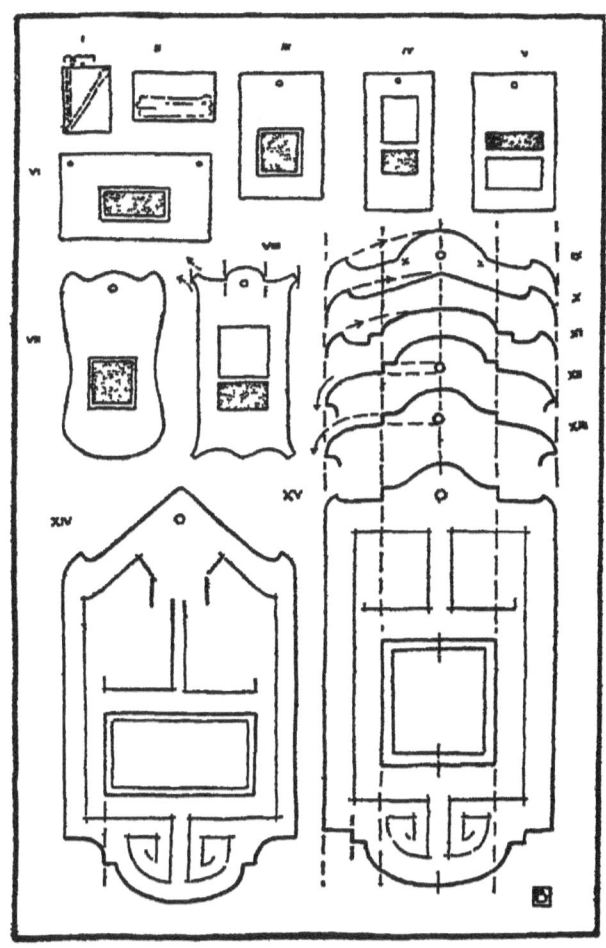

FIG. 86.

demanded by utility. The material employed may be wood. Two combative black cats seem appropriate as a decorative motif. The problem is now clear in its

M

development. We must first define the positions and relative proportions of the essential elements. The sandpaper may be on the box (iii), or below (iv), but not above it (v), because the matches within the box would be in danger of ignition. The scheme may be planned horizontally (vi), in which case two holes at the top would seem advisable. We have now to attempt a refinement of the structural elements and such an adaptation of the decorative motif that it shall be organically related in line and form to those elements in a unity of effect. For the sake of simplicity, let us first discuss the steps involved in a refinement of the essential elements. There are several errors which it would be well to anticipate. The first is in vii. Here there is no reciprocal relation between the curved lines of the back piece and the rectangular box. In viii the box is supported by the parallel side lines; but there are three weak points in this arrangement. There is not enough difference between the top and bottom of the design: the curves indicated by the arrow tend to lead the eye away from the center of interest; the division of the top into three equal parts is unfortunate, giving a result which lacks variety in proportions. In ix the second error is corrected — the curves keep the eye within the inclosing form. But there is another criticism here. At the points marked by the crosses the curves should be either continuous or the angles should

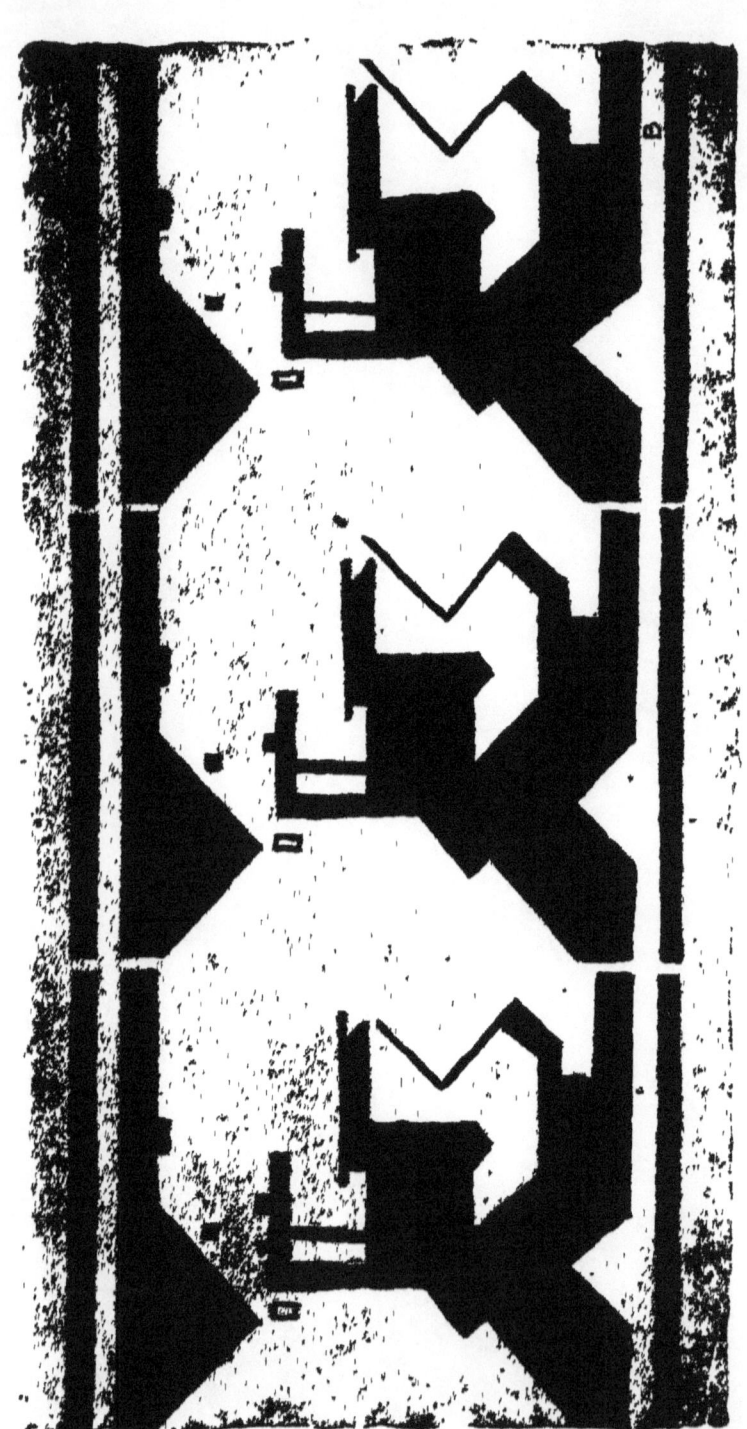

PLATE 28.

SQUARED ANIMALS IN BORDERS.

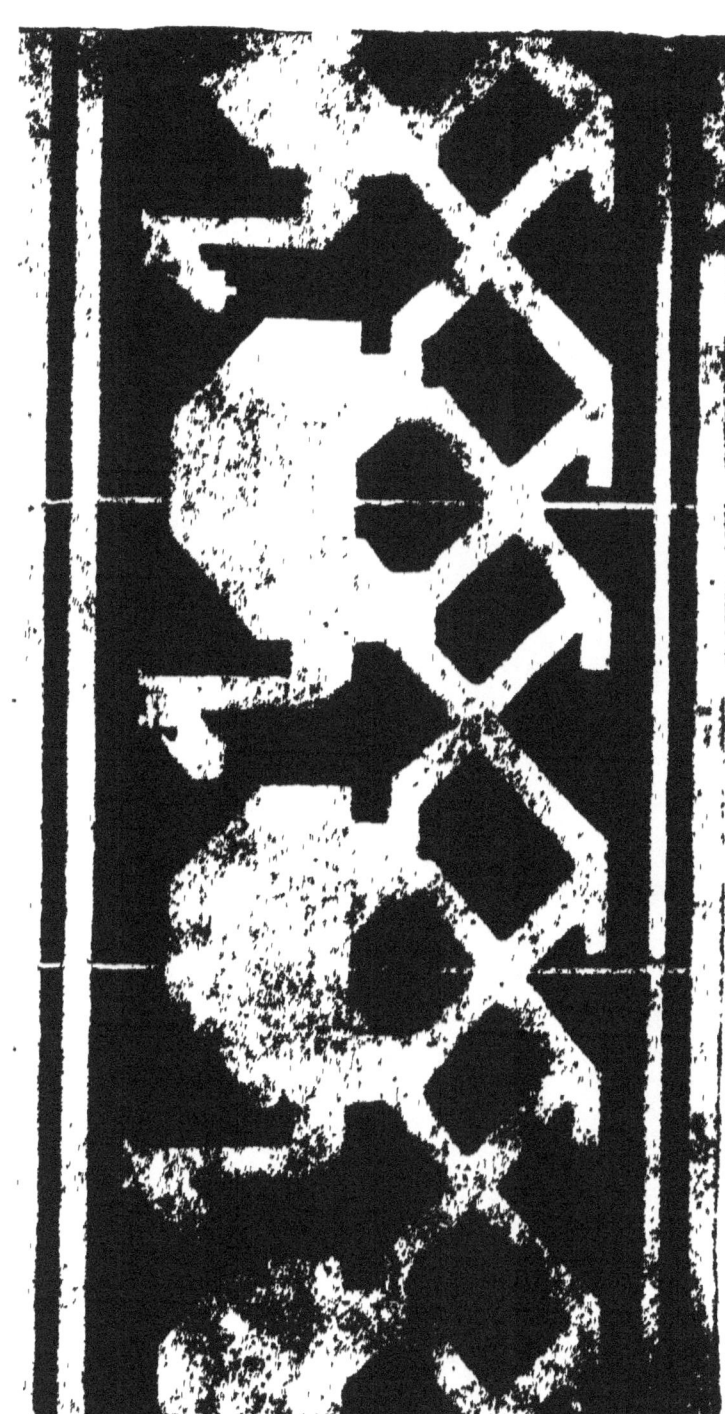

PLATE 29.

SQUARED ANIMALS IN BORDERS.

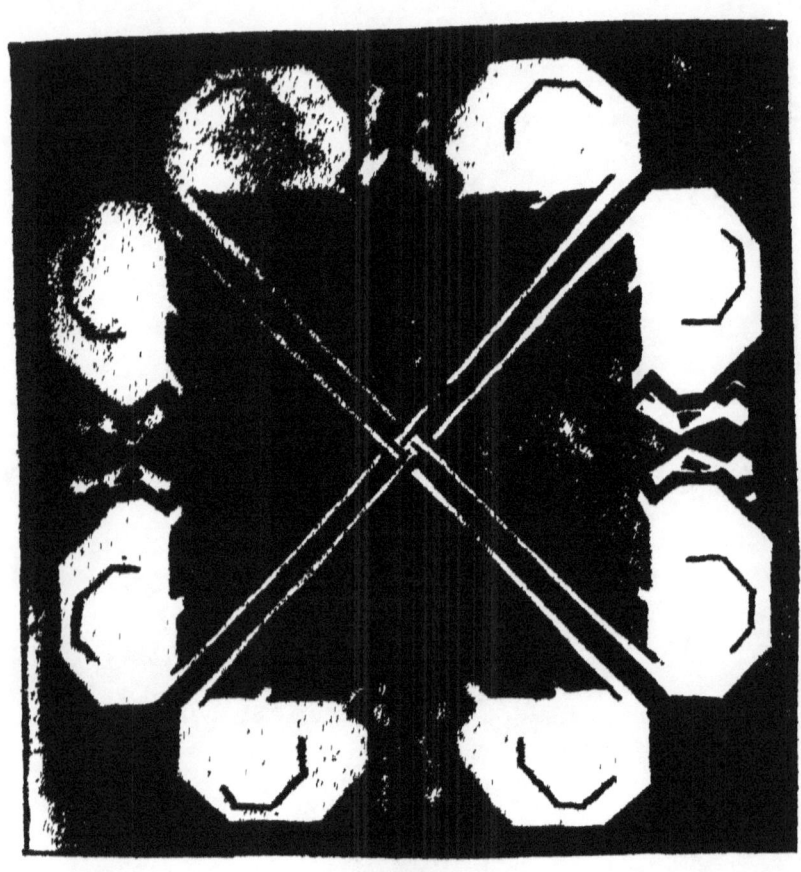

PLATE 30.

SQUARED ANIMALS IN RECTANGLE.

be more acute. In x, xi, xii, xiii are suggestions giving variety with unity in the lines and proportions used. Now, with these criticisms in mind, let us return to the point of the problem, the organic relation of the lines of the decorative motif to the structural elements. In xiv–xv are two sketches showing the adjustment of the proportions and the interrelation of all the lines of the design. These sketches emphasize the necessity of working from the whole to the parts. Ornament should never be added as an afterthought; it must always be developed with, and related to, the constructive elements of a problem.

PROBLEM. It would be difficult to devise a problem demanding clearer thinking than this one. Any student who has an idea that it is nothing more than the repetition of a " squared animal " should go back to the first problem of this series and take a fresh start. It requires the exercise of a wholesome play impulse under the restraint of orderly design. It seems unnecessary to recite again the conditions and limitations of the preceding problems as applied to this one ; mentality may be assumed. Study Figures 87, 88, 89, and Plates 28, 29 30, in the light of past experience; they are *dark* and *light*, space and mass, designs with additional interest imparted to them from Nature through the imagination of the worker. Figure 90, as well as Figure 81, may serve as the starting point.

Incidentally it may be remarked that, these figures being flat conventions, no perspective should be at-

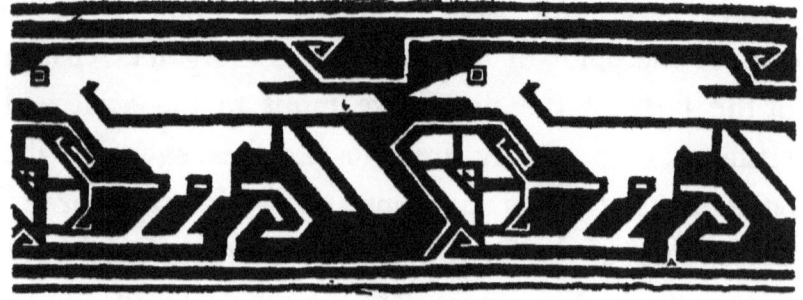

FIG. 87.

tempted; the feet, for example, should be on the same

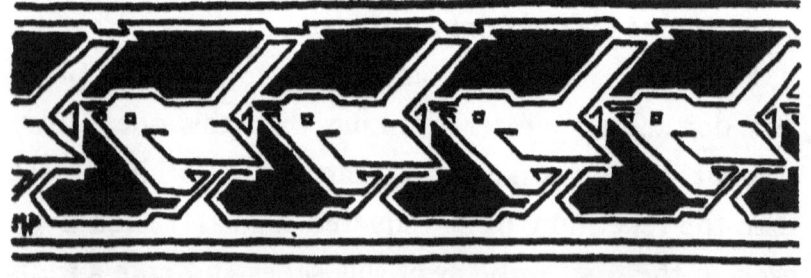

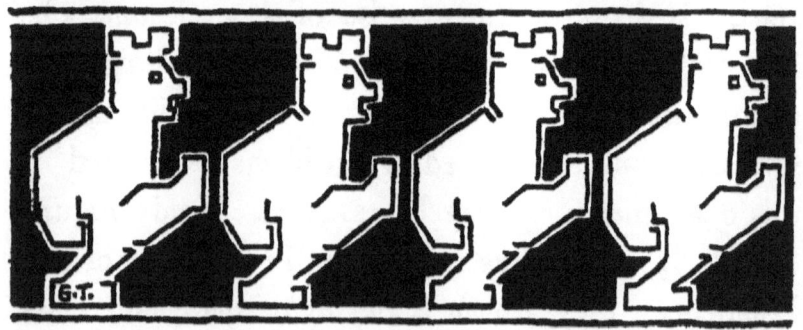

FIG. 88.

level, if the creature is walking, as in the first four instances of Figure 90. Figure 91 shows various

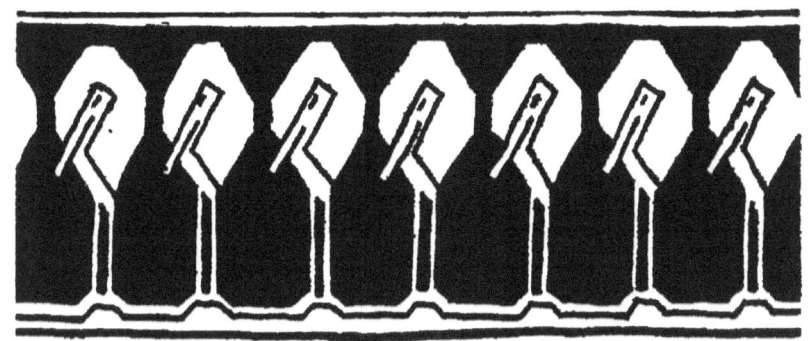

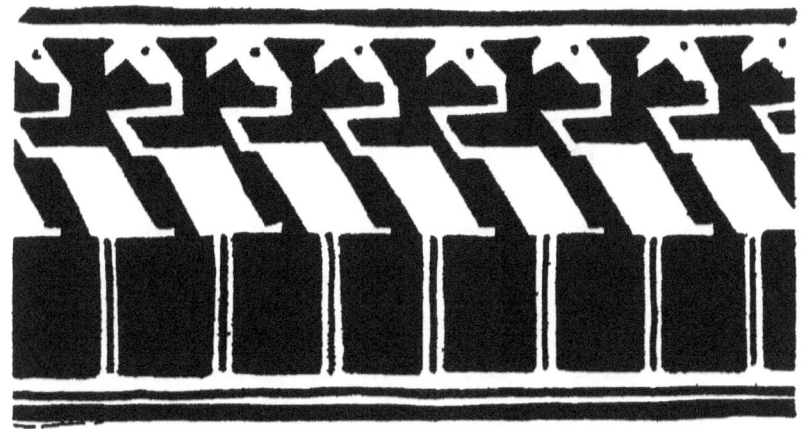

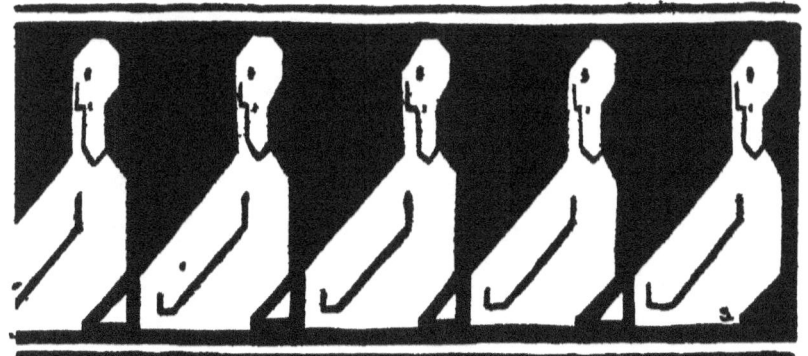

FIG. 89.

experiments with one of these forms in an effort to secure the best expression for sake of the design. Experience, assurance of judgment, may be hoped for

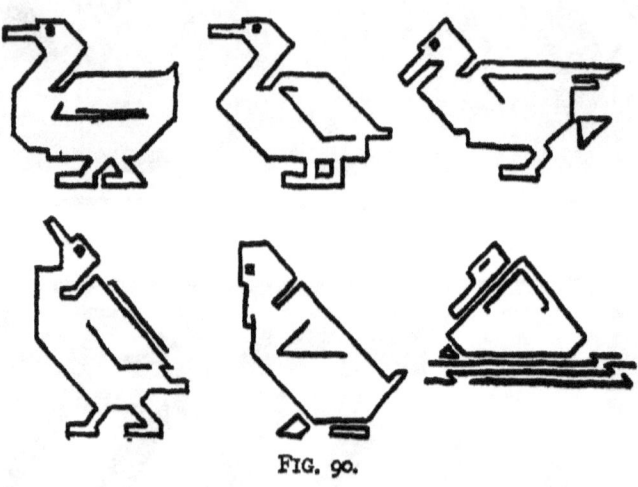

FIG. 90.

on the basis of many experiments and comparisons. The willingness to experiment must be accepted as part of a student's equipment for serious study ; it is the faculty that remains dissatisfied until the best possible expression of an idea has been demonstrated. In this case the final example may be accepted as giving the most interesting and complete relation of the different elements involved in the problem. As a final, though important, item of interest it may be said that in a design of this character the creatures should be doing something, going somewhere; they should enter into the spirit of the fun, not stand dumbly in a row as if waiting to be shot at.

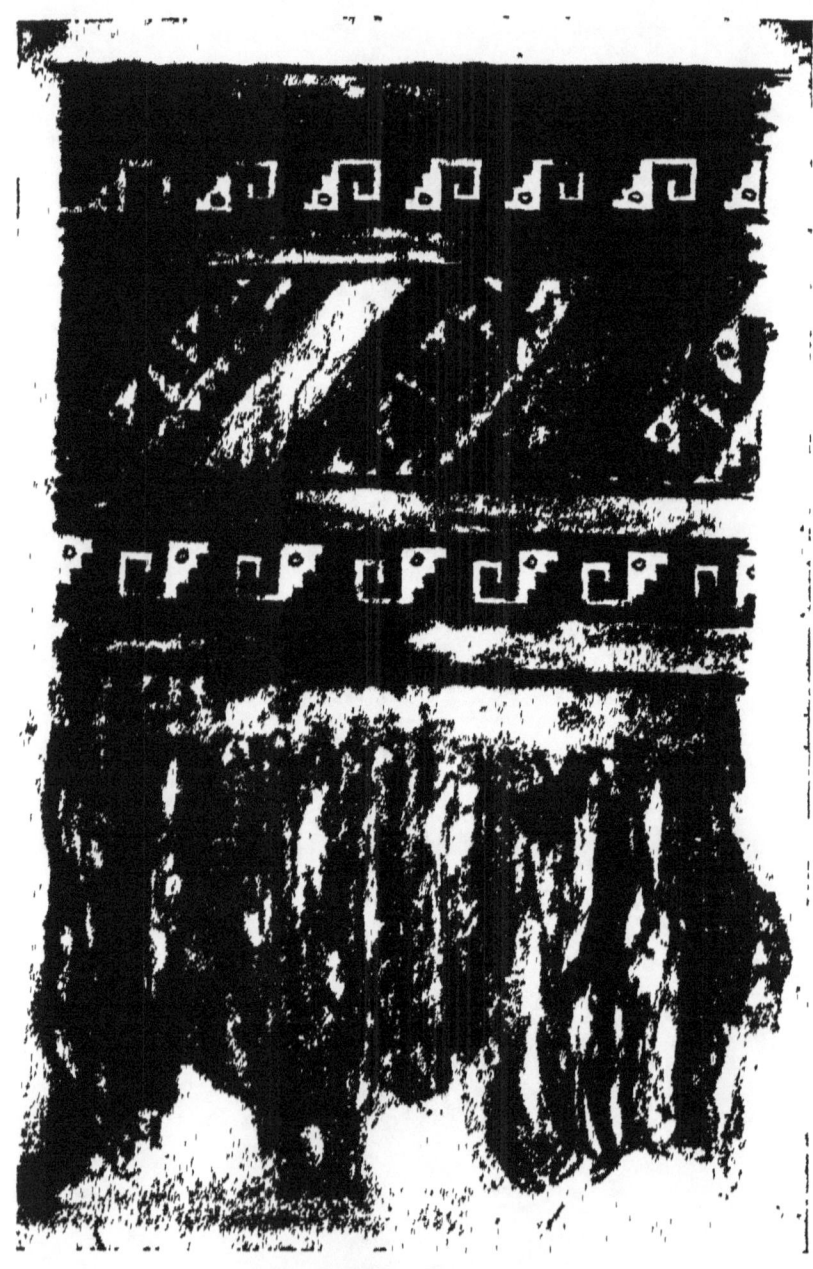

PLATE 31.

PERUVIAN TEXTILE. (BOSTON MUSEUM OF FINE ARTS.)

In the textiles of the primitive Peruvian weavers (Figure 92 and Plate 31) is a close approach to our problem. There is a simple and effective use of

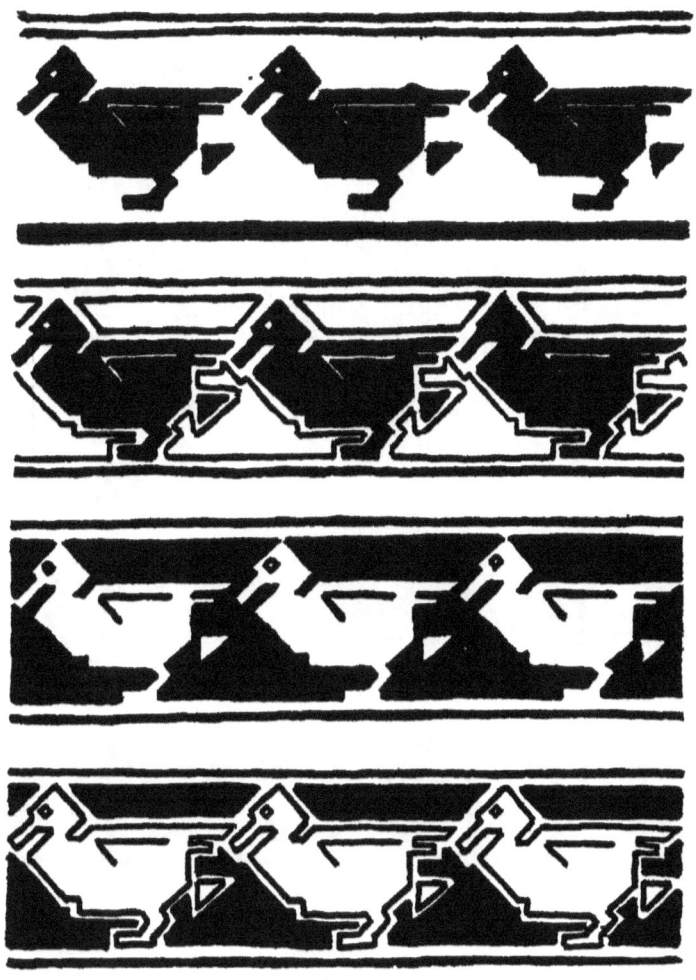

FIG. 91.

animal life to be found in all of this work. The particular forms are sometimes apparent; again, they become abstract symbols, as in Plate 31. But

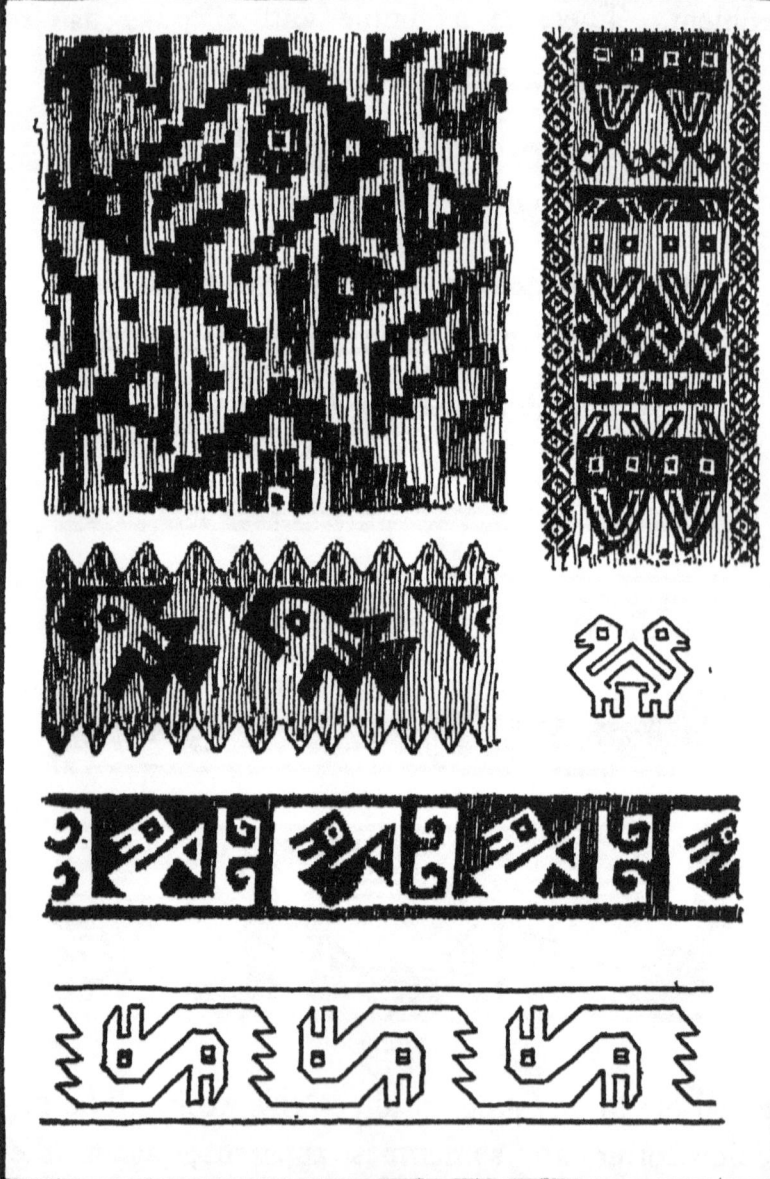

FIG. 92.

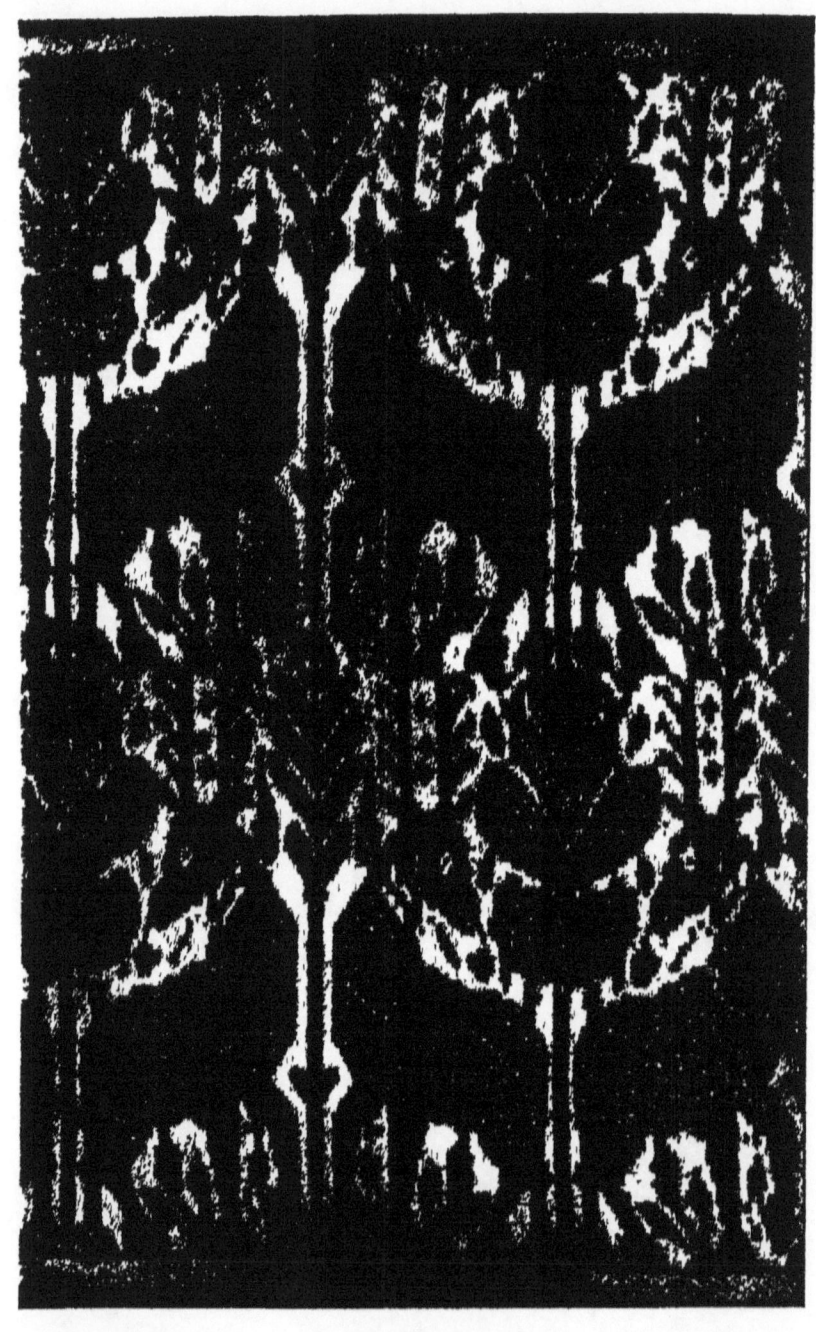

PLATE 32.

FIFTEENTH-CENTURY TEXTILE — ITALIAN. (SOUTH KENSINGTON MUSEUM.)

as designs they are invariably good. The student of design can find no more fertile field of suggestion at this stage than a collection of Peruvian art, or from a close study of illustrations of such work. The Peruvians were designers of consummate ability, shrewd observation; were endowed with a keen imagination, that play impulse which makes art a joy alike to the one who practices it and the one who studies it. In their textiles those weavers very frequently employed the exact duplication of space and mass known as counterchange.

Plate 32, a fifteenth-century textile from Italy, is also a close and interesting approach to this problem.

CHAPTER IX

THE IDEA AND NATURE

"There is little in nature that is ready made to the hand of the artist. A masterpiece of art is what it is in virtue of a something which was not in the natural motif of the artist, but in his treatment of it."— LEWIS F. DAY.

IF we look back upon the history of design, it will be found that the use of plant form through what is generally termed conventionalization followed upon long practice in the arts. Plant form in design has almost invariably been the last to suggest motifs to the worker. The development was much the same at the dawn of history as among the American Indians of to-day. The first designs were those that arose through technique; the first appeal from Nature was through animate life and through significant symbols of natural forces. It is not until men have passed a long way through barbarism into a higher state of culture that one finds an attempt to directly conventionalize plant form. It is not necessary that the student in his own work should pass through all the stages of primitive art and barbarism; to attempt it would be an affectation. But the principle involved in the historic development of design is important in the application to the individual student. This principle, in so far as it seems applicable, is followed through the problems of this book. It is the writer's belief that the direct conventionalization of plant life should follow upon long-continued study of principles.

To conventionalize Nature is to adapt a nature-derived motif to the structural demands of a problem, to the space and position which it is to occupy, to the tools, materials, and processes of execution. A man who has a thorough command over the technique of his craft, who possesses a refined feeling, good judgment, and common sense will inevitably turn to Nature for suggestion. If he has an appreciation of the elementary principles of line, form, and tone adjustment, acquired through persistent observation and experiment, he may be expected to adapt Nature to his purposes in a logical and consistent way. A paper-trained student who begins by seeking ideas in Nature and who essays the production of designs for wall papers that are never printed, textiles that are never woven, iron that is never forged, tiles that are never fired, with only a superficial knowledge of the tools, materials, processes, and constructive demands of these industries, cannot be expected to find in the word *conventionalization* any other significance than that involved in

the more or less formal rendering of a natural specimen. The most interesting conventionalization is
found in the work of a trained craftsman who turns to
Nature for a suggestion that will impart life and animation to the refinement and enrichment of his problem.
He can get along very well and produce beautiful work
without Nature; but with Nature as an ally he finds
his imaginative and inventive faculties stimulated and strengthened many fold.

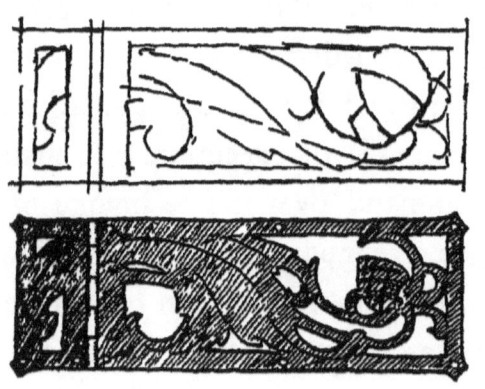

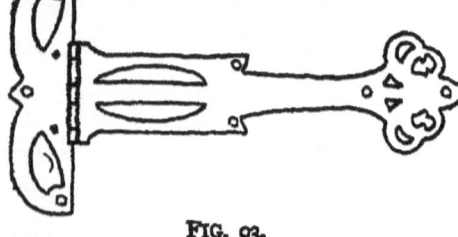

His treatment of the motif which he seeks may be such as is shown in the first example of Fig-ure 93, or such as is shown in the second example of this fig-ure. They were both suggested by the

FIG. 93.

wild teasel. One treatment is neither more nor less
commendable than the other, and any information as to
the source from which the suggestions were derived is
quite immaterial in a discussion of the results. We can
form no judgment as to the relative merits of the two

designs until we see them in position on the constructive problems of which they were merely structural elements. Each was adapted and related to a constructive
whole which led to distinctly different treatments of a
suggestion derived from the same source. As the designs stand, in this isolated form, there are but three
questions to be asked : Is each adapted to the tools and
processes peculiar to metal working ? Is each thoughtfully arranged in its line and form, space and mass ? Is
each consistent throughout in its treatment? It would
be inconsistent to place the formal, symmetrical ending
of the second on the rhythmic, flowing lines of the first.
The truth of this is so evident that it would seem unnecessary to mention it ; yet we find this simple principle, consistency of treatment, so often violated that
its emphasis never ceases to be desirable.

In the first example a rough, blocking-out sketch is
shown of the relation of lines, which was established
after the shape and measure of the hinge as an element
in the design, and the style of treatment were determined. A rhythmic relation of lines and forms was
desired; common sense and the material employed
demanded that all the loose ends of the design be
bound together into a compact whole. The question
of space and mass adjustment was decided, partly by
the application of elementary principles of composition,
partly by the saw and file.

The amount of conventionalization that is given to a nature-derived motif, then, is not in itself a basis on which any judgment may be formed as to the merit of the result. We may prefer the highly conventionalized symbols of the primitive weavers, or the less conventional treatment of Nature to be found in the Oriental textiles. In either case we can form an adequate judgment of the results only on the basis of line, form, and tone adjustment, and on the technique involved in the weaver's craft.

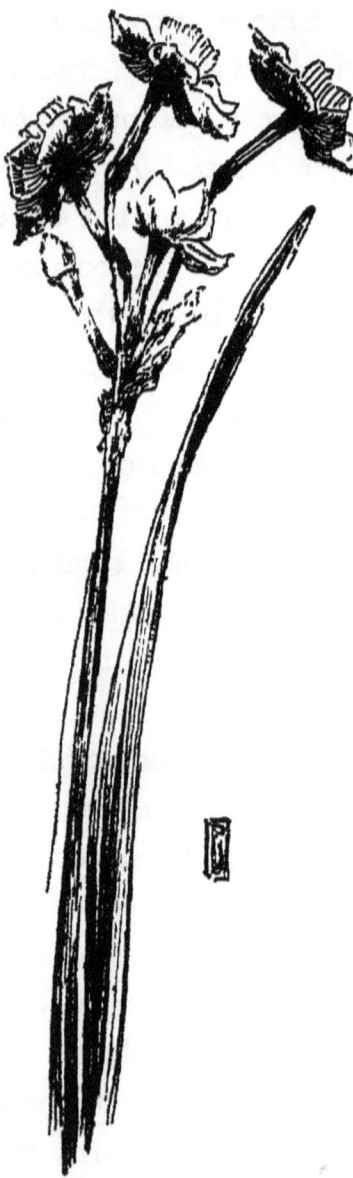

FIG. 94.

In Figure 94 is a pen sketch of a Chinese lily. In one sense even this sketch is conventional in treatment; it is an adaptation of Nature to the technique peculiar to pen-and-ink rendering. Its interest, however, is in light, shade, and texture, in the transient qualities which Nature has imparted to the Chinese lily. It is obviously unfit, in its present form, for purposes of design. Whether one prefers a naturalistic treatment in design or a formal, geometric treatment is immaterial. The essential point is that it is necessary to alter, rearrange, or in some way adapt the lines and forms here shown before they are suited to our purpose. The style or character in a design is the result of the treatment accorded the motif. The character which comes from treatment is, as we have seen, dependent upon the adjustment of several correlated questions. For the sake of simplicity we have isolated one of those questions for purposes of study. We are aiming at an appreciation of the æsthetic interest of a beauty that is expressed in abstract lines, forms, and tones, and of the application of some of the *principles* thus defined to constructive problems; simple problems indeed, but such as may be assumed to be somewhat within reach of our experience.

In the specimen shown we may find, in its typical growth and unique character, material for our ends; or we may seek in an analysis of its parts, bud, leaf, or flower, a suitable motif. But one thing is surely clear. If we cannot use the transient beauty with which Nature has endowed this flower, we must in our treatment of the motif impart to the work a beauty of another sort. Here, as in all things, Nature furnishes the raw material, but leaves it to man to convert this material to his needs by such processes as he may invent. It is a long step from the tree that grows in the forest, or the unquarried stone in the hills, to the houses in which we live. While Nature may furnish the

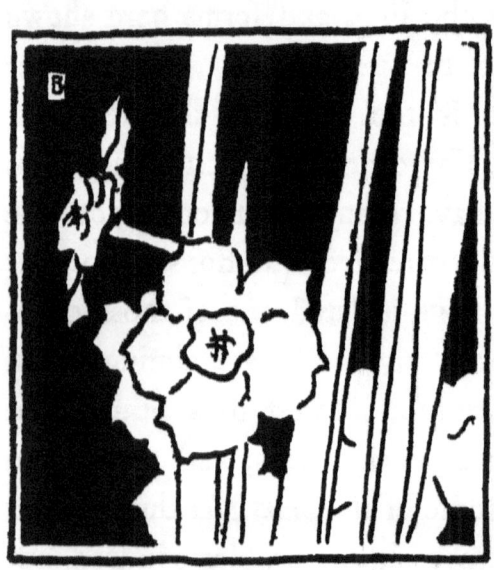

FIG. 95.

raw material, she does not furnish ready-made designs, and will baffle our efforts to find in her the clew to a beautiful design. The last is our part in the problem. *The beauty which we give to design must come from within us;* it cannot be found in a study of the specimen, however painstaking or analytical that study may be.

In Figure 95 is a treatment of a Chinese lily that may claim to be decorative in character. A specimen has been employed to express a definite idea with no other change than the elimination of realistic details. That idea was the decorative distribution of areas of black and white within a rectangle to secure interesting

space and mass relations.   To give decorative character
to a flower motif, then, is not merely to stiffen its
growth into formal lines or to
place it in a strait-jacket, but to
adapt it to the requirements of
a definite idea.   Let us *take an
idea to Nature*, — not seek an
idea in Nature.

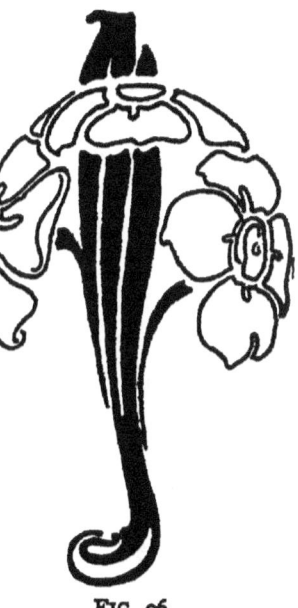

FIG. 96.

In Figures 96,
97 another idea
has found ex-
pression.   Here
the lily has served
as a basis for an
interest that is
dependent   en-

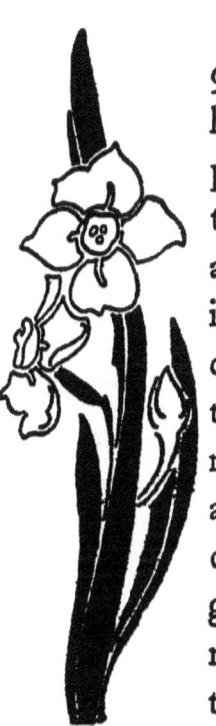

FIG. 97.

tirely on the rhythmic and balanced
relation of lines and forms.   The results
are sufficiently like the lily to demand a
consistent adherence to Nature's laws of
growth ; but to judge the beauty of the
results we must revert to the idea which
the lines and forms express, not to the
motif from which they were derived.

In Figure 98 is a line drawing of a single flower,
with two symmetrical renderings of that flower, one
in curved lines, the other in straight lines.   In the two

latter cases an effort was made to relate the petals to the center and to give some element of variety in shapes and measures to the areas into which the flower was divided. Beyond this, these conventions have no particular merit or distinction; in fact, we may well prefer the first sketch to either of the others. They should

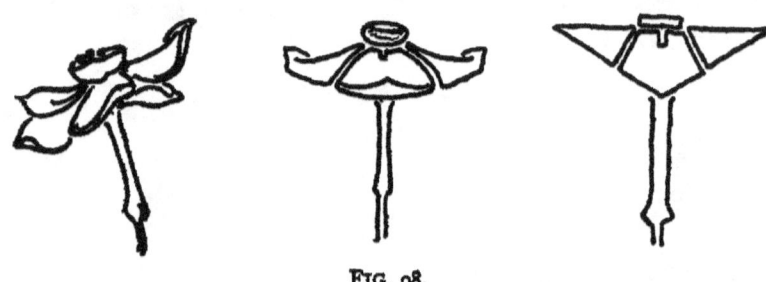

FIG. 98.

be produced by any one who has an understanding of the simplest of the elementary principles noted in the first chapter of this book. But these two conventions were made with a definite purpose in mind,—an application to a repeated design. In the completion of the idea may be found a justification for the treatment accorded the flower.

In Figure 99 the unit shown in Figure 96 is repeated at regular intervals, with a rhythmic, graceful movement from unit to unit. The design furnishes a pattern that is pleasing in character; it is an obvious and simple repetition of a unit interesting in itself, in which Nature was subordinated to a definite idea. As a *surface pattern* it demanded a comparatively small

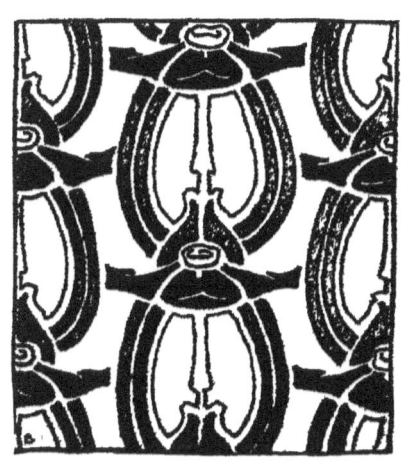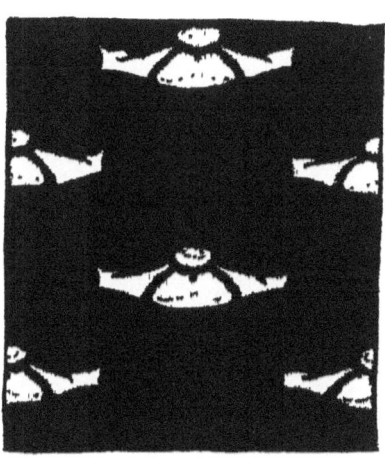

PLATE 33.

NATURE DERIVATIVES.

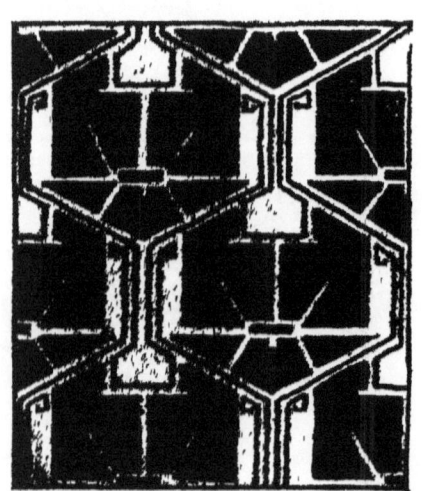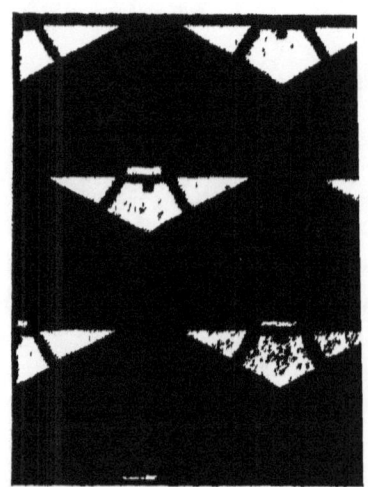

PLATE 34.

NATURE DERIVATIVES.

amount of skill, however.   The importance of a design increases in ratio to the number and variety of elements that have been disciplined into a unity of effect.   In

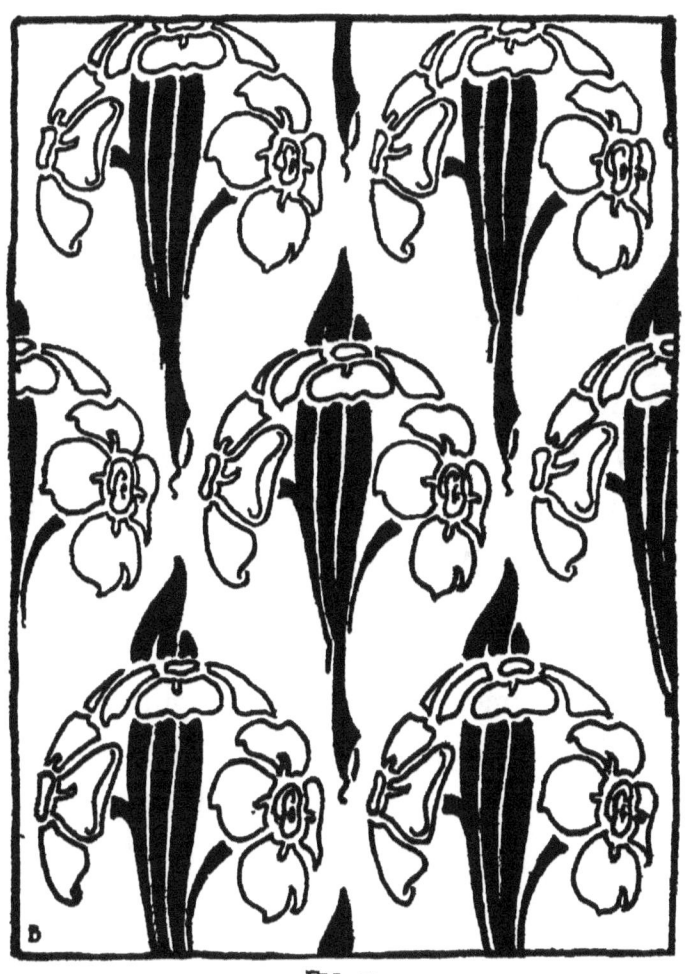

FIG. 99.

Plates 33, 34 are surface patterns that demanded more skill and a greater concentration of thought.   While Figure 99 involves the mere repetition at regular intervals of a pleasing unit, these two plates represent the deliberate building up of a surface pattern with " malice aforethought." The background has been accepted as an element in each design; an effort has been made to adjust three tones, black, white, and gray, into a unity to which each shall contribute. The achievement, or, rather, the effort, is to this extent more important than in Figure 99. In Plate 34 one would probably never suspect the motif from which the pattern started. The leaf form is not that of the Chinese lily; — and why need it be? It is here that the idea sought in the design overrides the specific character of the Chinese lily; invention takes precedence over selection. The design is consistent in treatment throughout and justifies the departure from the particular forms of the motif.

So we find that we may accept the growth and character of Nature almost literally, as in Figure 95, or may seek in Nature suggestions which, when adapted to our ideas, leave merely an incidental trace of the motif in the result. It matters not from what source the motif is derived, so long as the result is consistent throughout in its adherence to or departure from the specific character of the motif; and least of all is an identity of the motif essential in a discussion of the merit of the design. If the treatment has any claim to be called decorative, it must be based on an interpretation of the elementary principles of line, form, and tone composition.

PROBLEM. Instead of attempting a free conventionalization from Nature let us approach the subject from an abstract point of view and seek to bring to our first studies of plant life another expression of the same principles that have been defined through straight-line problems. We shall endeavor to develop a rhythmic, balanced composition of blacks and whites, suggesting plant growth, though not bound to any specific specimen from plant life. First, let us again thresh out the question of space and mass. It is ten to one that the student who has approached the study of design by accumulating sketches from Nature, and by seeking in Nature a justification for the principles that are to govern the structural development of his design, will feel that the problem of conventionalization is solved when he has adapted the lines and forms of a specific specimen to a definite shape. His attention is absorbed almost entirely by the lines and forms of the specimen with which he is working; it is difficult for him to depart from the specific character of his motif to the abstract consideration of his design in terms of line, form, and tone. If we are ready to accept the assertion that the beauty of a design is dependent, in the final analysis, on its structural fitness and the relation of lines, forms, and tones, rather than upon its relation to Nature, to historic ornament, to " style," or to pictorial interest, then, whether the designer wills it or not, the background, or space in his design, whatever it may be, must be considered as an integral part of his composition. Seek where we will through the wall papers and textiles of modern production, we find, with very few exceptions, motifs derived from specific natural forms, arranged in more or less ingenious patterns. The backgrounds enter into the composition as mere accidents, holes left after the pattern is repeated. In the worst of these designs sad efforts are made to imitate Nature in color and form, and to hide the very structural lines on which the finest ornament has ever depended for its beauty ; in the best of them we find a consistent and thoughtful treatment of Nature ;—and yet we turn with increasing admiration to the simple, dignified, soul-satisfying texiles of primitive men and to the product that came from the looms of the Orient, from Persia, Italy, Sicily, and Flanders during the palmy days of weaving. We discard modern carpets for plain floors and Oriental rugs. We prefer an unpapered wall to the restless, naturalistic patterns of modern production. What is it, then, that imparts so much of unrest to our papers and textiles, so much of restful simplicity to the older product ? Aside from the all-important question of color, it is this: modern patterns are imposed *upon* a back-

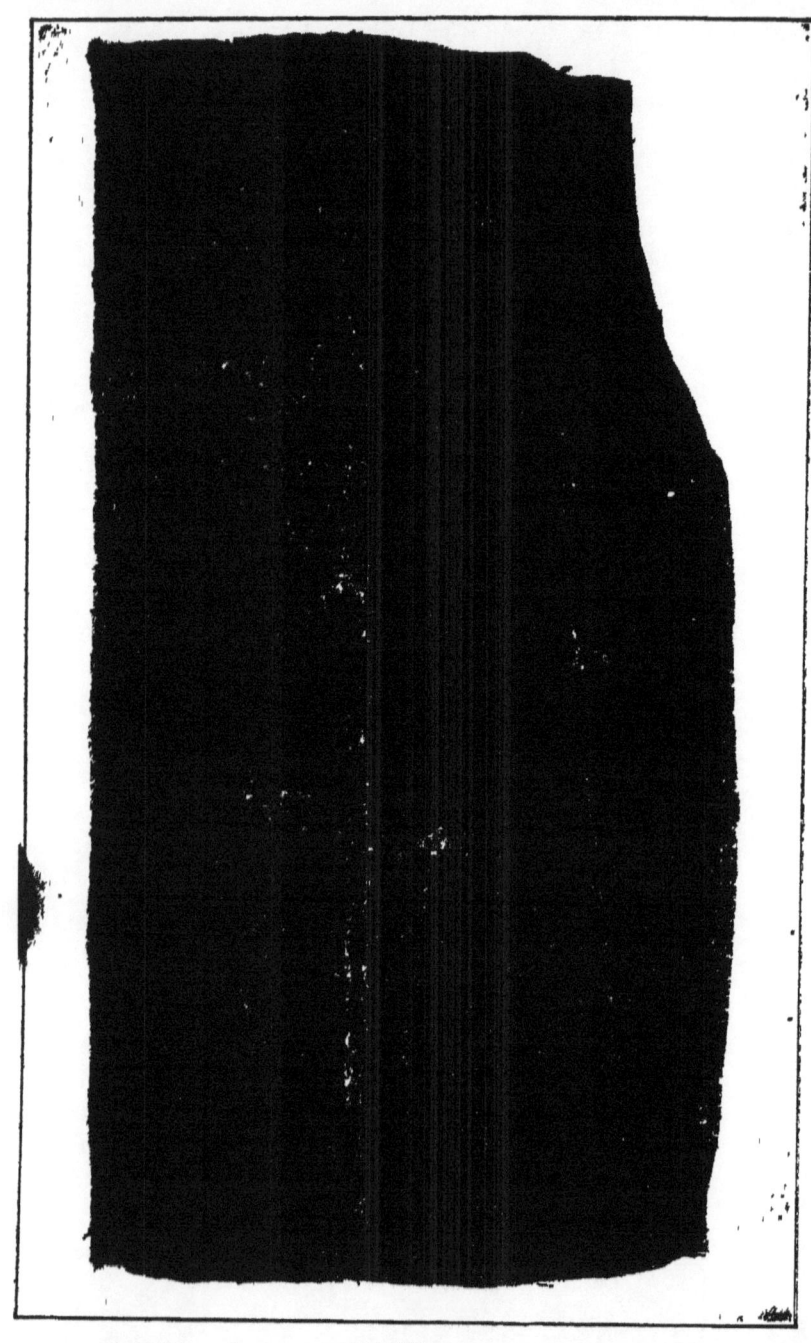

PLATE 35.

BROCADE. (METROPOLITAN MUSEUM.)

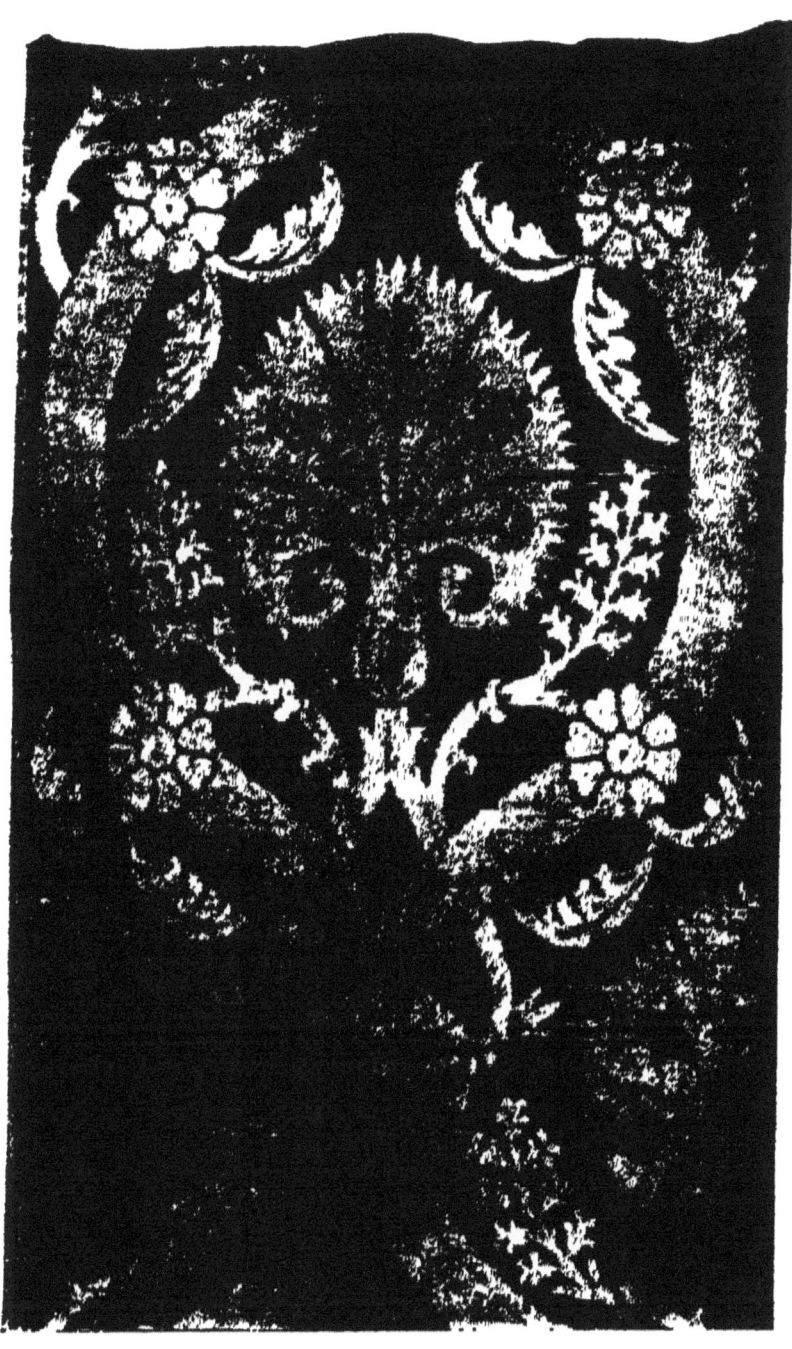

PLATE 36.

VELVET BROCADE. (BOSTON MUSEUM OF FINE ARTS.)

ground; the older patterns are incorporated *into* a
background. The modern designer works from
Nature toward technical demands; the old worker
proceeded from a knowledge of technical demands,
backed by the traditions of generations of weavers,
toward Nature. It is difficult to find a modern figured
wall paper that will harmonize with any environment;
the old product lends distinction to any environment
in which it may be placed. The first creates holes
through the wall; the second remains *on* the wall.
The clew to the character of the designs found in the
best of the old textiles (Plates 35, 36, 37, 38) was not
discovered in plant life. The designers possessed an
intuitive feeling for beautiful space and mass relations,
for the principles governing line, form, and tone adjustment. Nature gave to their work its final touch
of distinction.

It is our problem, then, to define the meaning of
rhythm and balance as expressed in curved lines.
The most interesting interpretation of the principles
of rhythm and balance in line and form applied to
Nature is to be found in the flower compositions
practiced in Japan, and explained by Mr. J. Conder in
his valuable book entitled " The Flowers of Japan and
the Art of Floral Arrangement," from which Figures
100, 101 are adapted. To us a mass of flowers thrust
into a vase, or bound together as a bouquet, is suffi-

cient. But to the Japanese the leaves and stems, their arrangement and grouping, are quite as important as the flower itself. They endeavor to adjust a few lines and forms into a rhythmic and balanced composition. They assist

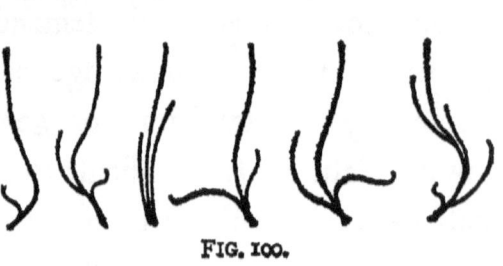

FIG. 100.

Nature, so to speak, to achieve the ideal toward which she seems ever striving. This type of composition has become with the Japanese an art, governed by definite principles. By careful selection of flowers, pruning of leaves, subtle bending of stems, they attain the desired effect. Mr. Conder

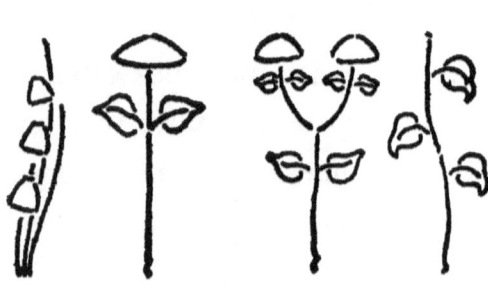

FIG. 101.

describes and illustrates these laws and principles with thoroughness and completeness. Figure 100 illustrates some of the movements to be desired in two, three, and five-stem compositions. It will be noted that the unity of the composition is dependent primarily upon the reciprocal relations of the stems, then upon the grouping of leaves and flowers. Figure 101 illustrates a few of the many things to be avoided, — formal symmetry, — equal height, — equal stepping, — " dew spilling "

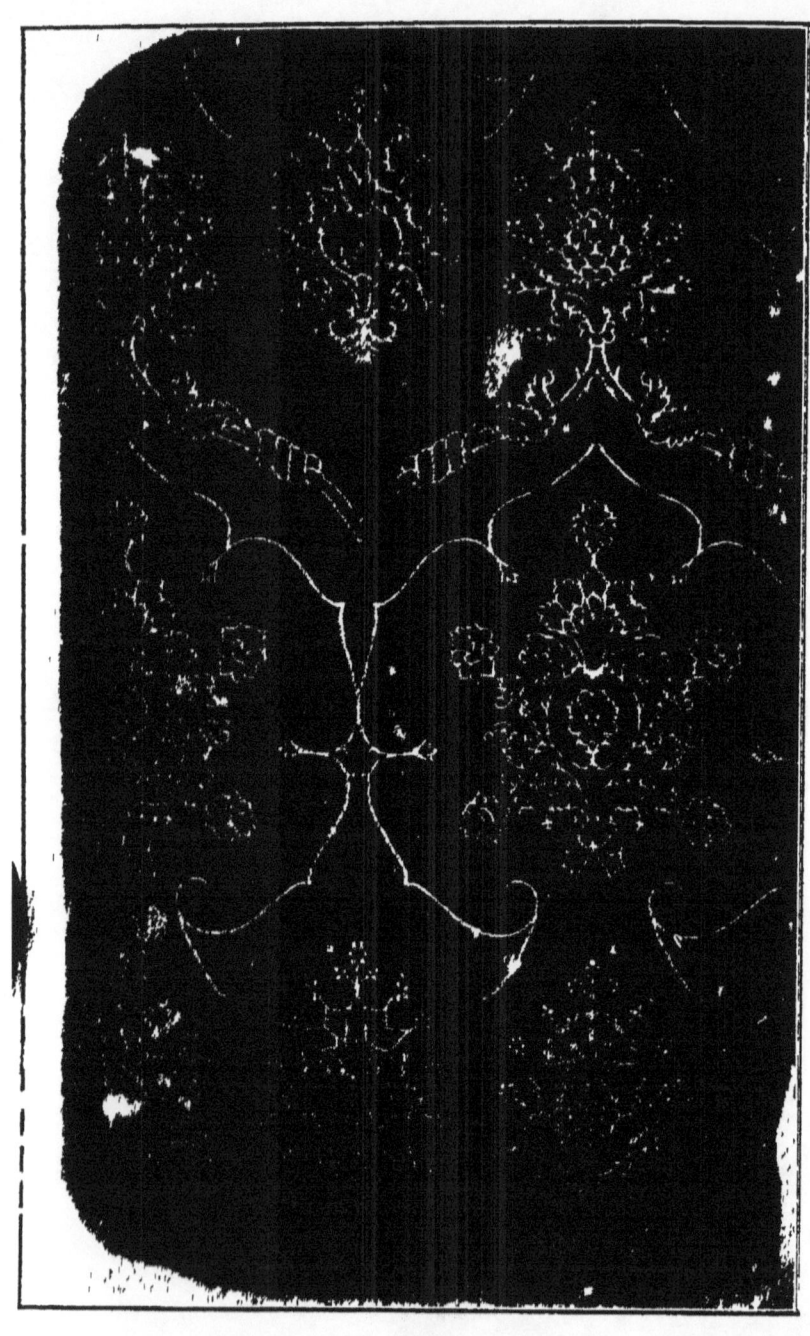

PLATE 37.

VELVET. (BOSTON MUSEUM OF FINE ARTS.)

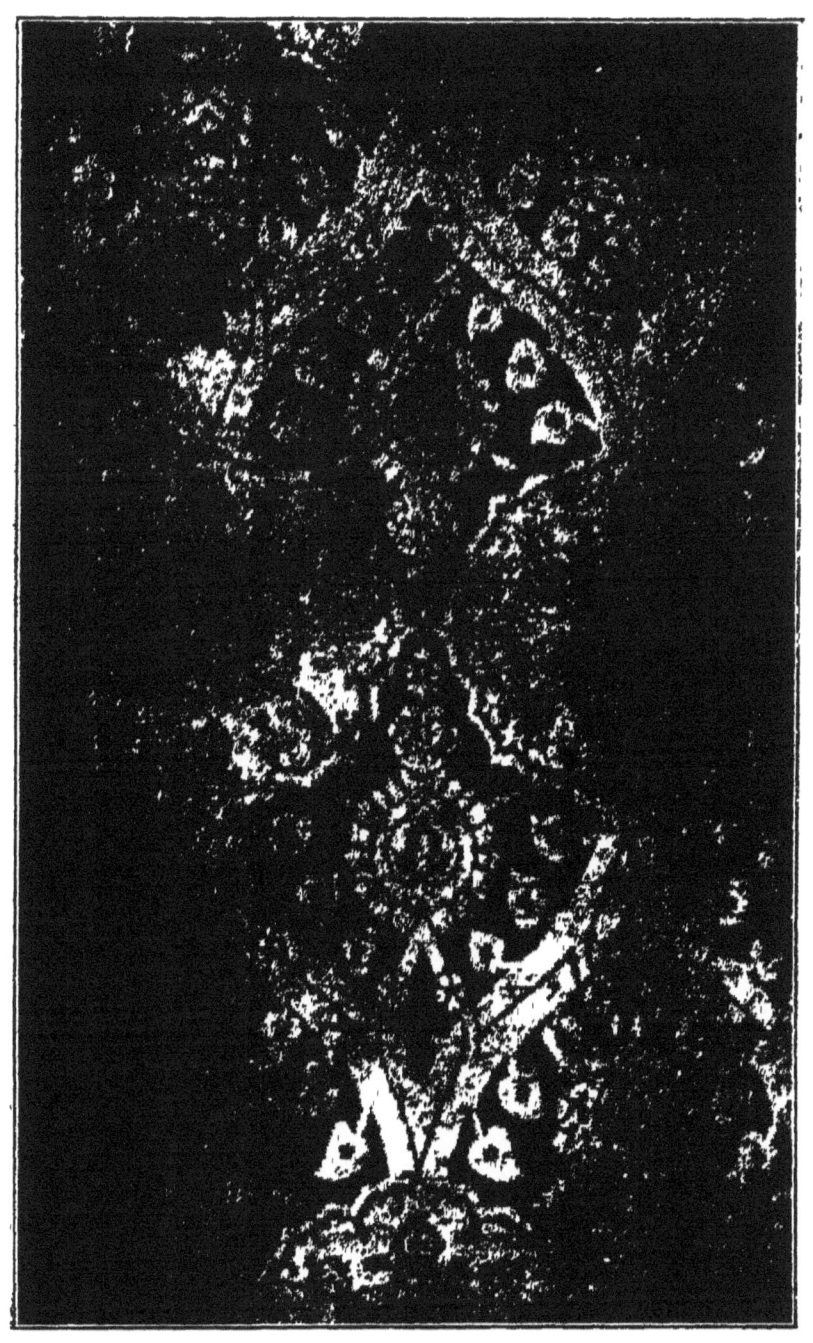

PLATE 38.

SCUTARI VELVET. (BOSTON MUSEUM OF FINE ARTS.)

leaves which carry the eye out of the composition. The ideas thus briefly noted are the same that must guide us to the achievement of any interest or unity in the present problem.

As a simple demonstration of these principles let us choose an abstract form such as is shown in Figure 102. This form may represent a solid of three dimensions rather than a half circle. To a grouping

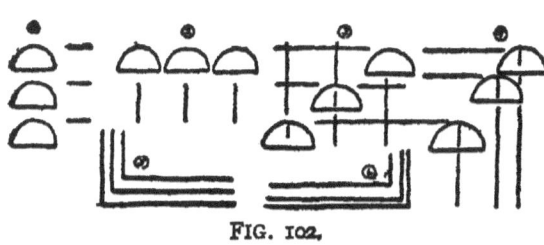

FIG. 102.

of three of these forms we shall first seek to impart variety with unity. In the first case there is variety on the horizontal lines; in the second, variety on the vertical; in the third, variety on both horizontal and vertical. But in the association of three objects similar in shape and measure the most obvious thing to do would be to break them into groups of two and one, as in the final example. Here is as much variety as is consistent with the unity of effect. The thought brings us back to the elementary demonstrations of proportion in the spacing of lines. There is more interest in the sixth than in the fifth grouping of lines.

In Figure 103 the first example lacks this element of variety. In the second the grouping of forms and stem lines is unquestionably more interesting. In the

third, fourth, and fifth examples another factor count‑
ing for variety is introduced, — variety in the direc‑
tions of the movements of growth. Considering these
forms as elementary flowers a breaking of each form
into petals must be attended with the same regard for
variety; in the sixth example each form is subdivided

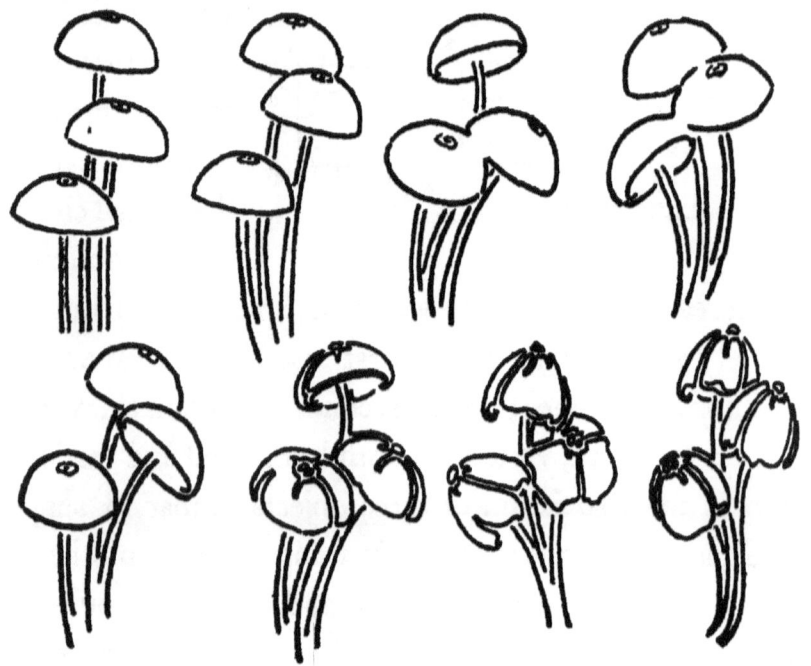

FIG. 103.

into equal but related space relations. This breaking
has been done without disturbing the rhythmic move‑
ment of all the details. In the following example it is
apparent that the balance is lost; also that the lines
which break up the big forms are not in good rhyth‑
mic relation to the rest of the lines. In the last case

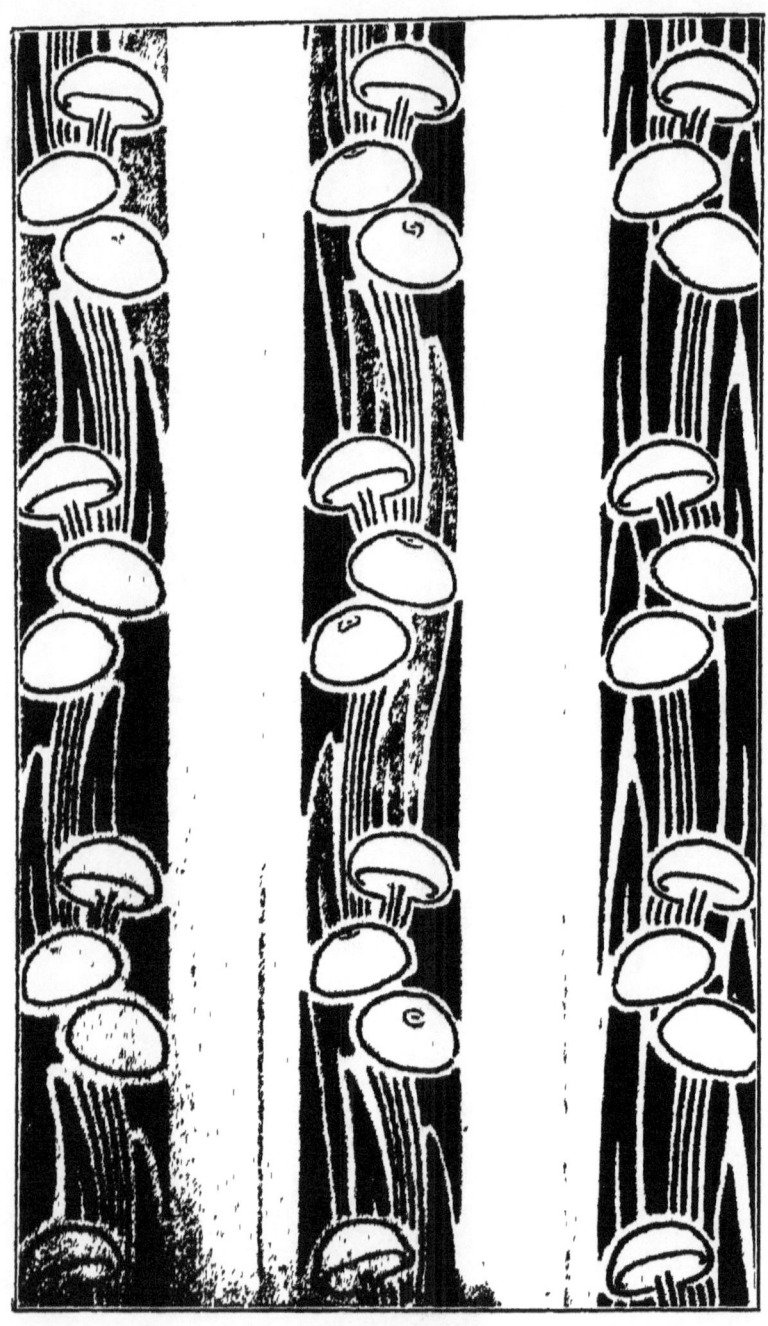

PLATE 39.

NATURE SYMBOLS.

a few slight changes restores the balance of the whole and the rhythmic movement of all the details.

In Plate 39 the same abstract lines and forms are studied for the sake of repeated patterns. The leaf form employed is quite arbitrary, chosen because it seems in keeping with the end sought. Compare these simple borders with the straight-line designs that have preceded them and it will be seen at once that their interest is due solely to their structural character. Every element within the borders, space and mass alike, has been made to contribute its share to the effect. In Figure 104 a surface development is shown from a clew suggested by one of the borders, and in Plate 40 is another step in which the reciprocal relation of space and mass is readily seen. The background is composed of dark and light leaves working in unity.

A study which strikes a happy middle ground between Nature and the abstract in its treatment is shown in the Japanese textile of Plate 41. Note the grouping and breaking of the flower forms and the charming treatment of leaves and background.

Problem. It is not proposed to develop the idea of decorative composition from Nature along the line indicated in Figure 95. Rather, let us seek in Nature a stimulant for the inventive faculty in the composition of abstract forms; the best time to go to Nature is

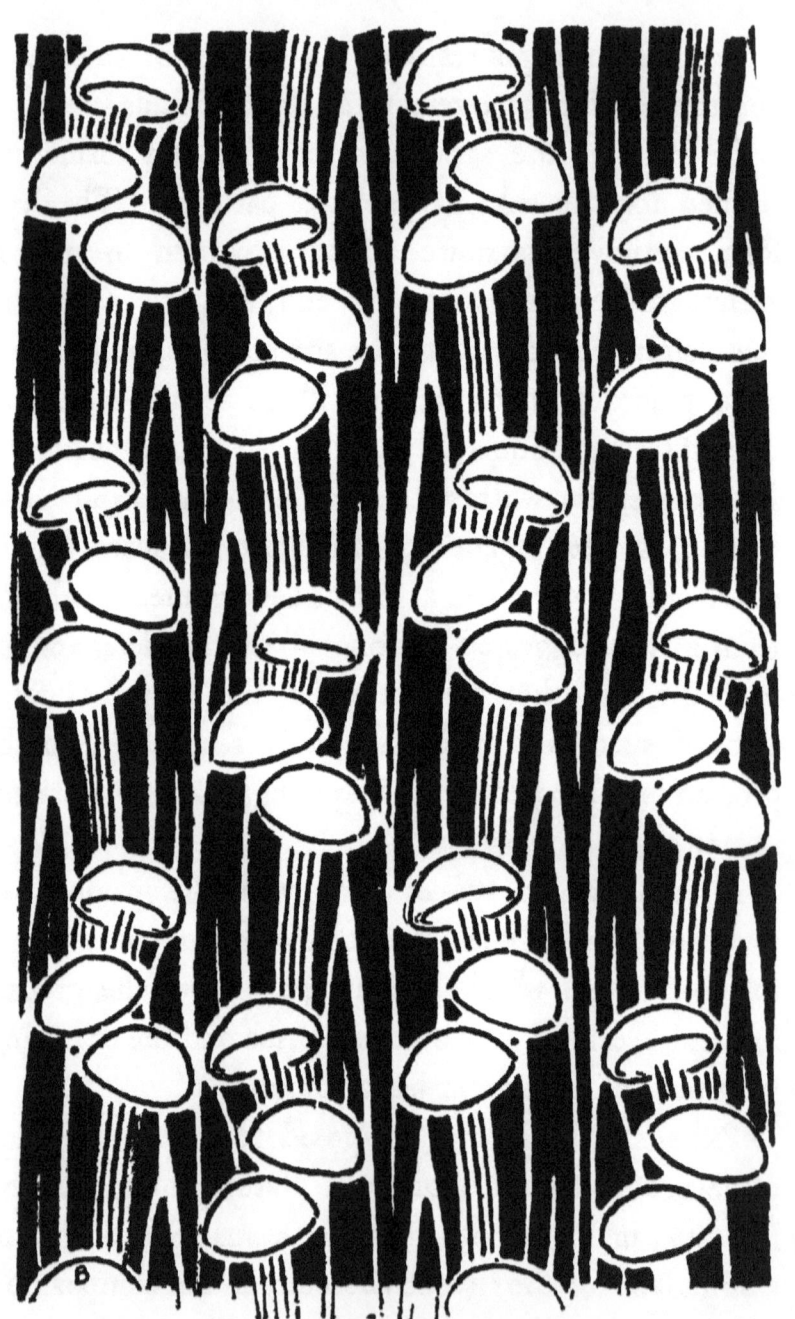

FIG. 104.

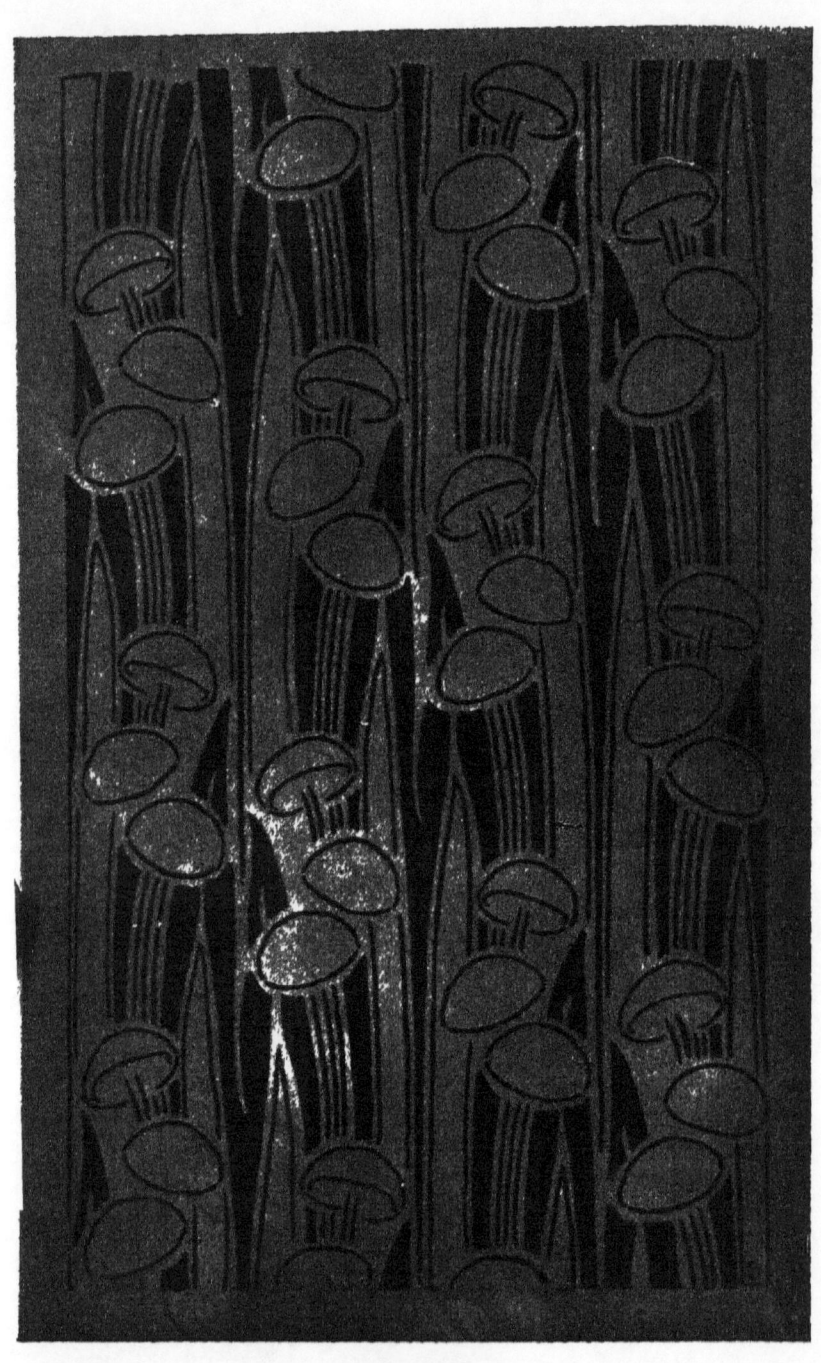

PLATE 40.

NATURE SYMBOLS.

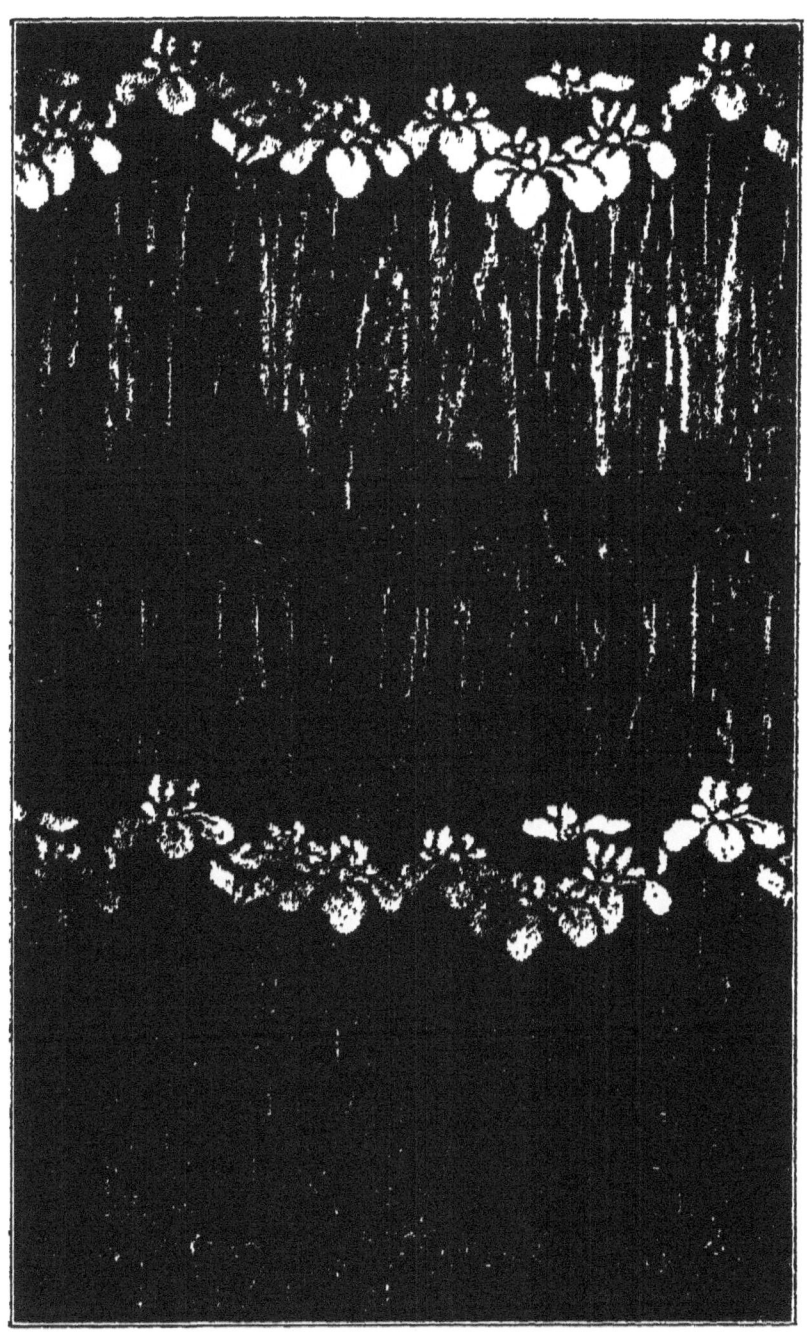

PLATE 41.
JAPANESE TEXTILE.

when the imagination falters. As a preliminary study for this problem it would be well to analyze a flower of careful selection,—say, a rose that is set with particular beauty upon its stem. Let us pass the rose of symmetrical growth for one which offers a variety in petal curvature, with a balanced disposition of lines and forms of growth. Study it in outline and in mass, in different positions; note the relation of the petals to the center and to each other. Detach a few of the petals and draw them from different points of view.

With these forms as a keynote let us try the construction of similar forms suggestive though not imitative of flower petals. As areas their beauty will be dependent on the relation of contour lines. It is then the purpose to build up an abstract flower form from the garden of the imagination. Its beauty will be a test of the feeling for rhythm and balance that is within the worker. Figure 105 may serve to indicate the start. A few tentative lines may define the general form of the flower and the subdivision of the parts. In shaping the petals into which this general form is to be subdivided, it is essential to bear these points in mind: each petal must be graceful in movement, pleasing in shape; there should be variety with unity in the shapes and measures of the different petals; they should be united in a movement toward a common center; should hang together as a whole; and, last, you are compelled, under pressure of necessity, to study the whites as well as the blacks. If you are able to attain the desired result in a single flower, it

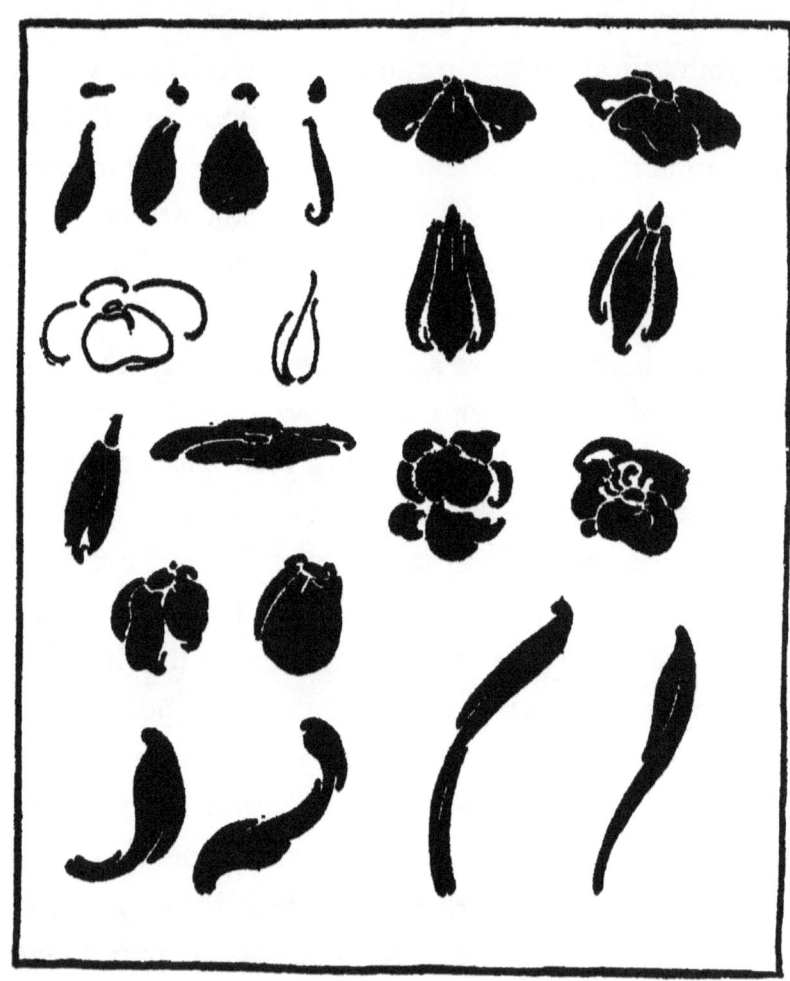

FIG. 105.

will not be difficult to combine lines and forms suggesting two flowers, or a flower and a bud, in a common movement. The demands of balanced composition,

rather than a symmetrical arrangement, will naturally
lead the designer to give dominant height to one flower.
Then see if you can strike a few well-curved lines
having a common growing-point and related by a
movement in harmony with the movement of the
blacks and whites represented by the flower heads.
In the same way see if you can develop a simple,

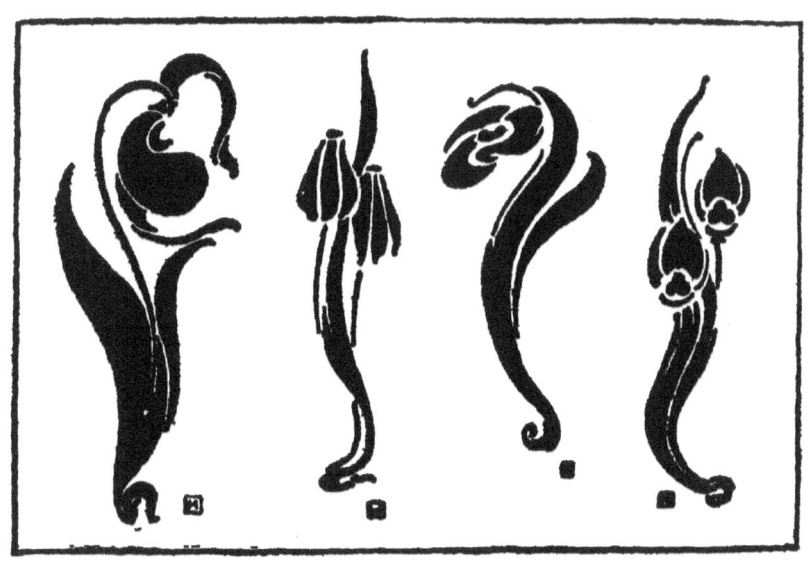

FIG. 106.

abstract leaf form. The leaves suggested are of the
simplest possible kind; it should be noted that the
growing point of each leaf is different from its ending.
"Parts which differ in function should differ in appearance." The movement of the entire forms, stems,
leaves, flowers, should be felt out together, subject to
change, for sake of the whole, in any of its details.

Figure 106 shows such results as might be expected from this problem.   Each example, like a good story,

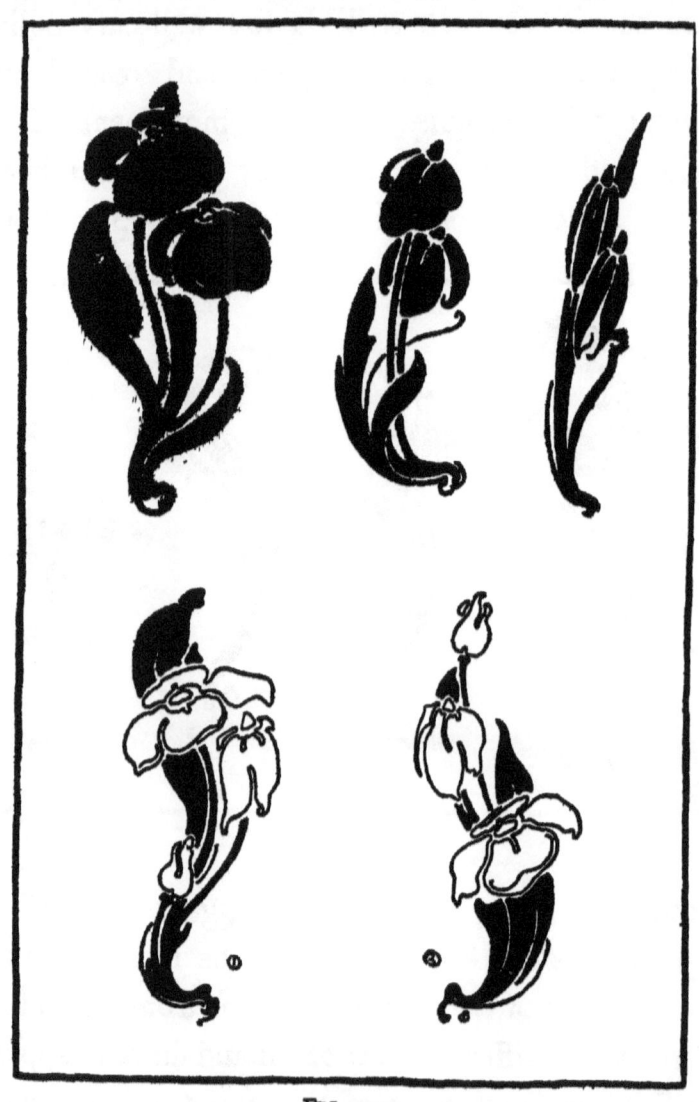

FIG. 107.

has a definite starting point, a gradual unfolding of its movement, and a conclusion with a concentration of

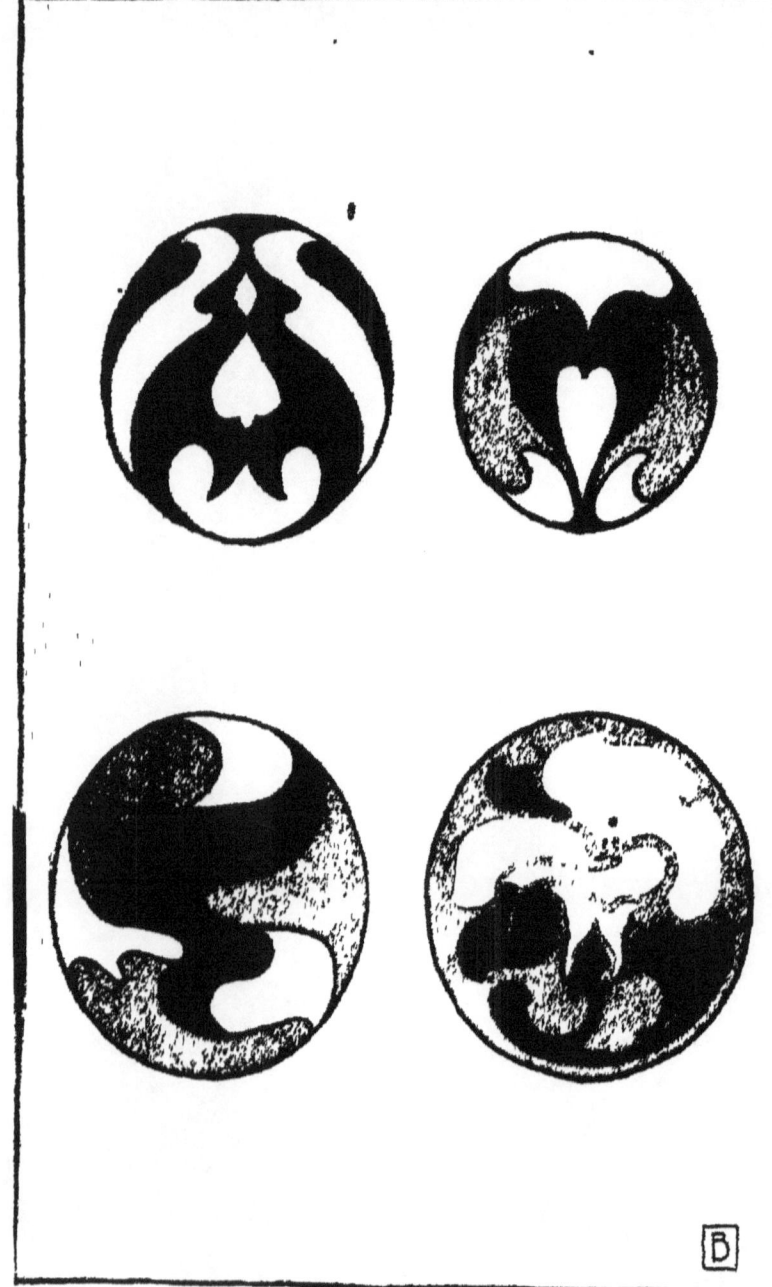

PLATE 42.

ABSTRACT RHYTHMS.

interest in the flower forms.   For sake of continuity
of movement a tangential union of all lines is necessary;
the movement may be sinuous and slow, or rapid,
depending upon the relations of lines (Figure 107).
The eye moves most rapidly along lines closely related
in curvature.   Not only in lines and shapes, but in
measures as well, we may seek to gain command of the
rhythmic movement of these studies.   In the lower
part of this figure measure rhythm has entered into the
problem.   In the first an upward increase of measures
in both blacks and whites imparts dynamic force to
the conclusion.   In the second the downward increase
of measures adds strength to the beginning of the
movement.   To borrow terms from music, the first is a
crescendo; the second a diminuendo.   To acquire complete command over rhythmic forces is the end sought.

PROBLEM.   Let us continue the thought of the
last problem under different conditions, a development
of either an abstract or Nature-derived motif within an
inclosing form.   A simple version of the problem will
serve to define the intent of the treatment (Plate 42).
Within a circle of about three inches diameter see if
you can swing a series of live curves, breaking the
circle into space divisions in which each line is rhythmically related to the circumference of the circle.   If
you will follow with a pencil the lines in any of the
figures of this plate, you will have the essential point

o

of the problem. There is a natural and easy flow of lines from the circumference of the circle back to the circumference. As these lines are made it will be found that areas are formed. Each area must be interesting in its contour and related in measure to the other areas. It will be found, almost invariably, that one area persists in remaining as a mere accidental hole in the result, refusing to come into the same plane with the others. To subdue this obstinate area and keep all of the spots in a single flat plane demands more skill than a mere statement of the difficulty may imply.

Now let us develop a motif within a circle. Plates 43, 44 serve to illustrate the intent of the problem and an application of the idea in the work of designers who were masters of their materials. Note in both the way in which variety with unity has been achieved. Of special interest is the grouping of the kernels of

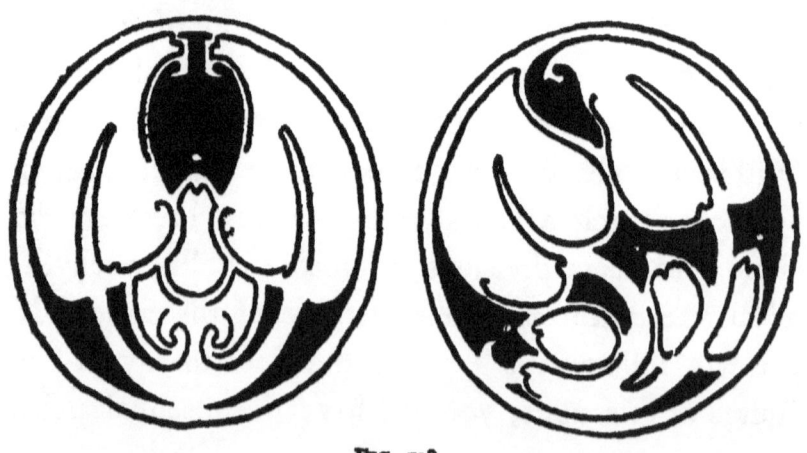

FIG. 108.

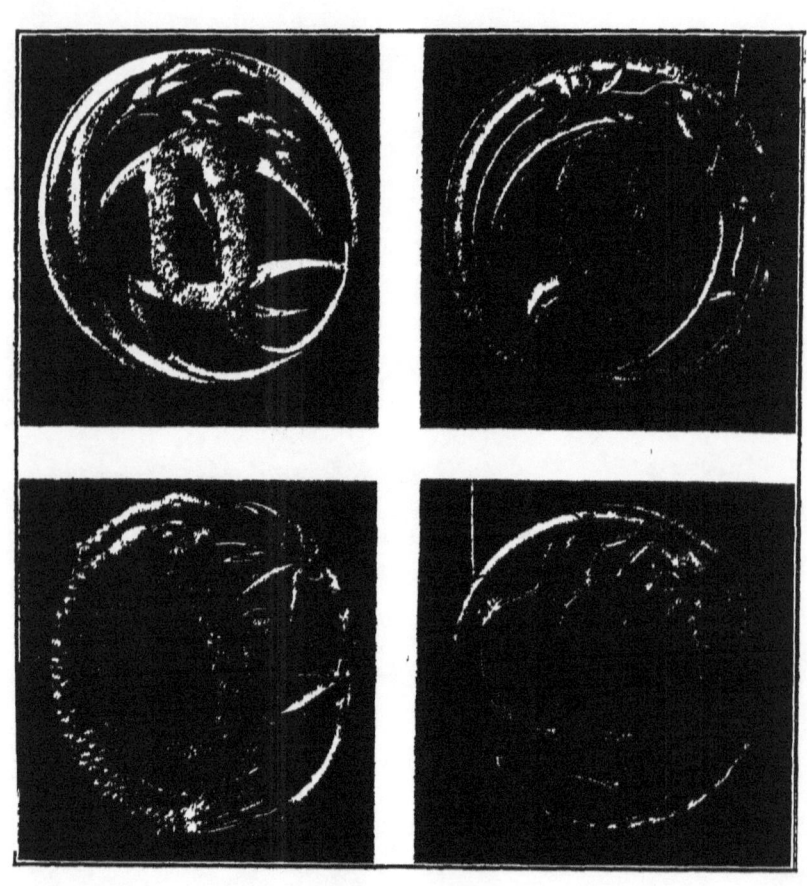

PLATE 43.

JAPANESE SWORD GUARDS. (BOSTON MUSEUM OF FINE ARTS.)

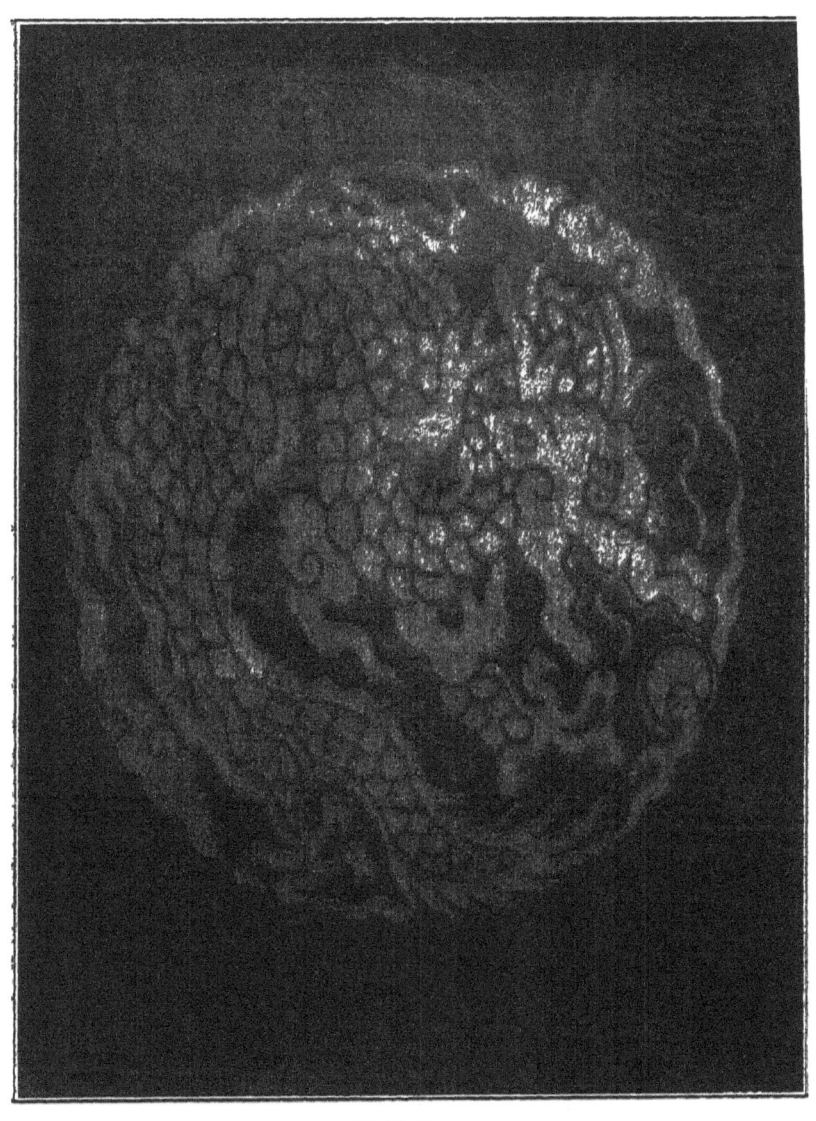

PLATE 44.

CHINESE TEXTILE. (BOSTON MUSEUM OF FINE ARTS.)

grain in the first plate.   Here alone there is evidence
of a master's touch,
of a refined feeling
that does not stop
short of the last
minute detail in the
finished product. In
Plate 44 the dragon,
a creature of the im-
agination, has been
chosen as a basis for
the arbitrary break-
ing of a circle into

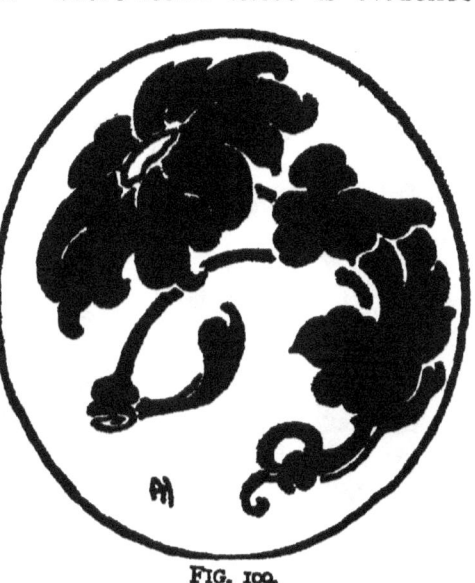

FIG. 109.

space and mass rela-
tions of dark and
light.

Figure 108 repre-
sents the simplest
version of the prob-
lem we are now to
solve.   Here   the
lines and forms of
natural growth have
been fitted to the de-
mands of a rhythmic

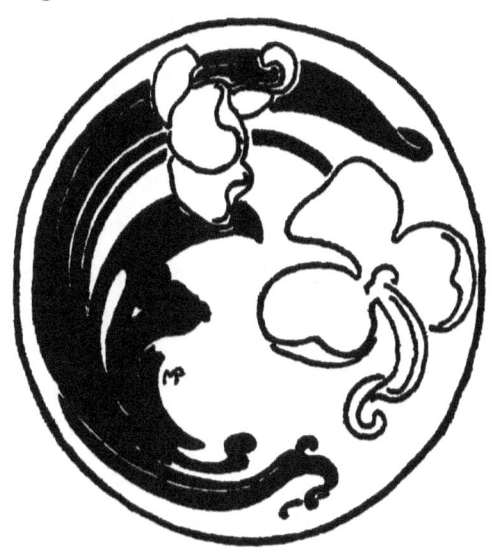

FIG. 110.

composition within a circle.   Figures 109, 110 indicate
good feeling for related movements of line and group-

ings of forms. The problem will be found sufficiently difficult if we eliminate details and treat the growth in

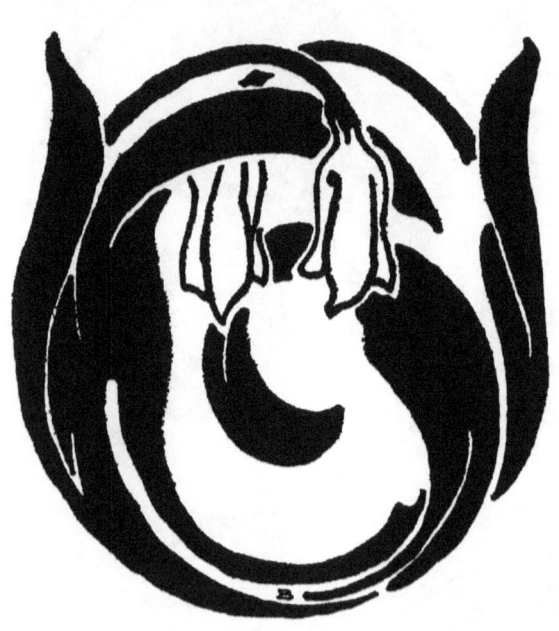

FIG. III.

one simple flat plane. In Figure 111, from the yellow adder's tongue, is a more difficult expression of the idea. In the opposition of two specimens there is always serious trouble involved at the growing points. The trouble was averted by approaching the problem from the point of view of a black-and-white composition, subordinating Nature to the principles governing such a composition of lines and forms. In Plate 45 another difficulty is added to the problem by attempting to secure a balance of three values in the result. In this acceptance of another element the importance of the effort increases. In Figure 112 the orange has been adapted to the form of a triangle. The idea involved in the problem remains unchanged. If you will refer to Figure 84, you will find the same problem expressed

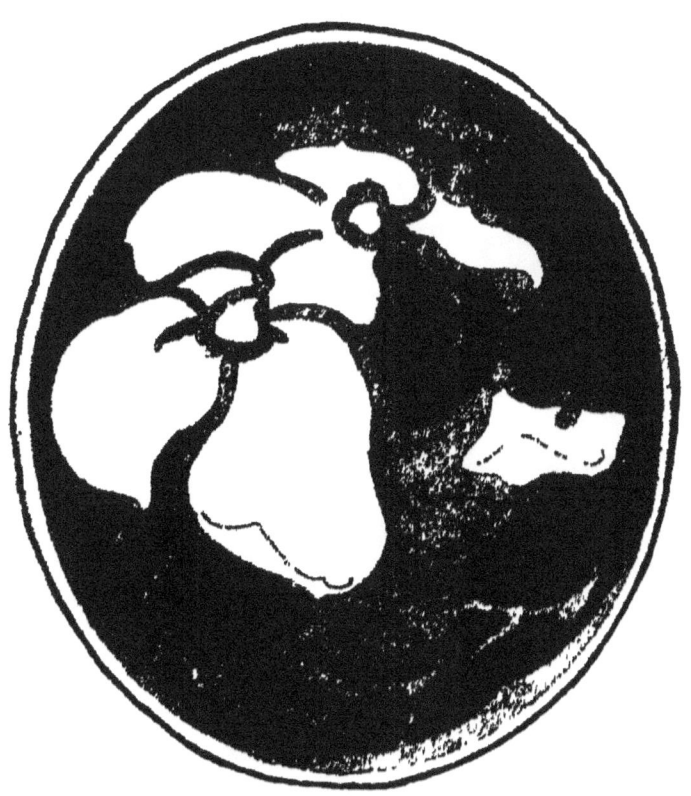

PLATE 45.

NATURE SYMBOL. — RHYTHM AND BALANCE.

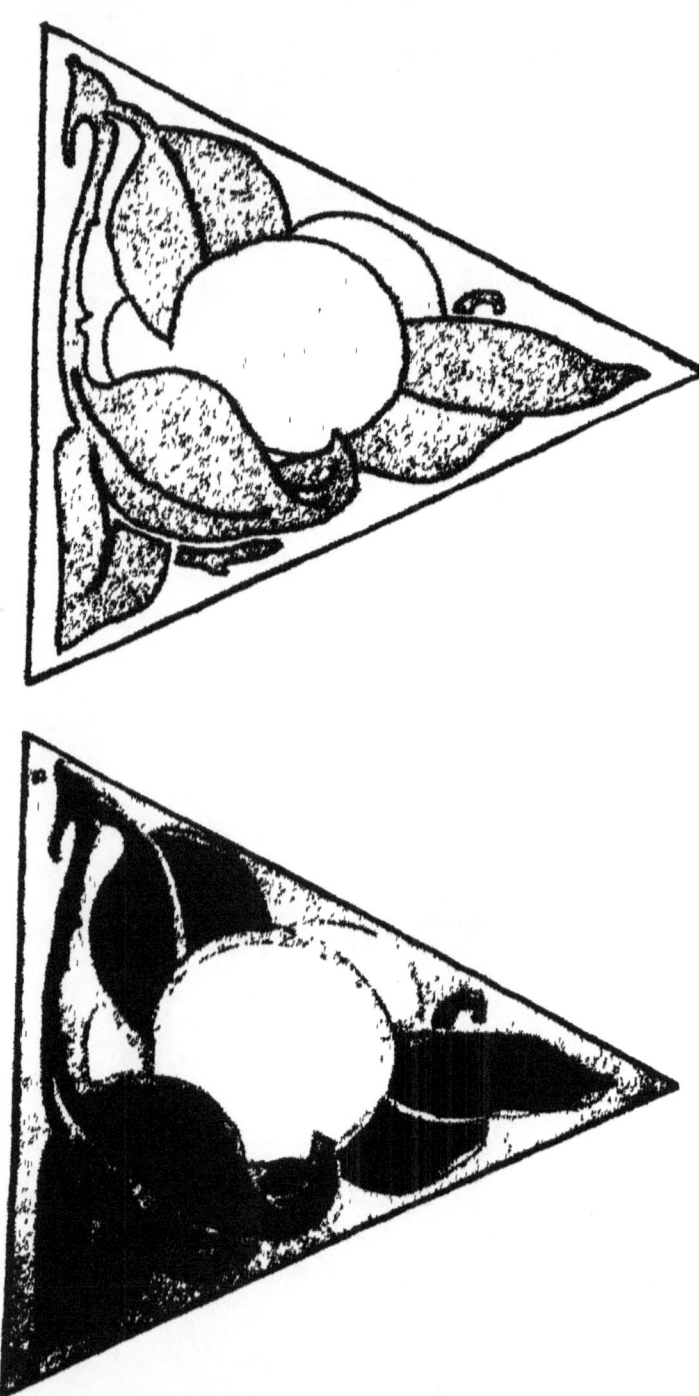

PLATE 46

NATURE DERIVATIVES — RHYTHM AND BALANCE.

in simpler terms. If the simple, geometric statement of the idea was understood, it will be seen that the present problem merely multiplies the difficulties by re-

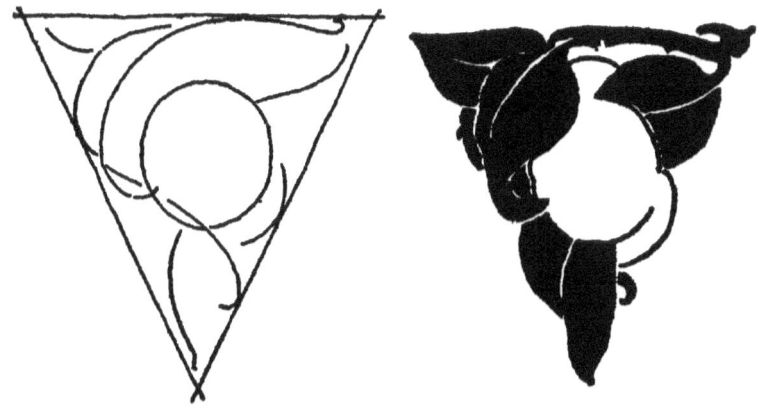

FIG. 112.

moving the props furnished by the squared paper and a limitation to straight lines. The design must proceed from the whole to the parts, from a tentative blocking out of the lines and forms to the final touches of refinement of execution. It is unnecessary to enslave one's self to a "leading line." There may be many shifts and changes of the first tentative lines as a solution develops; but not for a moment must one lose sight of the necessity for relating all of the lines and forms in a common purpose. In Plate 46 are two renderings of the result. In one is a balance of three values; in the other a dominant contrast has been given to the leaf forms.

Incidentally it may be asked: Why should one

commend the treatment accorded Nature in Plates 43, 44 and condemn the naturalistic character of the iron work shown in Figure 57? Here in one of these plates the scales of a fish and the leaves of the bamboo are detailed with painstaking exactness. But if we give more careful thought to a consideration of the motives underlying the work of the Japanese artisan and the rococo blacksmith, we shall find a fundamental difference in the aims and results. To suspend a naturalistic iron festoon of beribboned flowers from a bracket is quite feasible if the worker has sufficient technical skill to imitate with more or less exactness or through technical mannerism a carefully arranged model placed before him. There is no great amount of mental exertion evident in such a piece of work. The French potter, Bernard Palissy, in his fervent plea that the beauty of Nature alone was sufficient excuse for its unrestrained application to design, went so far as to make casts from frogs, shells, and fishes for use in his work, giving to these casts all the realistic character that his glazes permitted. And the closer he came to Nature the less interesting his product became. He expected Nature to do his designing for him. In his work, beyond the admirable technique involved in the execution, there was no evidence of system or orderly thought; the idea was wrong. While a motif from Nature may be beautiful on its own account, any effort to beat that beauty into iron, weave it into cloth, chisel it in marble, or model it in clay can end in nothing short of disaster. In the work of the Japanese artisans each detail is made to conform to the *idea* that the worker had in mind to express. Not in the demands of utility alone, nor in tools or materials, much less in Nature, can be found the key to a beautiful and distinctive product. A designer's work will inevitably form an index to the soundness of his judgment, the strength of his imagination, the depth of his feeling. From within him must proceed the idea that stamps his work as beautiful or ugly, distinctive or commonplace, worthy or unworthy. Nature stubbornly refuses to do his thinking for him.

CHAPTER X

FROM THE PARTS TO THE WHOLE

"Criticism is easy. But Art is difficult."
— *Inscription, Beaux Arts, Paris.*

LET us build up a surface repeat, assuming as a motif the three berries and two leaves with which acquaintance was made under the limitations of straight-line work. As in the former case, we are not bound to any particular specimen from Nature, though here, as at all times, it is assumed that a study of Nature has stored the mind with numerous available forms. In the demonstrations that follow purely abstract forms are employed.

Let us begin with the first detail, Figure 113, A. The grouping of the three berries first claims attention. The bottom group, considering these three groups without the addition of other details, seems to possess greater variety in the relative positions of the berries than the top one, and suggests a more consistent growth than the middle one. Any of these groups might be justified, however, in the arrangement of other details of the unit. Let us choose the bottom group. With this simple suggestion as a start it is now desirable to bring the two leaves of the motif into some rhythmic relation to the berries.

A few tentative lines might result in some such movement as is shown in B. There is now a reciprocal relation of these minor details. In completing the

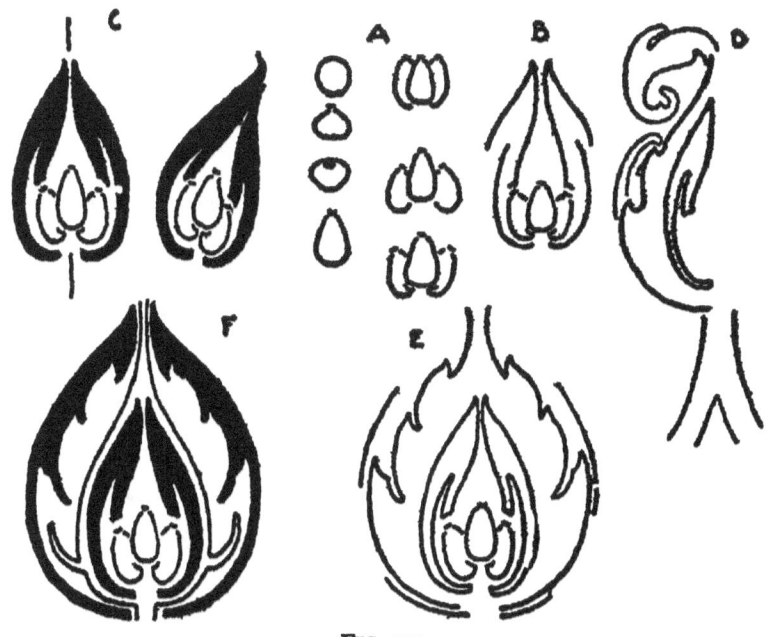

FIG. 113.

symmetrical adjustment of these elements, as in C, it must, of course, be decided whether the widest part of the unit shall be at the top or at the bottom; for the sake of variety it seems better that it should be at one or the other rather than at the center. It must also be kept in mind that the *symmetry of white within the unit is just as important as the symmetry of black formed by the leaves.* In the present case it is perhaps the more interesting of the two. So. much for the unit; its lines and forms have been determined.

It is now necessary to gain a reciprocal relation from unit to unit with a space and mass composition that will bind the repeated pattern together into a unity of effect. Experience enables the designer to foresee, in the shaping of the unit, the possibilities that it may possess for a repeated pattern. He shapes the details with the whole in mind. But the present aim is experimental in character. As a next step, draw the center line of the unit as indicated. Then on a full sheet of the transparent paper draw another center line. Place the unit in the center of the paper, underneath, with the two lines coinciding; trace the result. We now have the first element of the pattern. How can the unit be repeated at regular intervals to

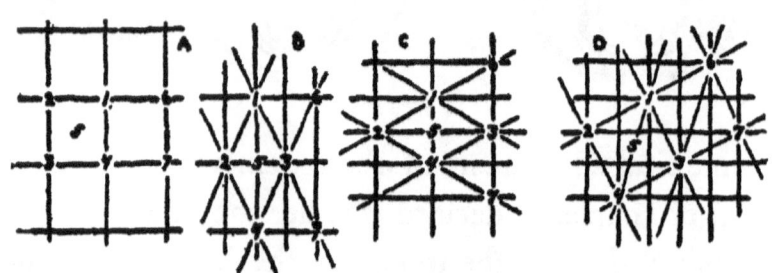

FIG. 114.

furnish the most satisfactory result? In the various diagrams shown in Figure 114 it may be assumed that the first unit is represented in each diagram by the figure 1. It becomes necessary to decide upon the position of the second unit of the repeat. By moving the original unit about under the transparent paper the relation of the two units as well as a forecast of the final effect may be obtained. For sake of illustration it may be assumed that a decision is made as in the diagram A. A second center line should be drawn on the paper and the second tracing made. A symmetrical unit almost invariably demands a symmetrical

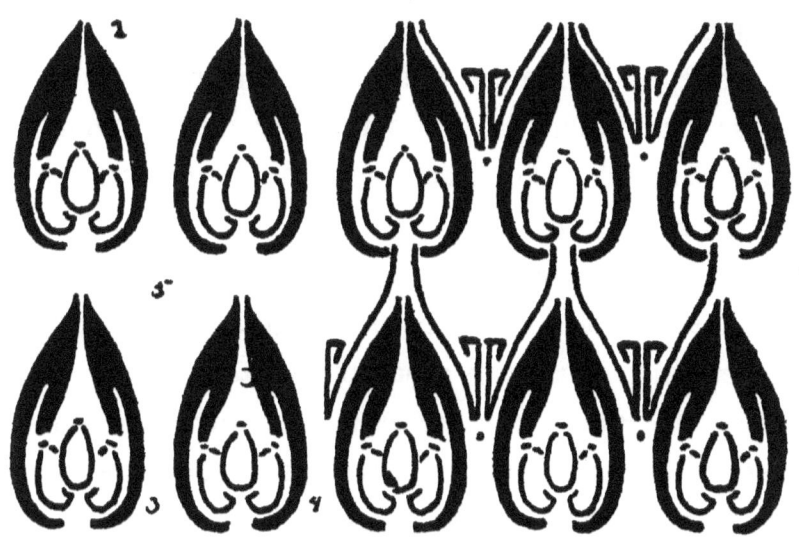

FIG. 115.

repeat; hence an indefinite number of center lines may next be drawn on the paper with the distance between these two as a key. Now when the units numbered 3–4 have been given position, the solution of the problem as a design has only begun. The two questions of most importance are to be solved now. The units must be bound together into a compact whole, with some rhythmic interrelation of all elements; the space, indictated in each diagram by the figure 5, must be accepted as another element in the pattern, — its shape and measure must be developed as an integral part of the design. Figure 115 represents the steps up to this point. It is readily seen that in the first section of this design the space 5 is too large and empty; the units are not well related. In the second section a simple line serves to break in upon the large area of white, and produces a better balance of space and mass; it also binds the units together into a common movement, relates the blacks and whites, and produces a third subordinate tone.

That is designing with an eye to the principles that these problems have been defining. The method of repetition may vary; but the idea is exactly the same. In Figure 116, for example, another development of this same unit is shown based upon the construction indicated in the diagram B of Figure 114. It may appear that the unit is better adapted to this repeat than to the other; in which case the experiment has made it possible to look ahead, in planning another unit, to the completed result. It is thus that we learn, — by doing, by experiment, comparison, and selection.

It will be interesting to carry this unit through one or two more experiments, into results more complex, more important. The original unit may always be altered at will to suit the exigencies of repetition, as in Figure 117, for example. Here a slight additional enrichment given to the original unit, as indicated by the dark line in D of Figure 113, furnished a new unit which was repeated on the structural plan shown in

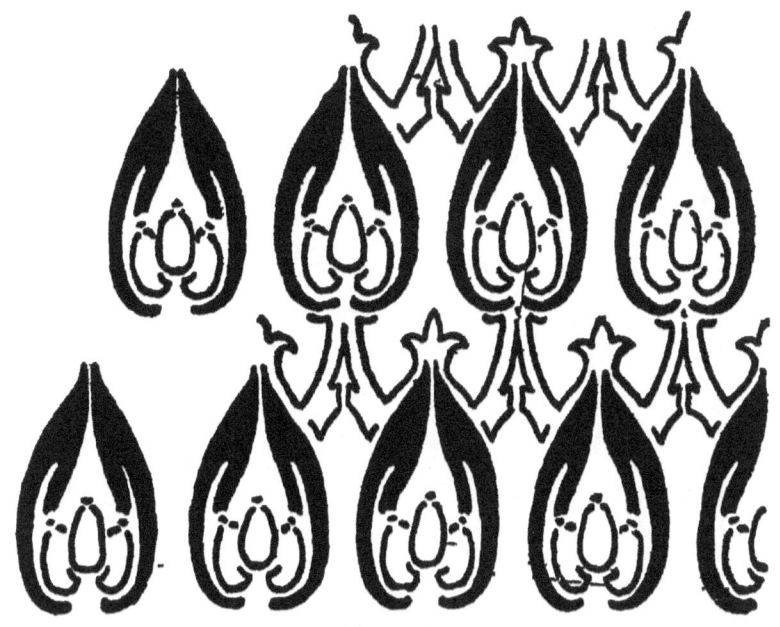

FIG. 116.

Figure 114, B. The development was quite the same as before,—namely, an interrelation of the units and a breaking up of the background spaces in order to bring them into the best possible adjustment with the units. To this end slight additions were made to the unit, as shown by the lighter lines in Figure 113, D. In the final result each shape and measure of black and white is made to contribute some element of interest to the design. It is not a black design on a

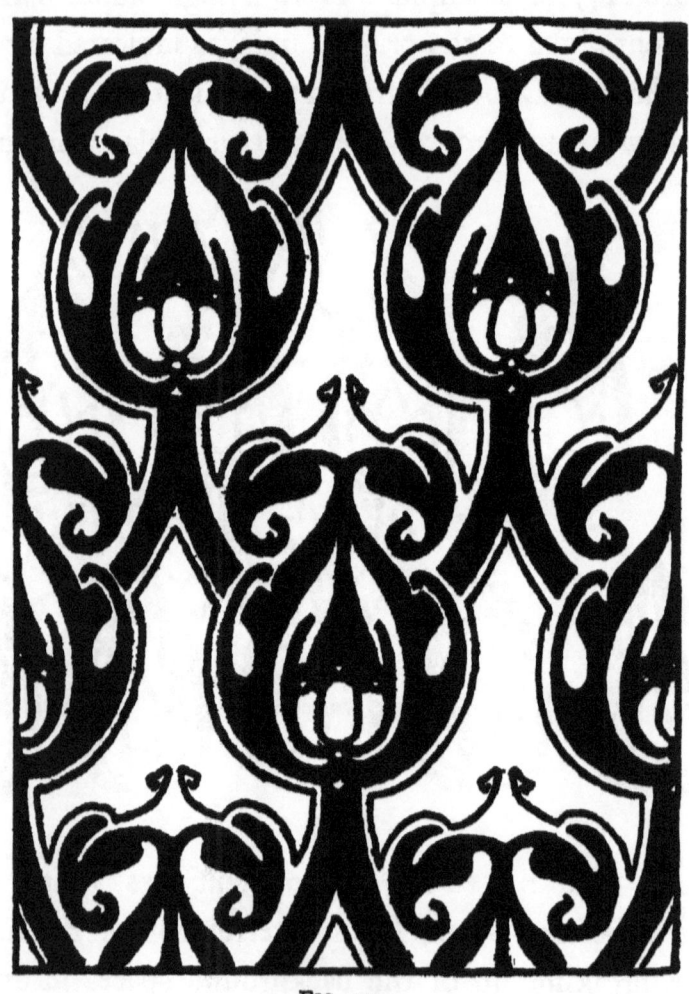

FIG. 117.

white ground; nor is it a white design on a black ground. It is a coöperation of black and white elements, of space and mass, of line and form, to a com-

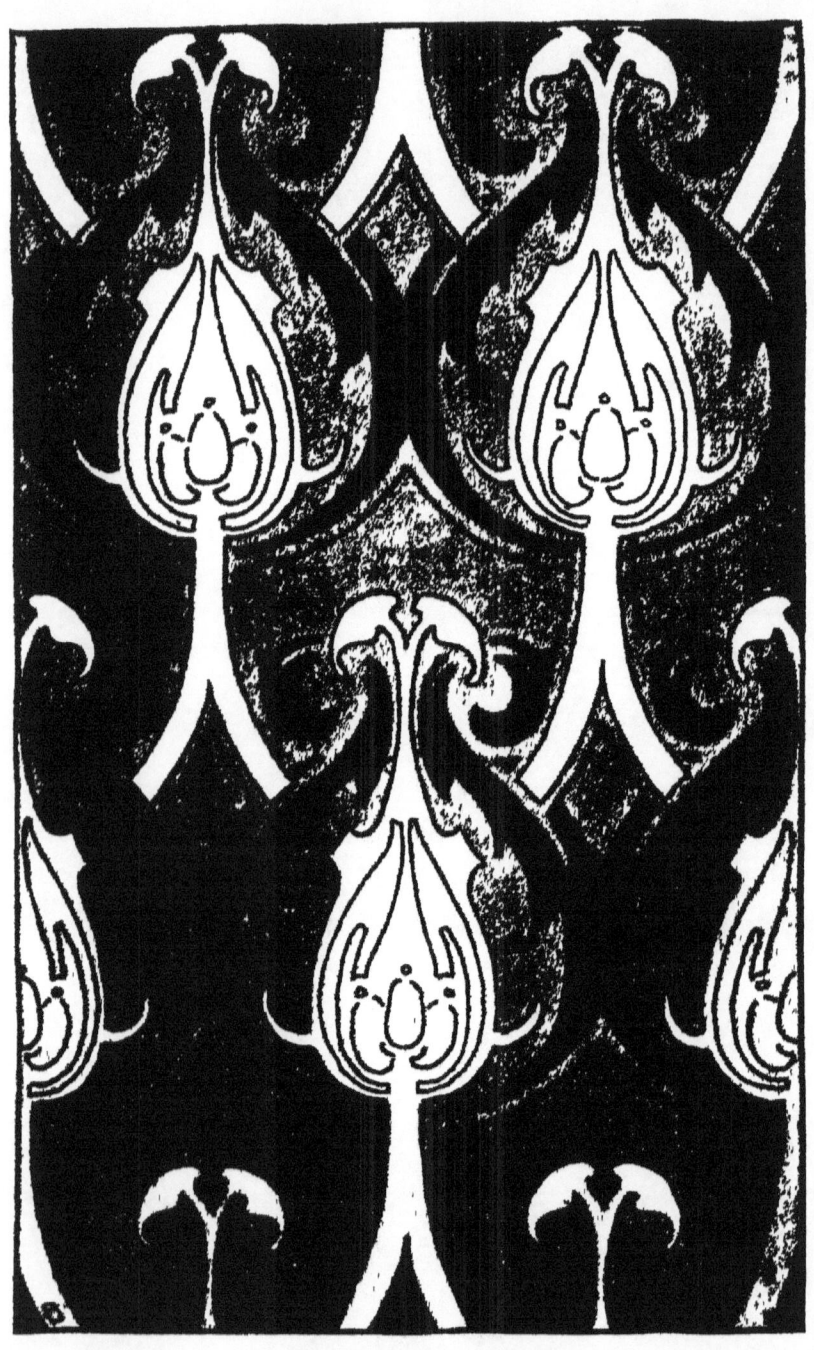

PLATE 47.

NATURE SYMBOLS.

mon purpose; all of which is a return to the original propositions with which these Problems were started.

In Plate 47 is a still more important effort developed from the same starting point. Here it has become necessary to discipline three tones, black, white, and gray, into a unity of effect, to which each must contribute its share. If you will keep in mind the demonstration to this point, the complexities of this pattern will be found to be more apparent than real. The first step is shown in Figure 113, E, F. It will be seen that the original unit with which the start was made has now become a mere incident in the breaking up of the space and mass areas of a more complex unit. Other experiments might, of course, produce units quite different in character from this one. The unit was repeated on the same structural lines as in the preceding plate, though the increased size of the unit naturally demanded a spacing at wider intervals. If a comparison is made between the unit as shown in Figure 113 and the completed pattern, several additions or slight alterations may be noted. If the demonstrations have been clear the reasons that prompted each change in the unit will be clear. The mere repetition of the unit is a minor question; the means adopted to bring unity to the result is the important question. And if the principles of composition are understood, the most prosaic and unpromising material may be developed into a pattern of interest and beauty. And, *per contra*, if these principles are not understood, material of rare beauty may be developed into a pattern devoid of any interest or distinction. Though the unit itself is comparatively unimportant, the use that is made of the unit being the important thing, the best design will always be one that shows a logical and distinctive construction down to the last minute detail, an interrelation to a definite end of every line and form employed.

Now, to return to the first statement of the motif, three berries and two leaves, Figure 118 represents other units equally dependent for interest upon the re-

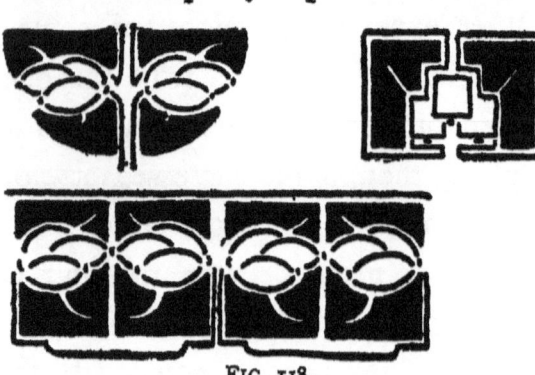

lation of black and white elements. They are merely masses of black broken by spaces of white,

FIG. 118.

the spaces of white being subdivided in turn by lines of black, all bound together into a compact and related whole. In one of these the squared paper of times past again appears. In Figures 119, 120 two of these units are repeated, with such additions in each case as will best serve to bring to the result the character that is sought.

The character forms, here as in the past, the basis of our experiments. Fortunately there are no rules or recipes in design, no method that will enable a lazy individual to achieve distinction, no process that will supplant orderly thought, hard work, and common sense. Such compara-tively simple designs as those shown in Figures 119, 120 demand orderly and concentrated thought. The finished product may, and should, have an appearance of sponta-neity; the drudgery that its completion may have entailed should be elimi-nated. None but those who have learned the true significance of the

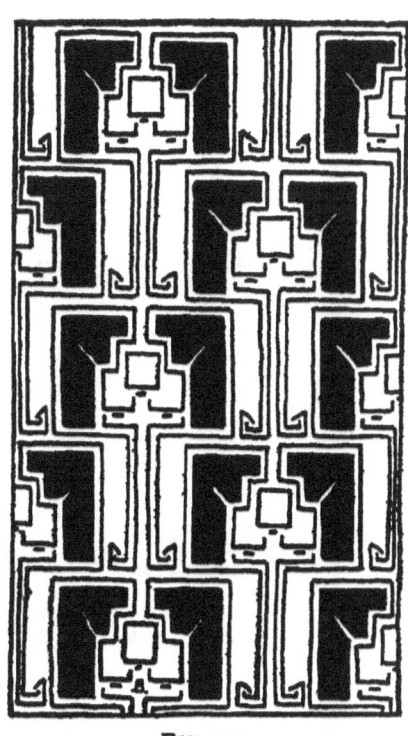

FIG. 119.

little word *study* will discern beneath the surface the many experiments, comparisons, and final selection.

To follow the path backward, then, through the analysis of a distinctive surface pattern we would ask : first, that its spotting of space and mass shall be inter-esting when viewed as a whole; that its structure shall be apparent to the eye; that each tone, measure, and

P

shape shall contribute something to the unity ; that all
of the lines and forms employed shall be intimately
and organically related, even to the last detail.

Thus it is seen that the same constructive principles
are involved in the planning of an abstract pattern as

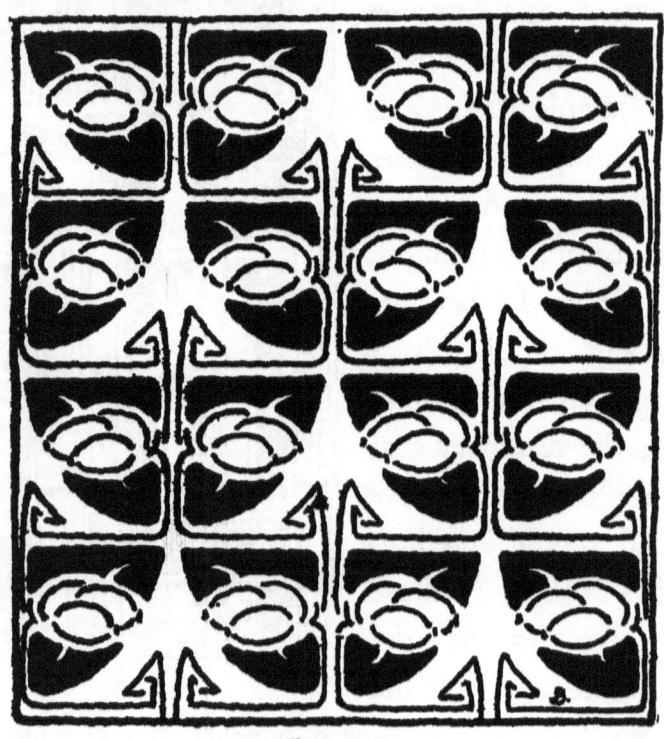

FIG. 120.

in the designing, for example, of an architectural composition. The beauty of either is dependent upon the
refinement and enrichment of a logical construction.
If the structural lines are weak or are ignored, are
buried from sight under a mass of superficial details,
then no amount of enrichment, whether it be " Greek

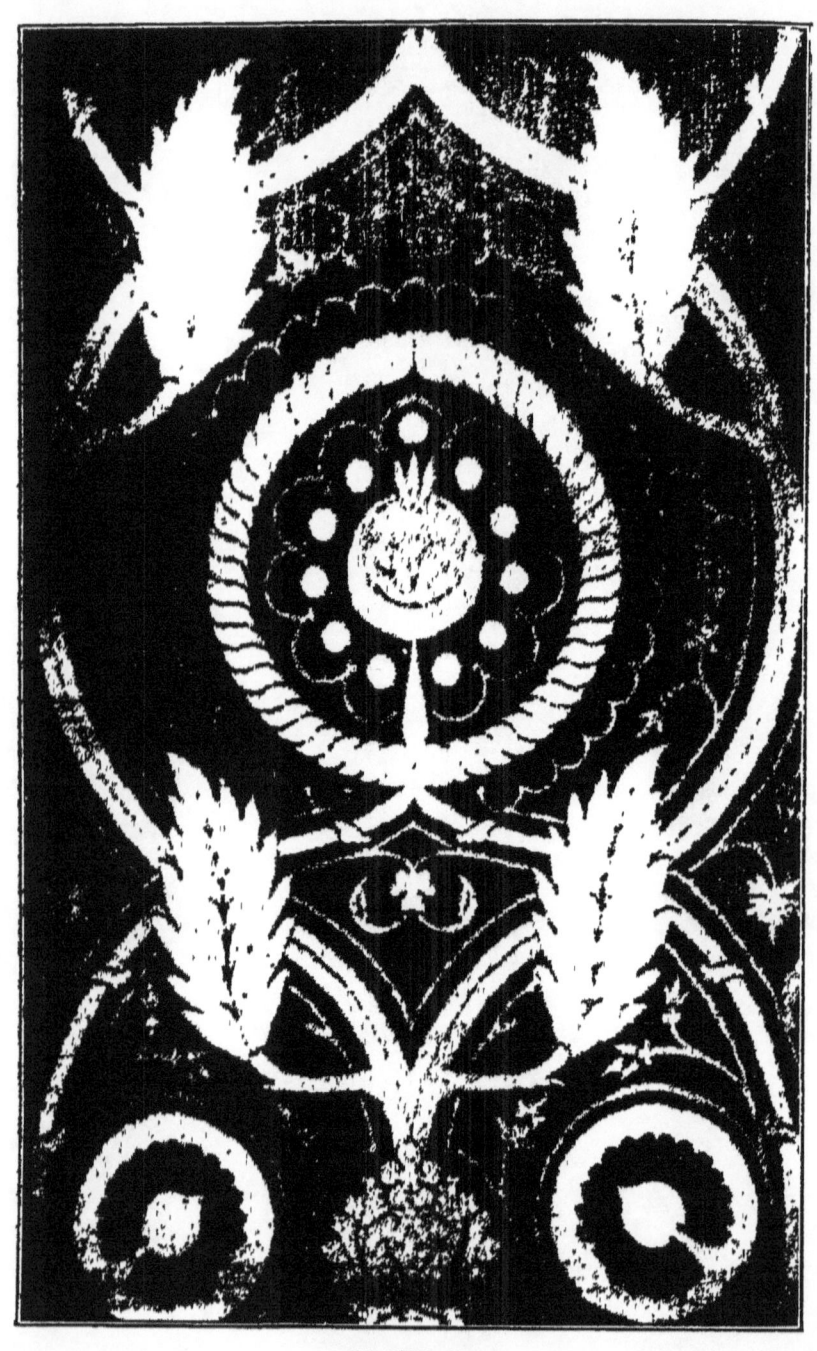

PLATE 48.

PERSIAN VELVET. (BOSTON MUSEUM OF FINE ARTS.)

style" or "Gothic style," or whatever the skill that may enter into its execution, will produce a result of character and distinction.

These experiments with surface patterns would naturally be carried on simultaneously with a study of textiles, wall papers, etc. In the development of textiles from the mediæval period on through following centuries is a profitable source of comparative study. It shows a progress from severe structural simplicity to a hopeless potpourri of lovelorn swains, cupids, ribbons, and flying garlands of flowers. One may note the gradual separation of the designer from the technical demands of the process; in later years we find the workmen vainly essaying the production of designs furnished them by painters who never saw a loom and knew little of its possibilities or limitations. Raphael himself had much better kept to his painting than designing cartoons for the weavers of tapestries. In the repetition of such a simple unit as that shown in Plate 48 there is bound to be a refreshing simplicity. It is a symphony in lines, forms, and tones. It has no pictorial interest, and needs none. There is a feeling of reserve strength throughout, however. The designer might have told more if he had chosen; but he preferred a simple structural treatment, in a broad, flat plane of light and dark. He broke his darks with areas of light, and broke his lights with areas of dark, each contributing to a unity. Of quite a different treatment, though of similar character, is the Japanese textile shown in Plate 49. Those who express a liking for Japanese work because it is "so informal" fail to understand the character of true Japanese art. All that was said of the preceding plate may be said of this wonderful textile. It is a simple, flat spotting of lights and darks, each contributing to the effect of the whole. Note how the legs break in upon the measures of dark, — the rhythmic movement of the bodies and necks. The measures of light are broken by the bills and wings. As in the other textile there is evidence of a definite idea, of orderly thought, and a treatment that is consistent throughout. It is the repetition of a unit on the structural lines of Figure 114, A, the units in the vertical repeat being turned alternately to the right and left.

If the unit is unsymmetrical one may be justified in giving it an unsymmetrical repetition, as in Plate 50. The structural basis of the repeat is always determined, in experiments of this kind, by the shape and measure of the unit. In other words the structure of the design is determined by the idea which it is desired to express in the repetition of the motif. In experimenting with this unit to the end that has been explained, it was found that the most interesting relations could be established by repeating it on lines

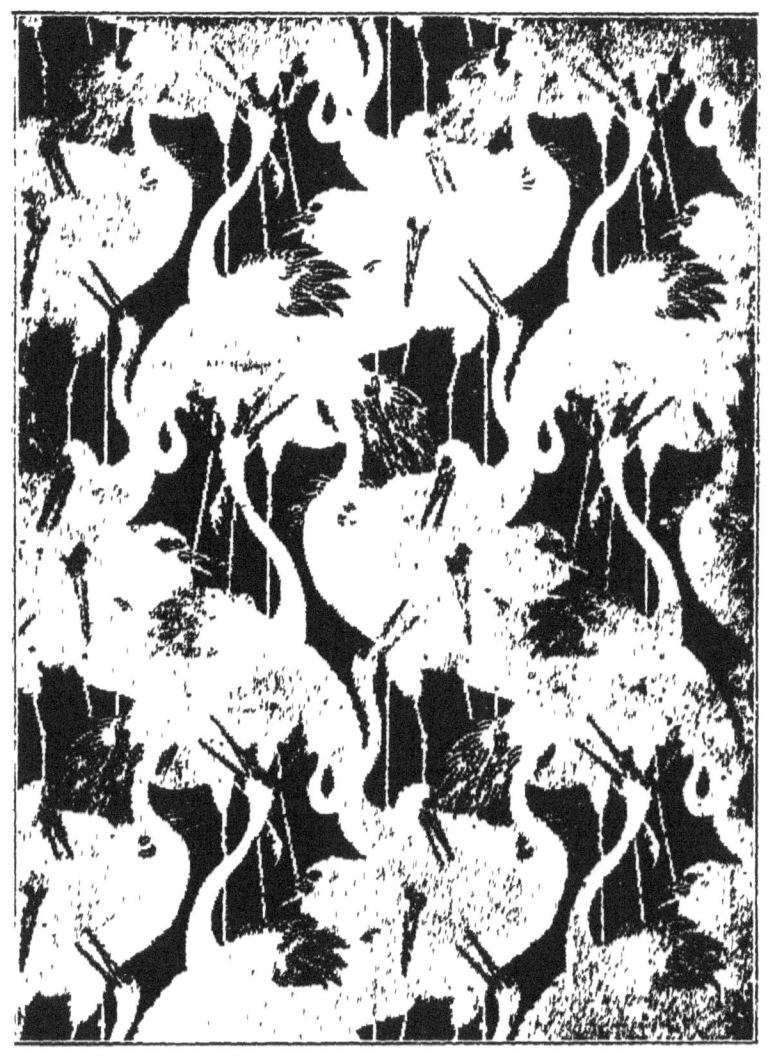

PLATE 49

JAPANESE TEXTILE.

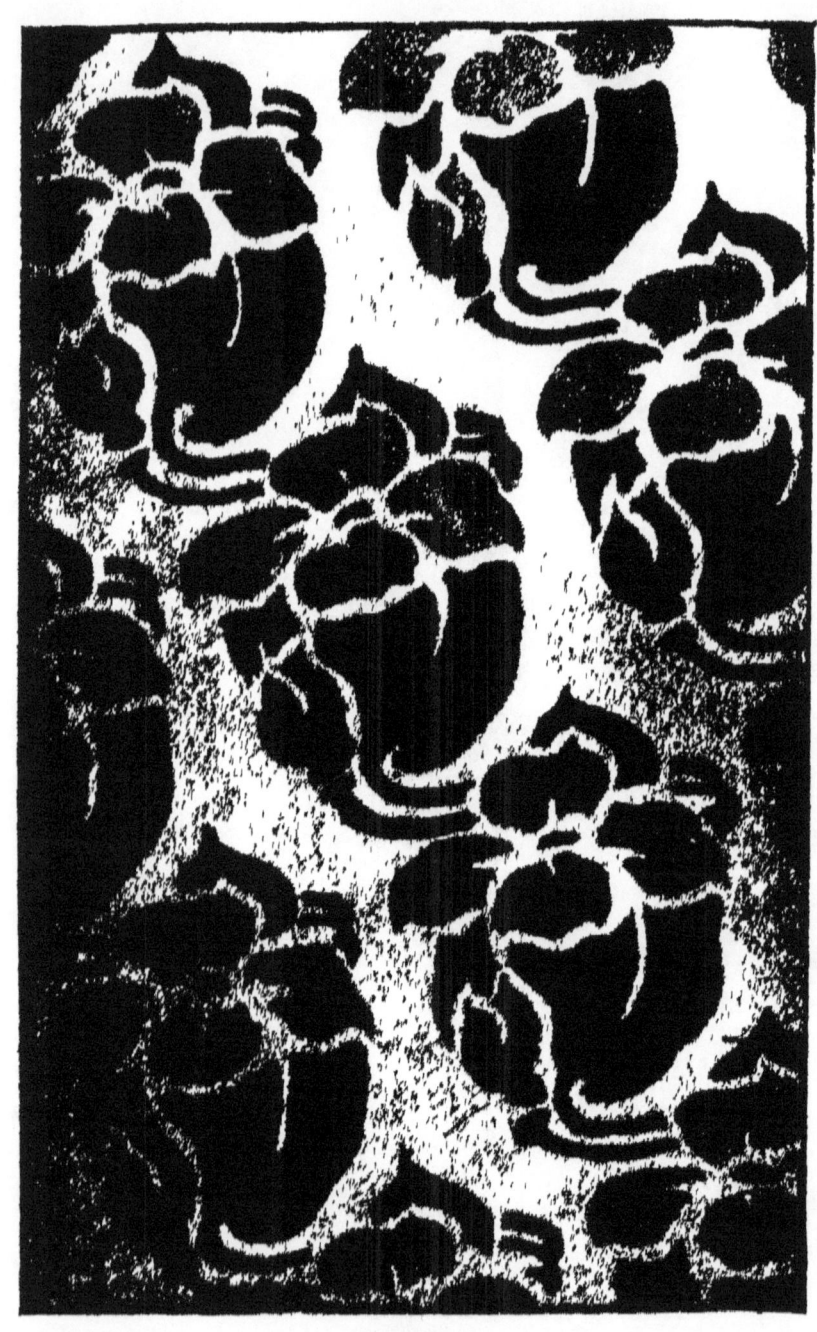

PLATE 50.

UNSYMMETRICAL SURFACE REPEAT.

indicated in Figure 114, D. Incidentally the motif chosen here was quite as simple as the other; it might be stated in these words,—*flower, bud, leaf*. Different individuals might render the motif in as many different ways as in the preceding demonstrations; and here, as before, one might seek assistance from Nature or develop a motif from imagination. It is a matter of choice and does not affect, for good or bad, the fundamental character of the result.

PROBLEM. This is another problem of the same character as many that have preceded it. Its purpose is the same, — namely, an adjustment of elementary forms into which Nature enters to impart additional animation and interest to a definition of simple principles. By the use of symbols such as are here indicated, one should in time acquire the ability to think in terms of design whether or not Nature enters into the question. The motif of this problem may be stated in two words —*fish, water*. The aim of the problem — to arrange these symbols within an inclosing form in such way that the various attractive forces will be rhythmically related in positions of balance. Before attempting a solution of the problem it would be well to refresh the memory by a reference to the abstract demonstrations that defined the ideas of rhythm and balance in a previous chapter. And a statement there made will also bear repetition, — the artistic interest in the result depends largely upon an *appreciative* application of the principles rather than upon a mere understanding of the formulæ through which they were described. We started to play our tunes, in the first problem of this series, on a primitive reed flute of a few simple notes. The range of possibilities of this instrument is now increased to the point where the personal equation becomes the important factor in the result. Imagination, and the ability to play under the restraint of orderly thought, will determine whether these little compositions shall be interesting and artistic or deadly formal and prosaic.

The character of the symbols for the problem are indicated in Figure 121. They are fishes reduced to the fewest possible lines. To these may be added

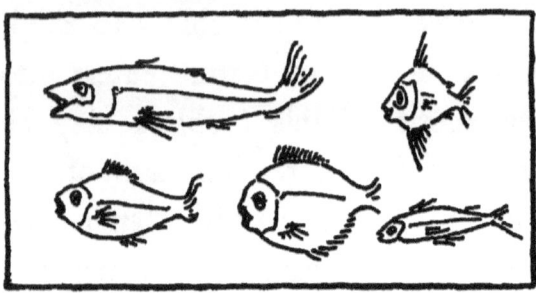

FIG. 121.

others based on an intimate study of fish life, or made from the imagination on a basis of general knowledge of such forms. It is desirable that there should be variety in the shapes and measures of the symbols. As a start toward the solution of the problem, the size and shape of the inclosing form should be established, although this form may be changed as

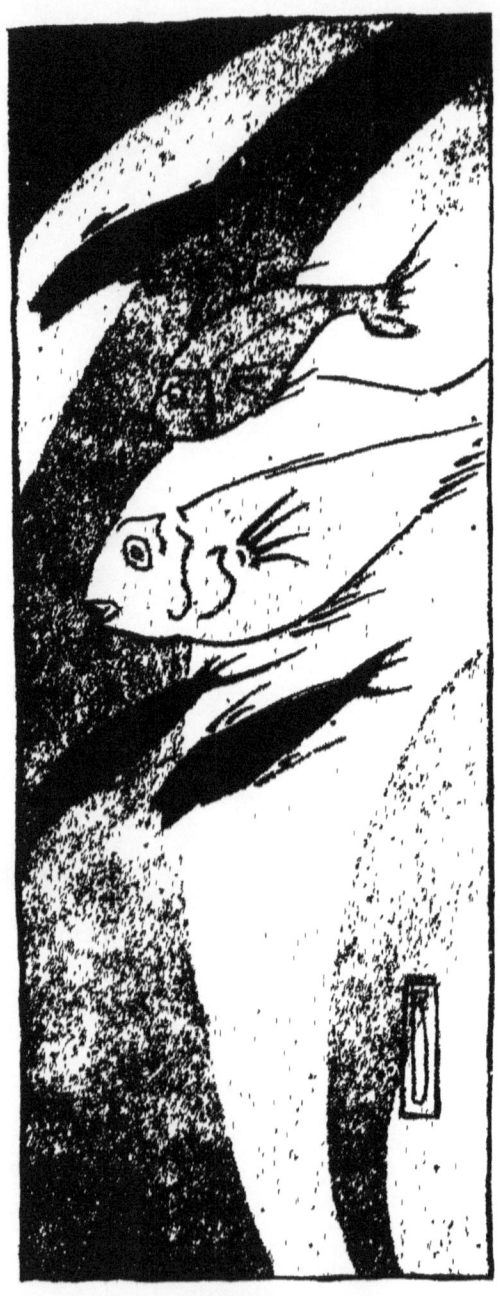

PLATE 51.

COMPOSITION OF TONES, MEASURES, AND SHAPES.

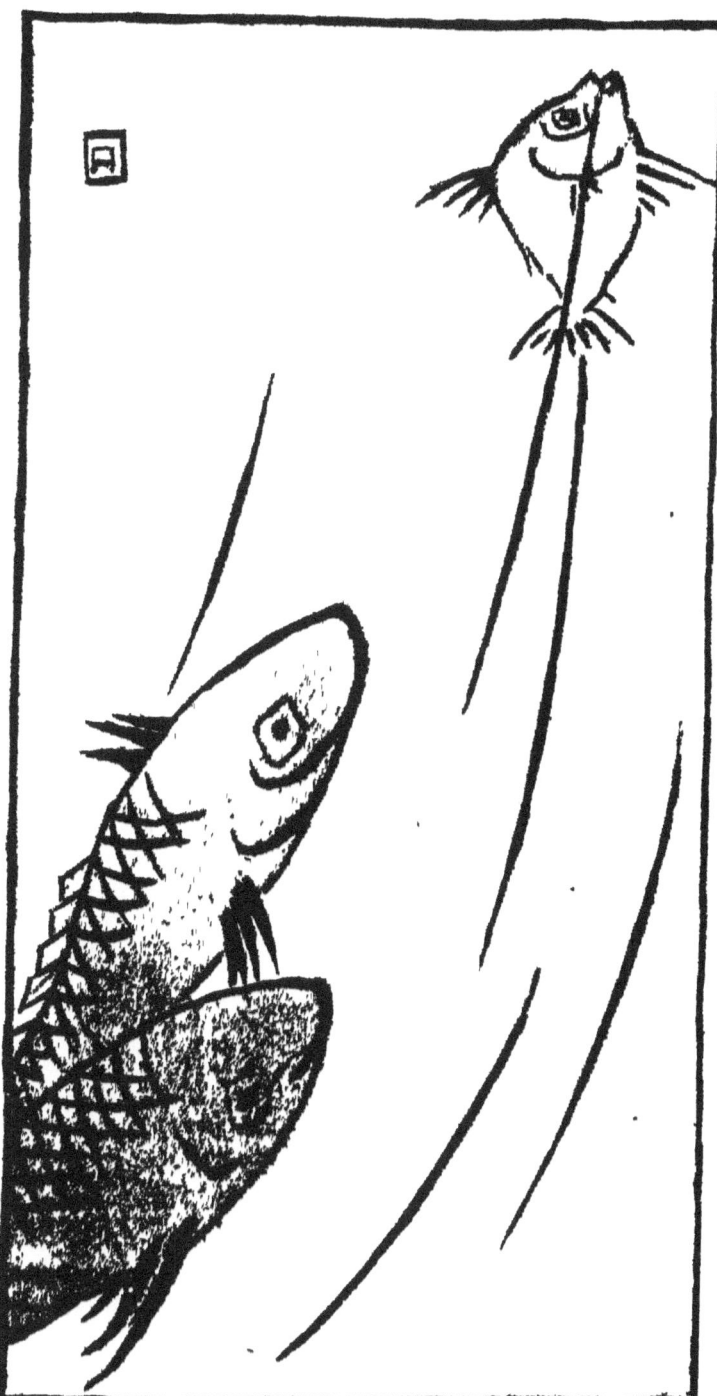

PLATE 52.

Composition of Tones, Measures, and Shapes.

the design develops. Then within this form it is our purpose to so arrange the terms of the motif that there shall be a rhythmic interrelation between the fishes and the lines indicating the water, and a balance of all the attractive forces involved in the problem. It is needless to say that this balance must result from sensitive feeling and good judgment, not from mathematical calculations. It would be well to make a first

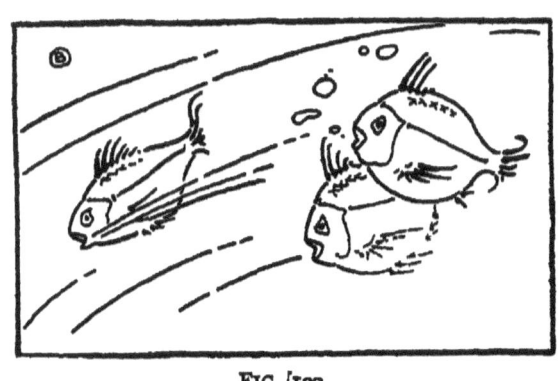

FIG. 122.

attempt through the limitations of a black and white composition, as in Figure 122. The water is represented by lines that may be used to strengthen or check the general movement of the design. The eye moves most rapidly along parallel lines, or slightly diverging lines that tend to meet at a common point.

With the addition of two or more values, the possibilities of the problem, and, by the same token, its difficulties, increase. A greater number and variety of attractive forces call for attention. The different tone contrasts that arise must be dealt with ; lights are to be broken with darks, darks with lights. Until one has given thoughtful attention to the solution of a problem of this kind, it is hard to realize the variations that may be given a composition of two or three flat tones. Let us attempt nothing of a pictorial nature. These are *designs*, not pictures.

As self-criticism is one of the chief aims in the study of a design, it would be well to enter into a more detailed account of the solutions of the problem shown in Plates 51, 52, 53, 54. Unity was the first consideration, a consistent relation of *all* the forces, a *reason* for each. Variety was sought in the shapes, measures, tones, and positions of the different elements. Note the grouping of fishes in each example, and the contrasts in each of shape, measure, and tone. Forces are related in movement though not pointed in the same direction. In Plate 51 the movement of the water adds a touch of variety to a result in which the fishes follow parallel lines. In this example, though, there is more variety in the measures and shapes than in the others. The measure of the large fish was neutralized by giving a greater tone contrast to the smaller ones. These three little fishes probably exert as strong an attractive force in the design as the two large fishes. These are all points that arise in a solution of the problem demanding an application of sensitive feeling and good judgment.

In rendering, the tones should be flat and clear in

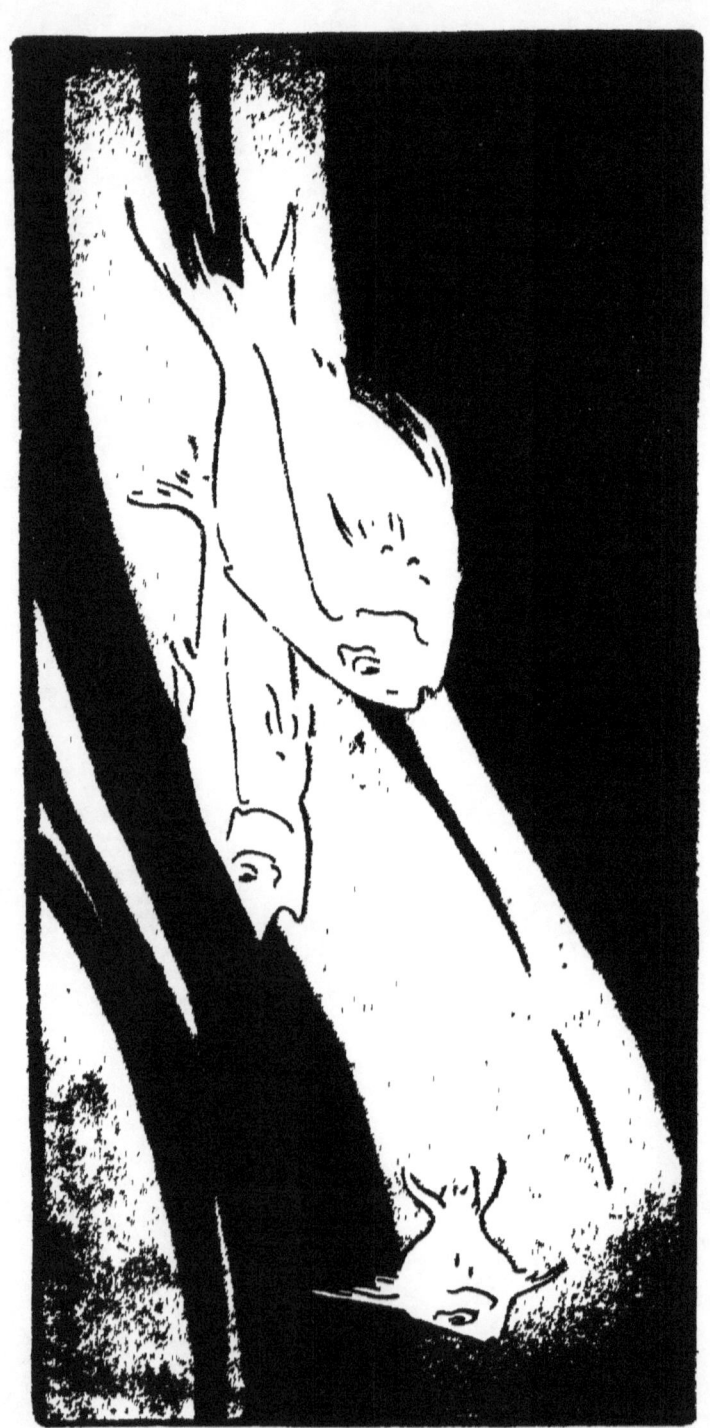

PLATE 53.

COMPOSITION OF TUNES, MEASURES, AND SHAPES.

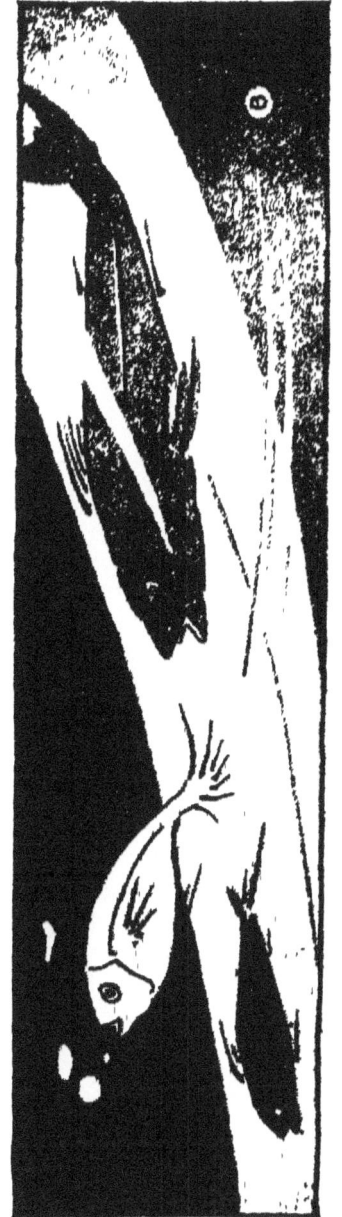

PLATE 54.

COMPOSITION OF TONES MEASURES, AND SHAPES.

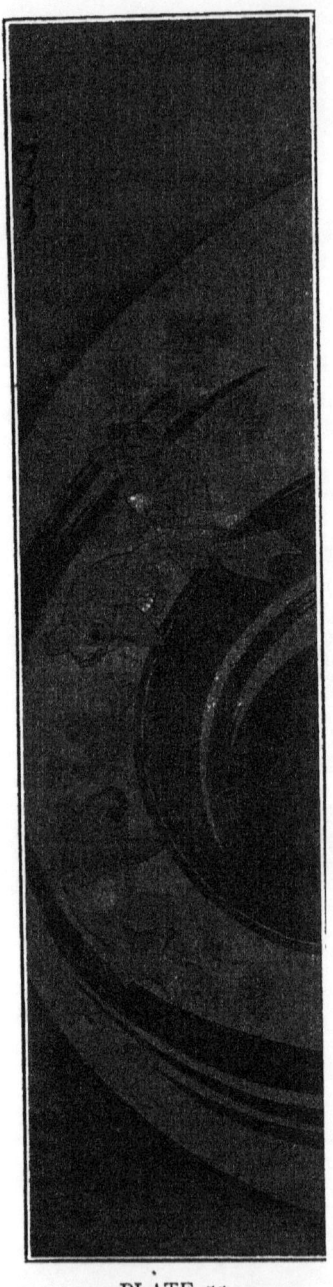

PLATE 55.
JAPANESE FISH PRINT.

statement. Lay a wash of the lightest value first over the entire figure. Then, keeping in mind the parts that are to remain in this value, lay the next wash over everything else.

If we seek examples of such work as this, decorative rather than pictorial, for purpose of study, it would be well to turn again to the Japanese workers (Plate 55). It is impossible for a man to understand all that such a piece of work has to say until he has tried to speak for himself in similar terms.

CHAPTER XI

FROM THE WHOLE TO THE PARTS

"Conventionality in ornament is the natural consequence of reticence or self-restraint, of doing, not all that the artist could have done, but just what is called for by the occasion."
                                        — LEWIS DAY.

IN the last chapter it was said that there were two methods of developing a surface pattern: one by starting with the details and working toward the whole through the building up of related lines and forms in space and mass; the other by striking at once for the big things and gradually breaking the measures of space and mass to the last details. But, though the methods differ, the aims are the same, — a unity of all the elements involved. The first method is valuable for experimental purposes and should precede the second in the study of design, as it is a logical development from simple to more complex questions. But it should lead to an ability to design by the other method. It is always desirable to work from the whole to the parts, to plan the big relations and forms first, and then, to the idea thus expressed, relate the minor details.

It is now proposed to discuss the development of

a pattern by the second method (Figure 123). A greater degree of skill and judgment is demanded than before. This is a rhythmic design of black and white elements, in which the white is of dominant interest, but in which the distribution, the shapes, and measures of black have demanded an equal amount of care. A description of this method of working with illustrations showing the evolution of the design from its first idea may be interesting and profitable. It may well be assumed that the method is in accord, aside from questions involved in the technique of weaving, with that pursued by the designers of the old textiles. We may be sure that they worked from the whole to the parts, from big, general forms to specific details. They had learned to think in terms of design, and Nature stood always at hand to strengthen their imaginations and suggest details that would add the final touch of life and interest to the work of their hands. We do not care to ask whether their designs are " based on the rose," or on any other particular specimen of natural growth. They are beautiful in all that counts for unity in design. They are based on a sympathetic observation of Nature and not on a painstaking analytical study of natural forms, as in so many of the conventionalizations of the modern worker.

The present design represents a problem of an abstract character into which Nature enters as fiction

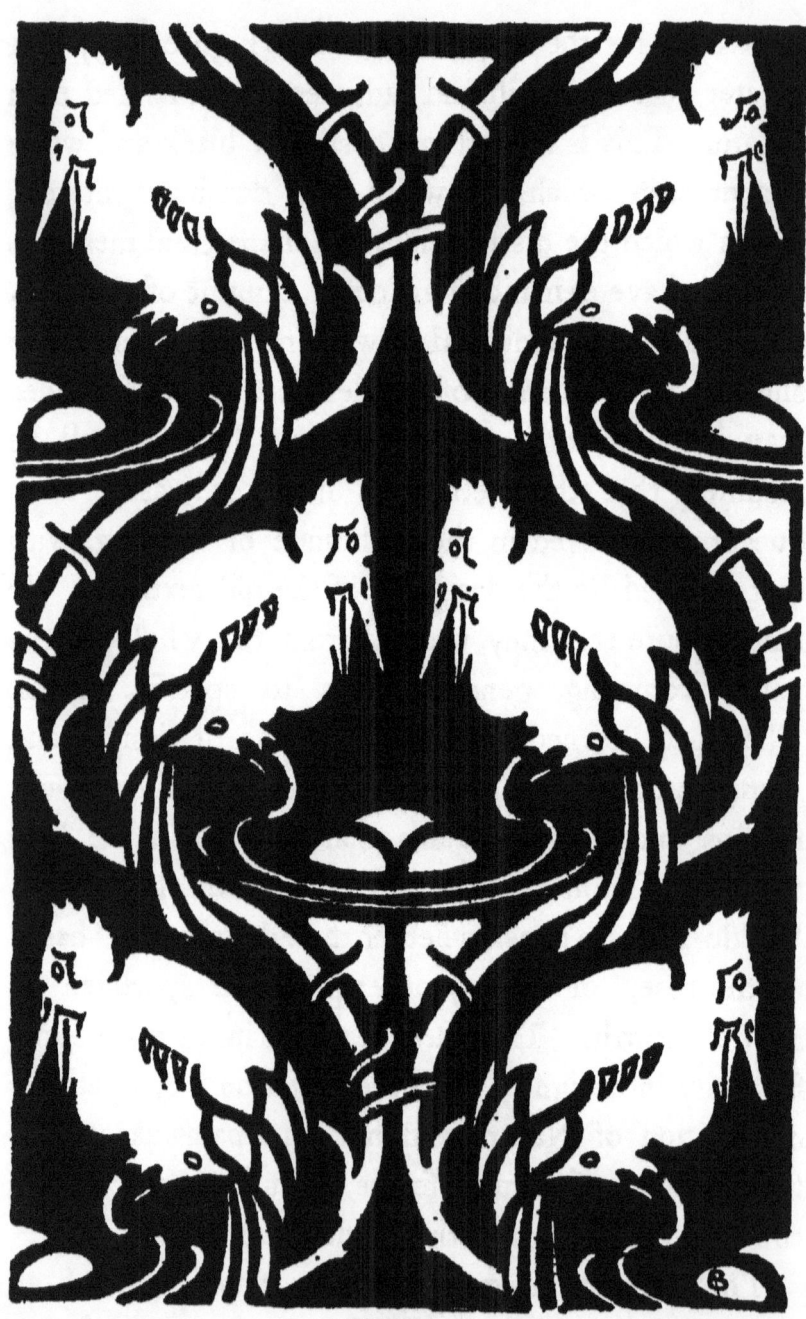

FIG. 123.

rather than as fact. If it has any style, it is the result of a thoughtful adjustment of tones, measures, and shapes, in accordance with the few simple principles that have been de-fined. It started with this motif, — *two birds and a nest.* There was no re-straint imposed by an adherence to the specific character of any bird or nest. It seemed better to allow the forms of the motif to de-velop as the de-mands of sound construction might suggest, leaving something for the imagination. With this thought in mind, the main construction lines were established first of all (Figure 124). To insure a regular repetition of a motif a geometric constructive basis must be accepted as the first element in the problem. Two geometric bases of a repeating character are shown in Figure 125.

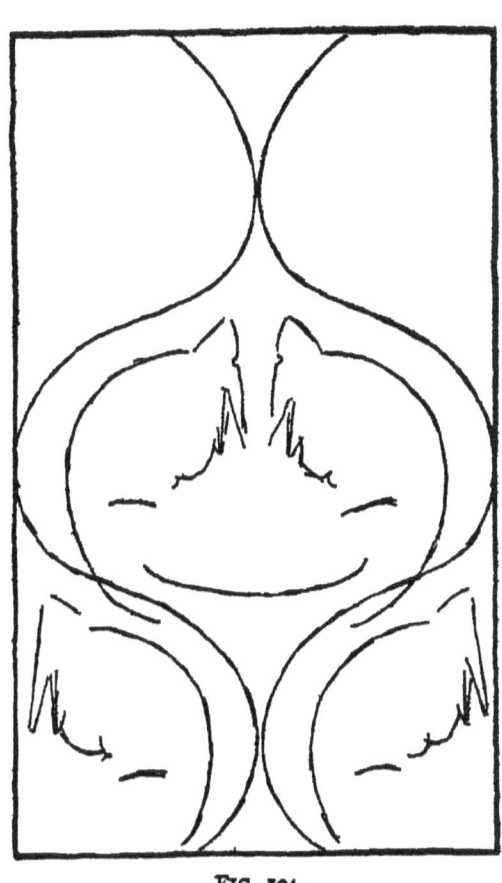

FIG. 124.

In the completed design this geometric basis may or may not appear to the casual observer. During the development of a pattern other interrelations of line and

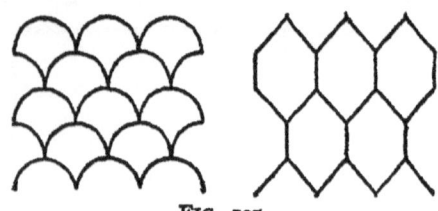

form, constructive in character, may be emphasized and the original basis subordinated or even lost entirely from

FIG. 125.

sight. In this example, though, the original basis remains as a distinctive feature in the result. The next step was to seek a few tentative lines to define the forms and positions of the birds, their relation to the big movement and to each other. The tails were planned to cross the line of this movement in order to break its monotonous length.

The succeeding steps are shown in

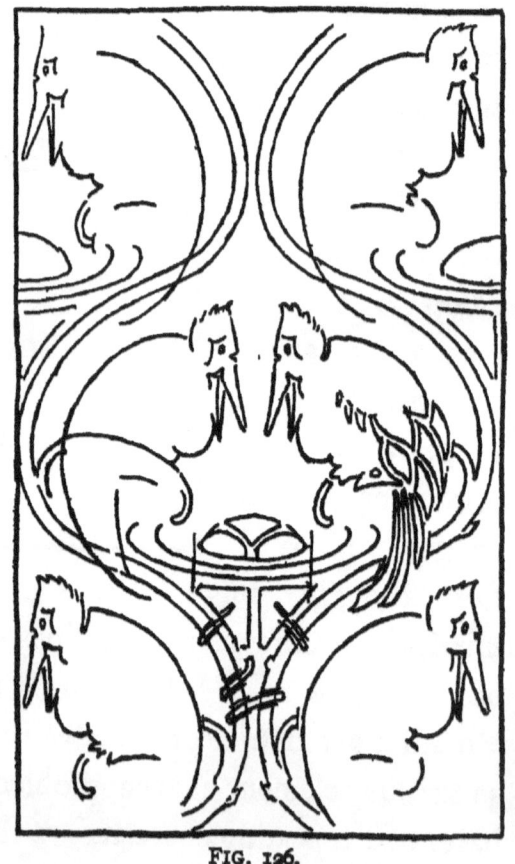

FIG. 126.

Figure 126. The birds were given a more distinctive character; a forecast of the tone distribution was made; each additional line was related to the other lines. The size and form of the mass represented by the three eggs were assumed, and the space of black below this mass was broken by the two simple leaf forms. Several experiments were tried with the nest; but the most consistent treatment of this element led to the adoption of an abstract symbol. It was a question to be solved on a design basis, not through a study of birds' nests. Then came the breaking of the large measures of white into related details, and a binding together of the lines of the movement by the twisted leaf stems. In the final breaking up of the forms, such things as are shown in Figures 127, 128 from Flemish, Italian, and Japanese textiles, and in Figure 129 some bits of Japanese metal work, may be studied with profit. In these it is less a problem of wings and feathers than of space and mass; not so much a question of Nature as of tools and materials.

Thus we have a result that may serve to again illustrate the difference between thinking in terms of design and in terms of Nature. It is this form or method of thinking that one should aim to acquire. A painstaking study of Nature, an accumulation of facts, will not necessarily lead to orderly thought in design or to constructive beauty with tools and materials. It may

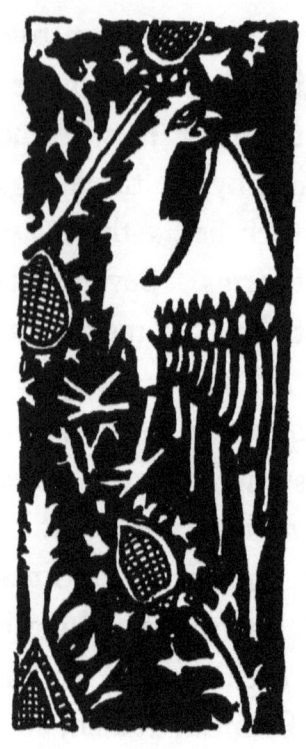
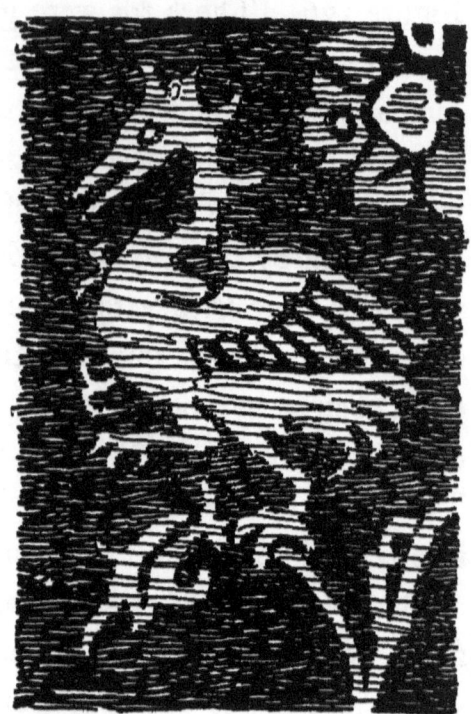

FIG. 127.

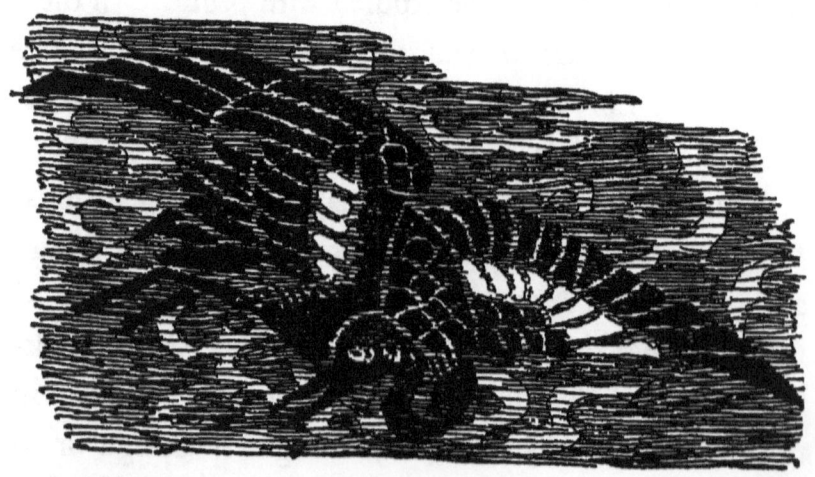

FIG. 128.

even be said that observation is often strengthened at the expense of imagination and invention. The character of the design is within us. There is no reason why one should not make a record of facts of natural growths and forms in pencil, pen and ink, and color. But without proper digestive assimilation, those facts,

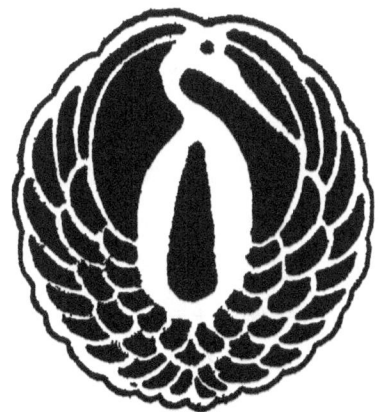 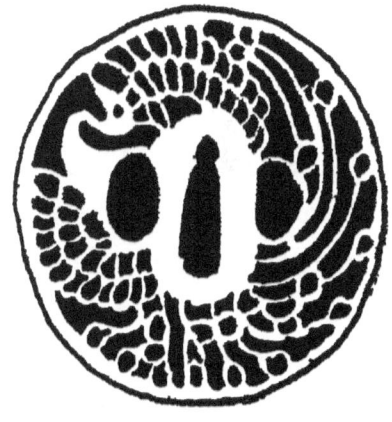

FIG. 129.

however interesting they may be on their own account, are of little use. The designer must be a keen observer of Nature, —but a sympathetic observer withal. We too frequently approach Nature with a scalpel and a microscope, thinking that we may find weird and unique forms that no one else has ever used in design, thus stamping our work with peculiar distinction. We analyze the wing of a fly, hoping to find there material of some sort that is ready-made for purposes of design without the interplay of imagination and invention.

To illustrate this point let us compare the work of

Q

two carvers who were probably about contemporaneous in point of time but widely separated in aims and methods (Plates 56 and 57). The first is the work of a Renaissance carver, the second of a Japanese carver. Each is fairly representative of the ideals toward which the craftsmen worked. If there is any distinction in words, the first might be called elegant, the second beautiful. Each is a piece of consummate craftsmanship, perfect in execution and finish.

The first is a bit of descriptive carving, an accumulation of facts of observation expressed in wood with remarkable skill. The foot with its hair and claws is wonderfully carved, leaves are exquisitely turned, feathers delicately executed. But the carver's imagination did not rise very far above the facts of form and texture. His hand was sure in the execution of such things. But he had very little to say beyond that. Lacking a sympathetic imagination, he sought to give distinction to his work by elegance of lines and an incongruous association of forms. In the history of design, the surest evidence of a declining imaginative power is to be found in this hashing together of unrelated facts and forms. This style of work, of which the carving here shown is a comparatively sane example, went, in times of later decadence, to absurd extremes.

In the second example, though, there is evidence

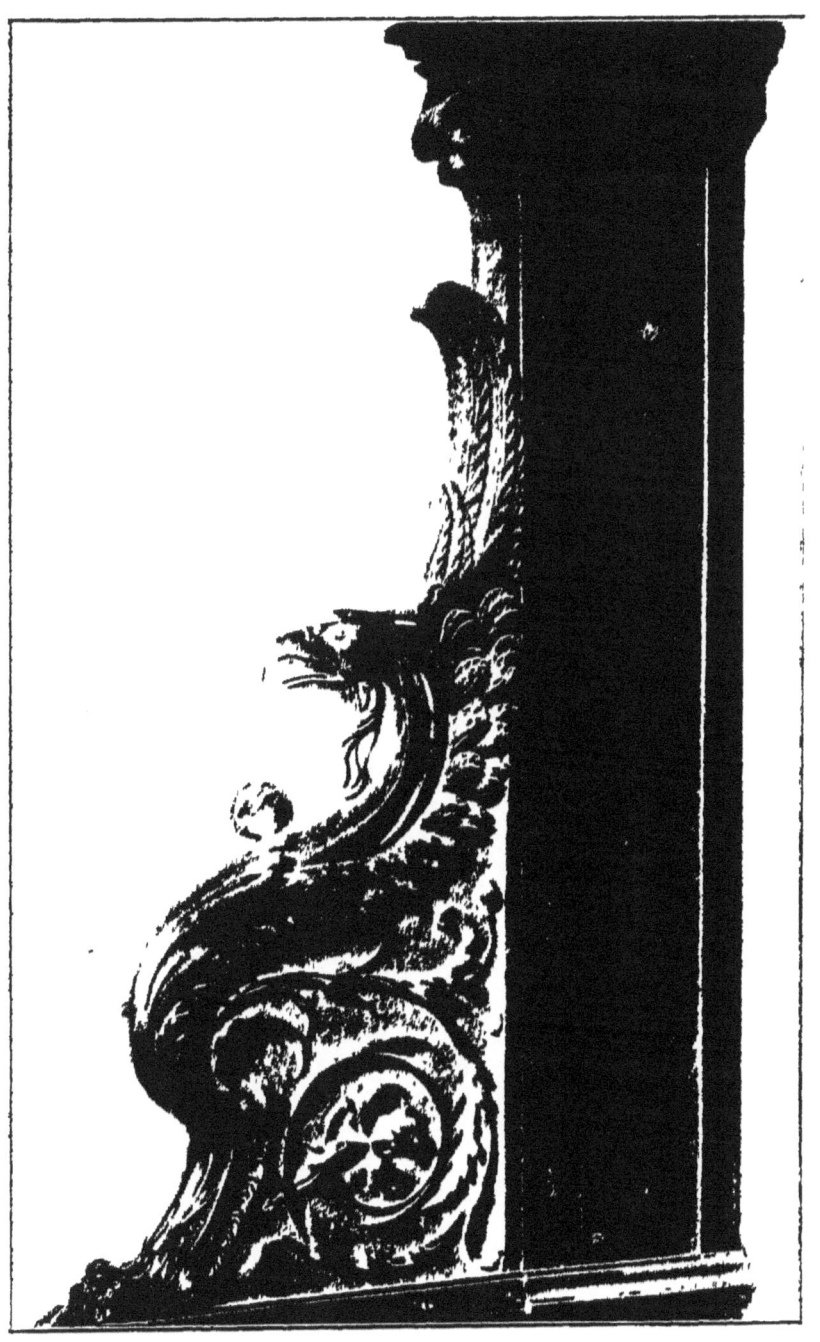

PLATE 56.

RENAISSANCE CARVING, FLORENCE.

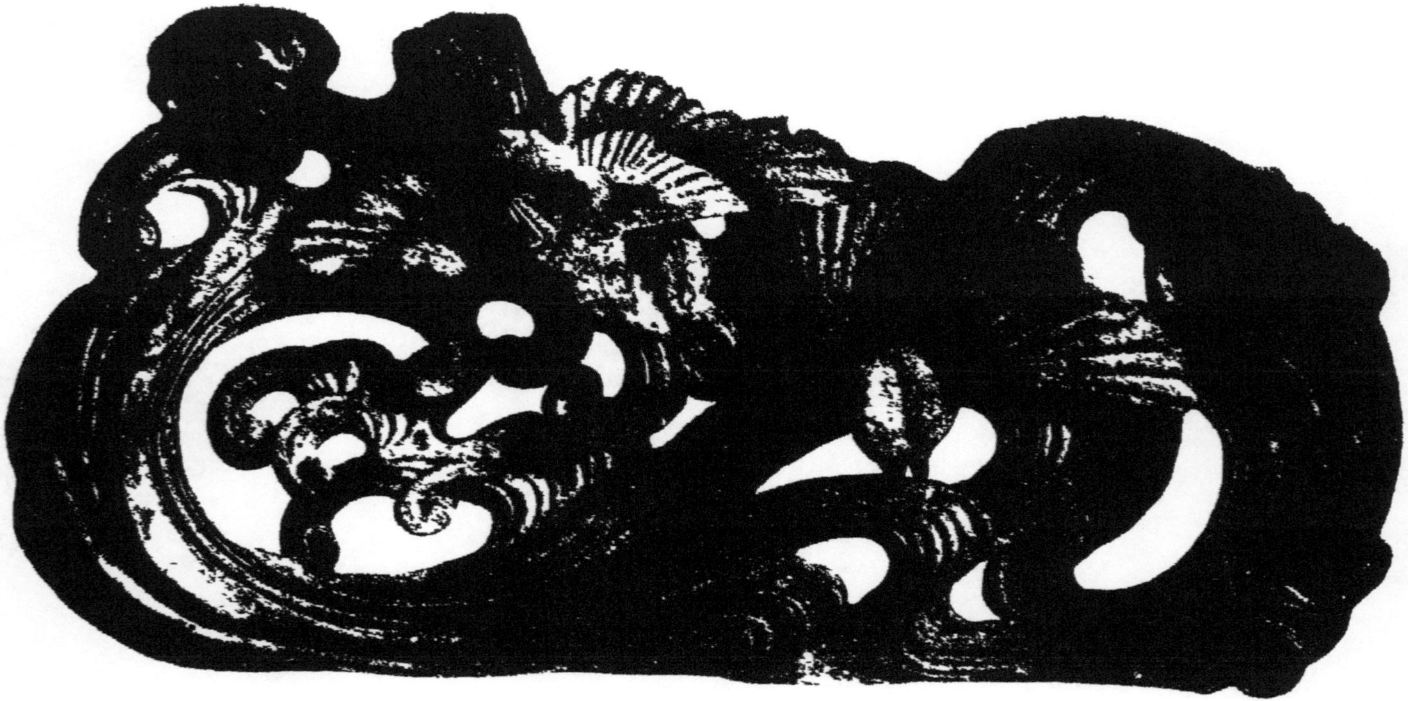

PLATE 57.

JAPANESE WOOD CARVING. (BOSTON MUSEUM OF FINE ARTS.)

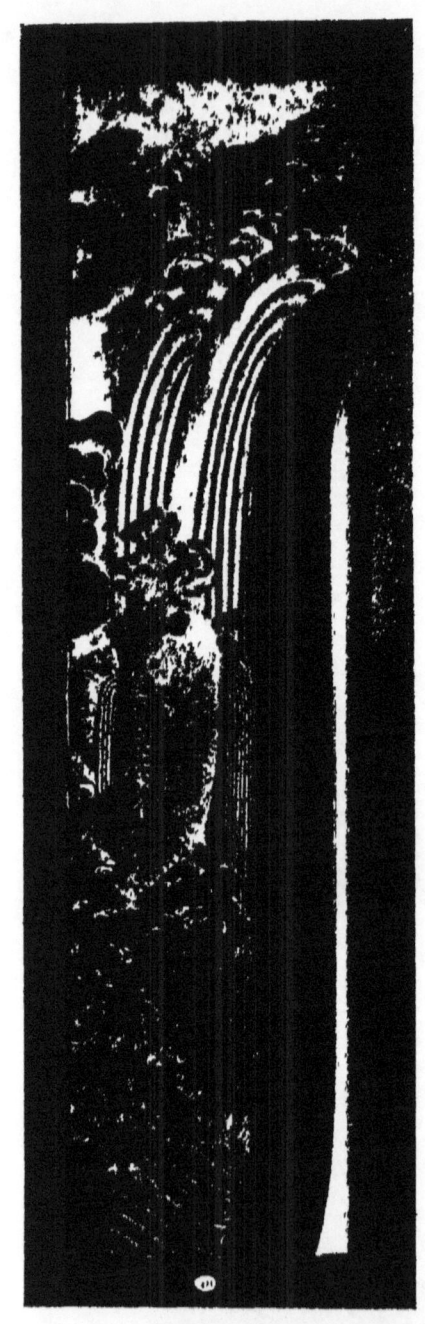

PLATE 58.
SIXTEENTH-CENTURY JAPANESE CARVING.

of feeling, emotion, imagination of the highest order.
We may admire the technical excellence of the first;
but in the second our interest is in the idea which the
carver has sought to express. He, too, must have
known all the facts of his motif; he was a keen observer; but he did not choose to tell all that he knew.
It was the spirit, the poetry of Nature that appealed
to him, the charm of the Mother Carey's Chickens
flitting back and forth through the wave crests. To
him the birds and the water became symbols, a mere
means to an end, for the expression of rhythmic movement. He sought an arrangement of lines and forms
that would give true character and style to his idea.
Note the beautiful line relations throughout, between
the birds and the water, the consistent simplicity of all
the details. "Not as I am," Nature might say, "but
as I should like to be."

Similar in character and purpose are the Japanese
carvings in Plates 58, 59. These things have real
"soul stuff" in them of a sort that comes from a sympathetic understanding of Nature. The strong personality of an artist is carved into every line and form.
It may be said that Plate 59 is too plastic in treatment
for a wood carving. One must see the original (Boston Museum of Fine Arts) to fully appreciate the
technical qualities of the work. Every line and plane
is turned to make the most of the grain and texture of

the wood. Moreover, as this carving was to be exposed to the weather, the craftsman foresaw the part that Father Time would play in his work and so adjusted his planes that storm and sunshine should enhance its beauty.

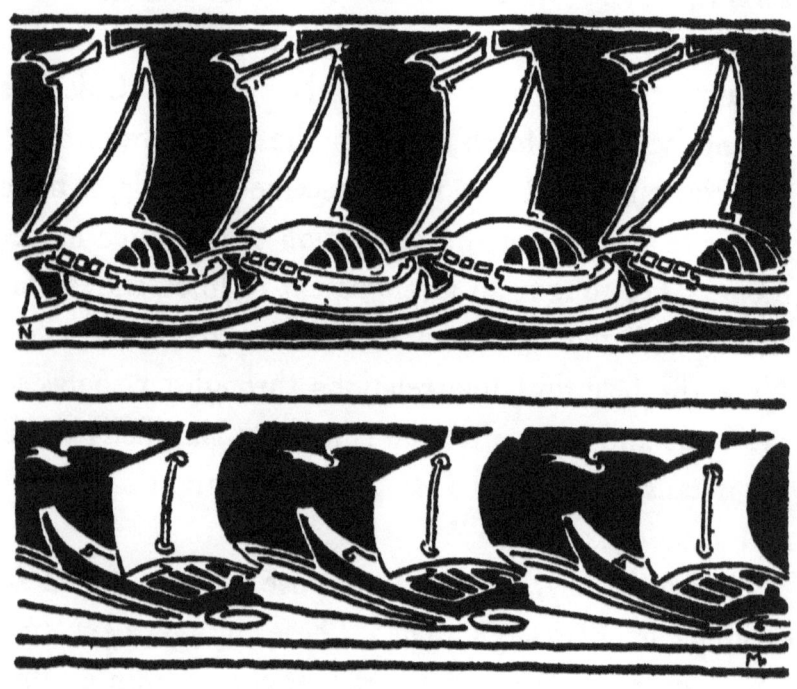

FIG. 130.

PROBLEM. In the presentation of problems like this one much is left to the imagination and invention of the worker. It is sufficient to suggest as a motif a simple statement such as *boat, sail, wave.* If the *aim of the problem* is understood, — namely, a constructive arrangement of lines and forms, spaces and masses bound

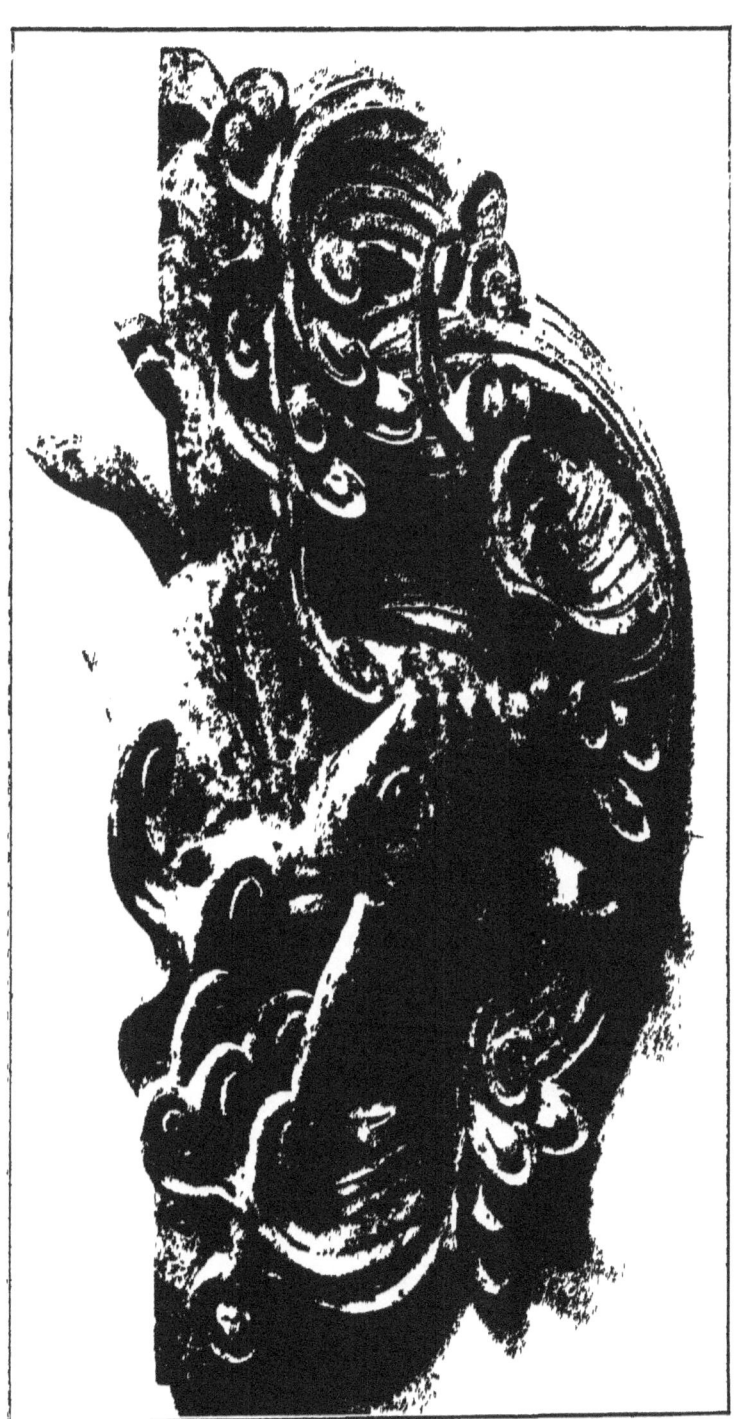

PLATE 59.

EIGHTEENTH-CENTURY JAPANESE CARVING. (BOSTON MUSEUM OF FINE ARTS.)

together through the reciprocal relation of the various elements into unity,— considerable opportunity occurs for individual application of the idea. *Definiteness* is the first thought, not a pictorial row of boats in a sketchy semblance to water. Each line and form has to be studied carefully, and the part it contributes to the oneness of the design becomes important. Lack-

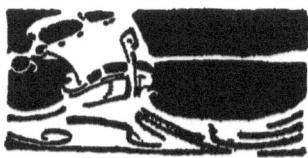
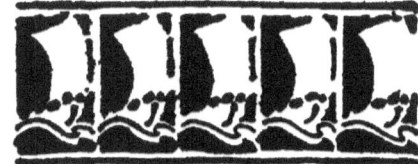
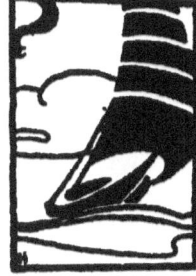
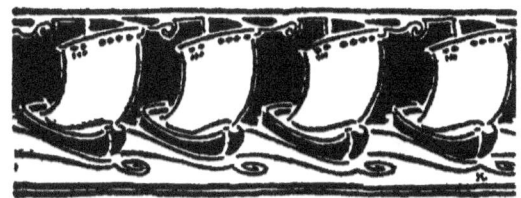

FIG. 131.

ing a thorough organization of all the elements involved, the result will be little more than a row of sail boats. In the examples shown (Figures 130, 131) one may note clearly the means employed to achieve unity. The boat itself may retain features peculiar to a particular type of boat, or it may become very abstract in its final rendering. This depends upon the individual and the clearness of his understanding of elementary principles. This motif, in its presentation, is typical of many others that may suggest possibilities of individual interpretation. Such motifs as *two birds in a cherry tree*, or *hen in the grass with corn* are sufficient to arouse latent ideas and give the imagination exercise.

CHAPTER XII

LINES OF STUDY

"The spontaneity of undeveloped faculty does not count for much. It carries us only a little way. Let no one believe that without study and practice in design he can recognize and appreciate what is best in design."

— DENMAN ROSS.

THE student will find it profitable to pursue his study at all times along four closely related lines. These lines of study have been indicated in the development of text and problems to the present point; it now remains to summarize them briefly : —

(1) A study of line, form, and tone composition for the definition of æsthetic principles.

(2) A study, through actual practice and constant observation, of the practical principles involved in constructive work. In the union of the æsthetic and the practical is the end sought.

(3) A study of the work of the past, not from a superficial historic ornament point of view, — rather to learn something of the principles involved in the production of work in the past, what design meant to the

people, what sort of life and thought it expresses, the conditions from which the work was an organic growth, in fact all the influences that contributed to give unique distinction to that work. More important than the outward forms of ornament are the questions of how, when, and why ornament was employed. To this study one would naturally apply the æsthetic and practical principles acquired through practice; an appreciation of the work of the past broadens with one's own experience.

The study along this line should be deep and continuous,— from the point of view of history, geography, archæology, ethnology. Many influences were combined in the development of what we term a style or period.

The needs of primitive people are very much the same,— food, clothing, shelter. These are obtained from materials immediately available with tools and processes of a simple nature. The resultant forms are much the same under similar climatic conditions and environments. The stone age, the iron age,— these terms have no special place in point of time; each has been repeated in widely separated places through the centuries from preglacial times to the present. As needs become peculiar, so the forms of primitive art become distinctive,— here a hunting people of the plains, there a fishing people; again a nomadic people of the desert with their flocks. There were those who dwelt on the mountains, on the lakes, in the cold of northern climes; each followed the line of least resistance in the development of art forms, each form the logical outcome of the environment in which the primitive man found himself.

Gradually at different epochs in history one people after another has settled into conditions insuring permanence in the practice of the arts. Shelter becomes building, and building in turn becomes architecture. Rude implements give way to better made tools; new materials are discovered, new processes invented; permanent institutions arise, the outlook upon the world broadens, ideas become crystallized, a language of signs and symbols appears. Those races which become most virile express their decided convictions in their art.

There comes expansion through conquest and commerce, each leaving its trace in the arts of different peoples. A powerful nation impresses its ideas upon conquered nations, or acquires, through conquest or peaceful channels, ideas and forms that are assimilated by its own workers. A raid upon an unprotected corner of the Roman Empire gives spoils to some barbaric tribe in Scandinavia, — and with the spoils comes a new influence that appears as a modification of forms which those people have developed. From Persia and India caravans brought wares which inevitably influenced in design and technique the work of the western world. The pomegranate, the peacock, the palm, the many symbols of Persian art appearing in the product of the Flemish weaver, may indicate an influence from afar. On the other hand, when the caravans wended their way home across the desert they in turn took products that leave an influence sifting through India even to Korea and Japan. But these influences were assimilated with ideas already well established, — and by practical workers who welcomed a fresh incentive. It was generally an indirect influence, or the new forms were soon interwoven with and lost in the creative work of those who borrowed them. It was a different sort of thing from the effort of the modern worker to achieve through scholarly research a direct imitation or adaptation of forms and symbols which have long since ceased to be vital.

At all times in the course of that which we call a style was a real need, a vital thought. The rugs of Persia were attributable to the conditions of that country, — with the hair of the goat and the camel, with a nomadic tent life, the weaving of rugs followed as a natural sequence, — and with these conditions prevailing for centuries the consummate skill and feeling came about naturally. Each individual had back of him the traditions of many generations ; into these traditions of a technical and artistic nature he implanted some little of his own personality. Changes of line, form, pattern were not radical; they were gradual, — slight changes sometimes covering many generations of workers. Things were not ordered on Monday to be done at 10 A.M. on Wednesday, whether or no.

Again, the wonderful creative work of the middle ages was fostered in the quiet of the monasteries. Each monastery was sufficient for its own needs; the inmates tilled the soil, practiced the building arts, and in their shops continued the practice of many crafts. As the conditions of life became more settled and prosperity came again to the land the operations of the monasteries broadened. But for many years in the cathedral building the individual was subordinate to the whole. Each individual tried hard to express the dominant idea about him, subject to the ensemble.

In Japan there came again a peculiar combination of circumstances which brought another creative period or style into being, as distinctive in thought and expression as was the mediæval from the primitive. But the lesson is ever the same, — a vital art has ever been the direct expression of the thought, feeling, environment in which it was created. Other things have merely influenced it.

Conditions have indeed materially changed. The term *local* has a broader significance. Cities that were once nations in themselves have long since been absorbed in wider boundaries. Transportation facilities, invention, mechanical processes, have contributed to spread the world's art on our library tables. The very surfeit of examples makes it more difficult than ever to build upon real needs. We follow the line of least resistance by appropriating whatever we find that seems adapted to our purposes.

The past should influence us strongly and deeply. But it should be known that the past has no patent on beauty. Many unworthy, positively ugly things are preserved for our inspection. It may be taken for granted that the work of the past as a whole is more beautiful than the work of the present. There were fewer inutilities; things were made because they filled a real need. The steps from producer to consumer were simpler; the bonds uniting them were more intimate, and the men who used tools had greater opportunity and incentive to exercise a creative faculty. Nevertheless there is decadence as well as true growth. It is for us to sift the good things from the bad, seek the principles involved in their construction, refinement, and enrichment. But let us not sneak in at the back door with a scrap of tracing paper and appropriate for our own use those things we find.

Can we not do as well as those old craftsmen? Probably not; but we can at least try hard to clothe such ideas as we have in a simple and consistent garb. The world's art that is loved best, — that which appeals to the heart with a human interest, — was done by craftsmen who were trying to give adequate and beautiful expression to their ideas. They lived their simple lives, met their daily problems, and passed away; now we treasure the things they did and call it art.

(4) A close, sympathetic study of Nature. Nothing is too small or trivial in Nature to pass unnoted. The hand of a Master designer is everywhere apparent, — nothing is left to chance. The art of the designer involves both selection and invention. He may select materials appropriate to the problem which he has in hand; but he must bring to bear upon them an artistic invention which comes from his own thought and feeling. He may select from Nature forms which seem suitable for his purpose in design, either through an almost literal interpretation or through complete conventionalization; or he may draw upon his own imagination for forms, which come perhaps indirectly from Nature. In either case the measure of his invention is what gives character to the result.

One may study Nature from an analytical point of view, — a seeking for pattern, for unique forms, for color principles. But the student should not always approach Nature with the question, " Can I use this in design? " He should not be possessed with the idea that Nature is something to be conventionalized. Many of the results of his study may never be directly used. It is enough that he has been in close touch with the spirit of Nature, the grace and beauty of the life about him. If he has caught the fleeting beauty of leaf and flower, he has added to his equipment something that will inevitably appear in his work; his mind has been refreshed, his imagination awakened. An effort to paint the flying cloud shadows on a pasture hillside may appear in a designer's work to quite as much purpose as a microscopic examination of a bee's wing in search of a pattern for immediate use. He will find his mind alert for suggestions, himself in intimate companionship with Nature,—and if his study has been of the right sort, his work will respond with fresh interest and vigor whether he "conventionalizes" Nature or seeks within his own mind for the desired forms.

PROBLEM. In studying the work of the past the student should keep in touch with those things most in accord with his own experience. Up to the problems of Chapter VIII primitive work offers the most helpful material. With the problem of Chapter IX a new thought in the use of lines and forms opens, and the student may profitably turn to mediæval work, to the products of the Renaissance, and to Oriental work. A study of mediæval and Oriental textiles opens one's

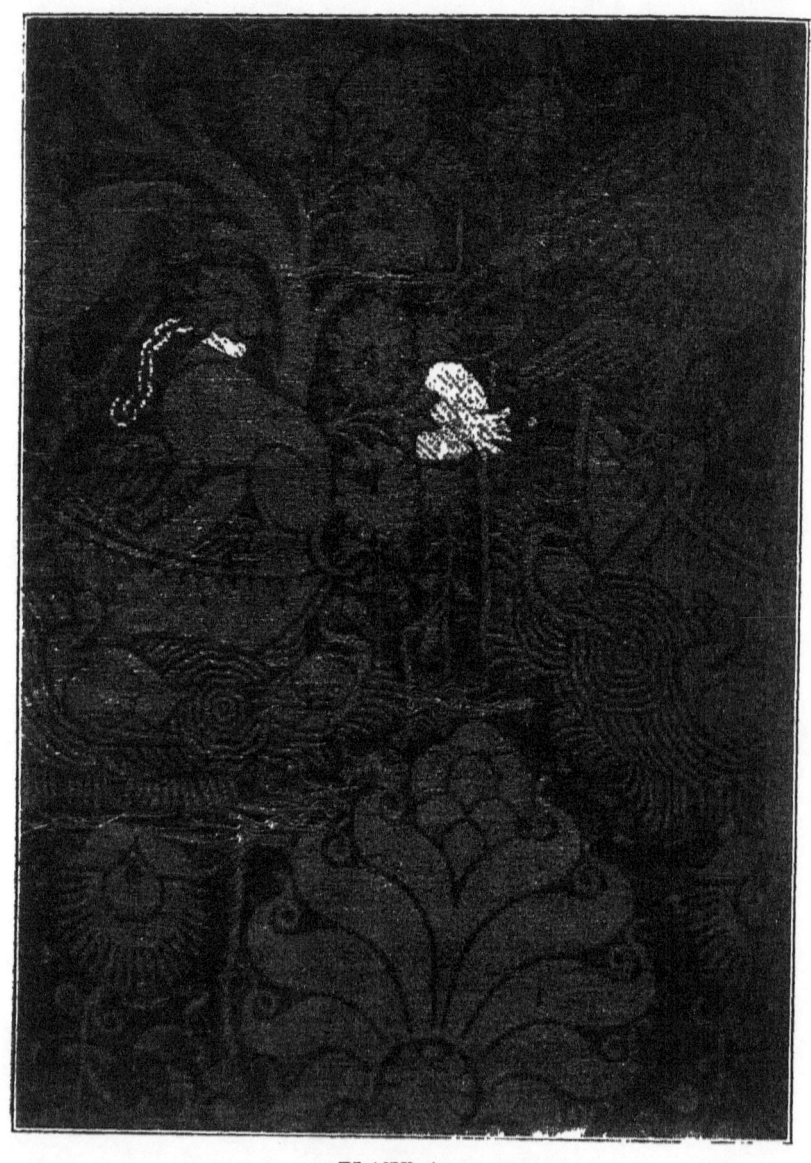

PLATE 60.

ITALIAN TEXTILE — FOURTEENTH CENTURY. (SOUTH KENSINGTON
MUSEUM.)

eyes to the fact that invention plays a greater part in design than mere selection. By study is meant, in this case, many careful sketches in pencil, ink, and color of motifs and completed designs in various materials. The purpose of such work is, obviously, to get into close sympathy with the products, study the motifs and the sources from which the ideas were derived,— to put one's self, in a certain measure, into the position of the old designer. Such a masterpiece of weaving as the Brocade in Plate 60 offers food for thought to the

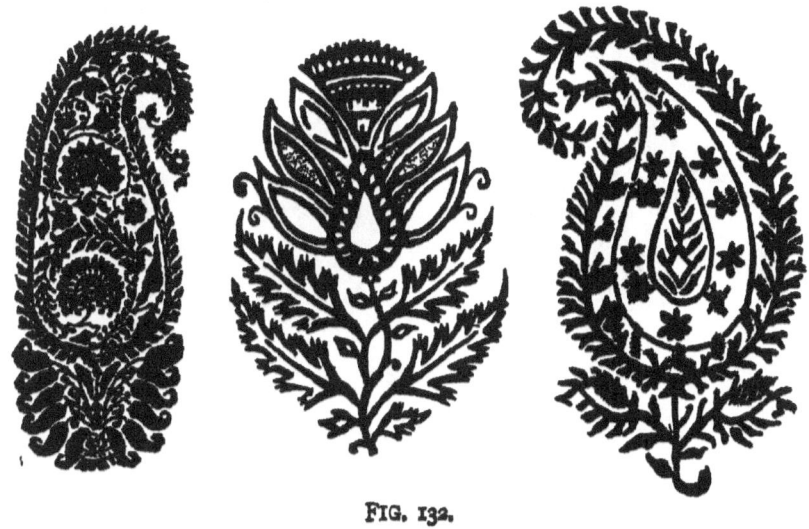

FIG. 132.

student who goes to Nature, expecting to find designs ready-made. The assistance furnished here by Nature is of an indirect kind; mere facts of observation have counted for little. The same may be said of the Indian motifs in Figure 132. There was no clew in any natural specimen that would suggest such patterns; they came from the designer, and any discussion as to whether they are "conventionalizations" of this or that natural specimen is of archæological rather than artistic interest. As motifs expressed in terms of design they may be considered from an abstract point of view, in line with the method of treatment in the prob-

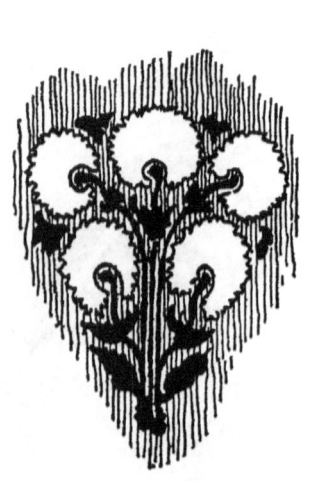 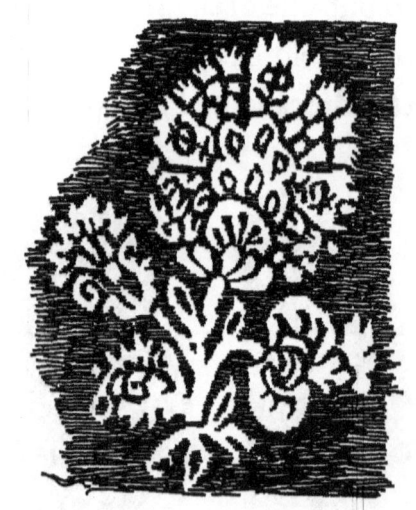

FIG. 133.

lems of this book. The sketches in Figure 133 are of the same sort; they are breakings of space and mass with lines and forms, the terms of design refined and influenced by a sympathetic observation of Nature. The pomegranate motif of Figure 134 shows how much the organization of the design depends upon the worker. In the first sketch is a literal pen study of a pomegranate cut in sections. The designer has retained the general form; but as a study in the spotting of lights and darks the problem came home to the personality of the worker, — it was his invention, imagination, feeling, expressed through a technique peculiar to weaving that shaped the design.

In studying such things it would be well to attempt to work for one's self in the *mode* of such productions; note always how the elementary principles of design

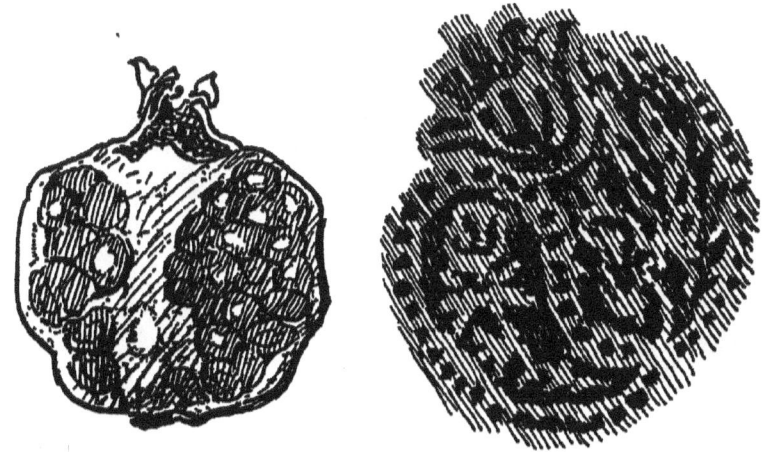

FIG. 134.

have received application and then endeavor to work from a similar point of view. As an instance, Figure 135 may serve to illustrate the thought. The first sketch is from a Persian textile; the second, made directly after the first, was a study of a similar big form broken into subordinate forms in a way that one may believe was followed by the original designer. The result is not far removed from the original; but

R

the second suggested the third, and this in turn a fourth, and so on through a series of six or eight studies, the invention of the pupil being awakened with each effort to new suggestions and variations. As an exercise the problem has served its purpose; it is not the intention to "adapt" a Persian motif,—rather, to find, if possible, how the Persian designer achieved such a result.

Following such a series of studies the pupil is in

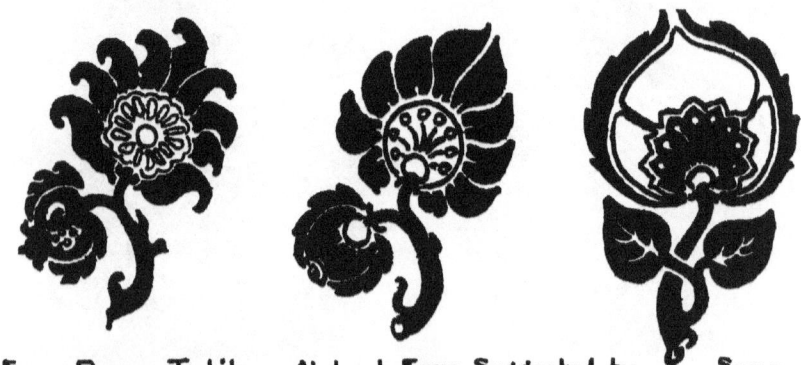

From a Persian Textile • Abstract forms Suggested by Same•

FIG. 135.

position to apply the thought to work of his own; his study of Nature will now assist him materially; his invention and command of principles through practice should lead to an infinite number of well-organized forms, breakings of light with dark and dark with light as the details develop. Figure 136 indicates a few from many such studies and shows the wide range of individual thought. They are "original," in the true

PLATE 61.

COPTIC WEAVING. (SOUTH KENSINGTON MUSEUM.)

sense of the word, intelligent efforts to work from the whole to the parts through abstract principles.

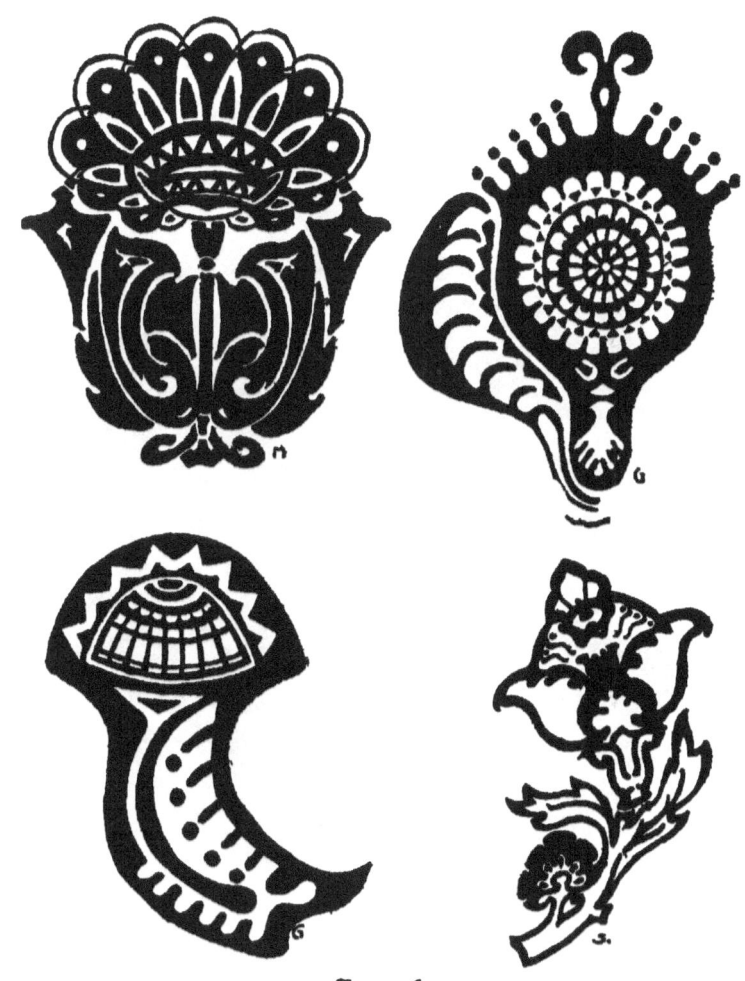

FIG. 136.

Continuing the thought into a result involving a more severe test, the Coptic weaving in Plate 61 may serve a purpose. It is a symmetrical, space-filling problem with flat areas and a grouping of dominant masses, with a consistent growth suggested throughout. The process is from the whole to the parts, as before. It should begin with the tentative blocking out of a few leading lines of growth, an indication of the shapes, measures, and positions of the dominant masses and a

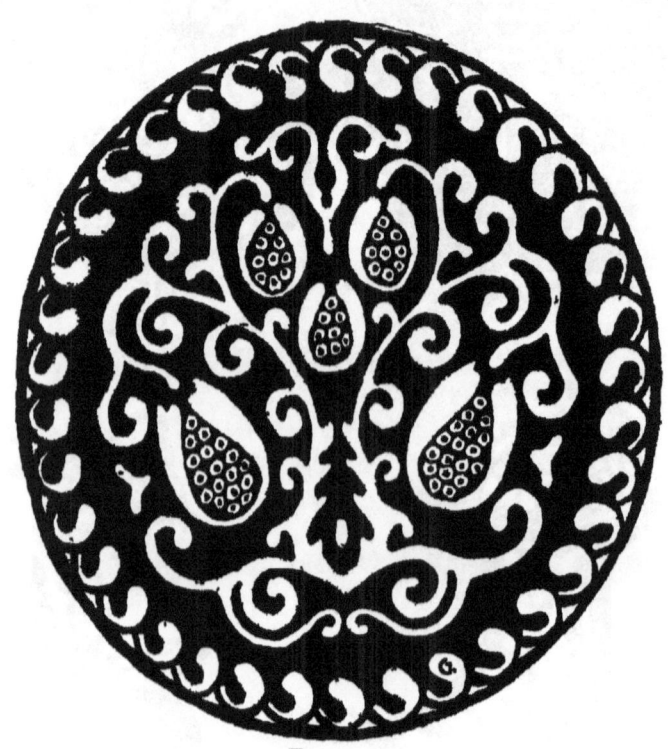

FIG. 137.

gradual subdivision of forms. It is necessary to keep both space and mass, dark and light, in mind at all stages, working from one to the other. This, like any other design, should be *felt* out from tentative suggestions to the completed result. With the blocking in of the first idea the worker should be alive to any change that suggests itself; he should be able to recognize and seize upon any variation that may lend additional interest or

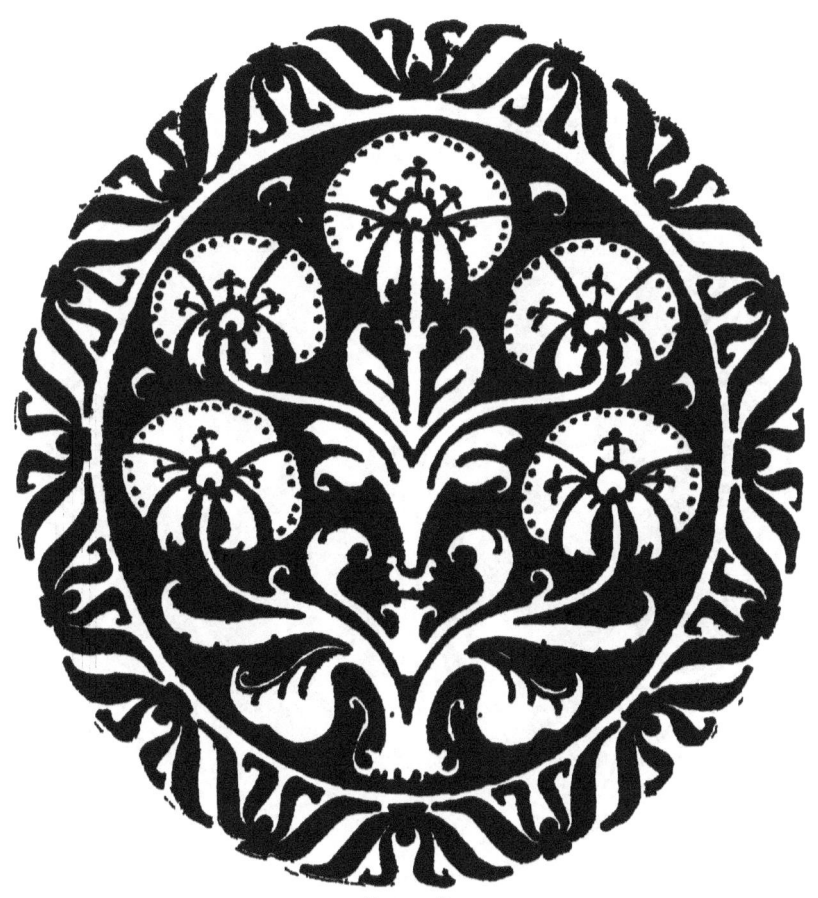

FIG. 138.

beauty to his work. The first tentative lines may give way to an entirely different adjustment as the design progresses. It is better to be able to adapt one's self to a new version of an idea that may develop with the process than to be enslaved to a "leading line," or to stubbornly push a first idea through all suggestions. Throughout the process there should be a measure of

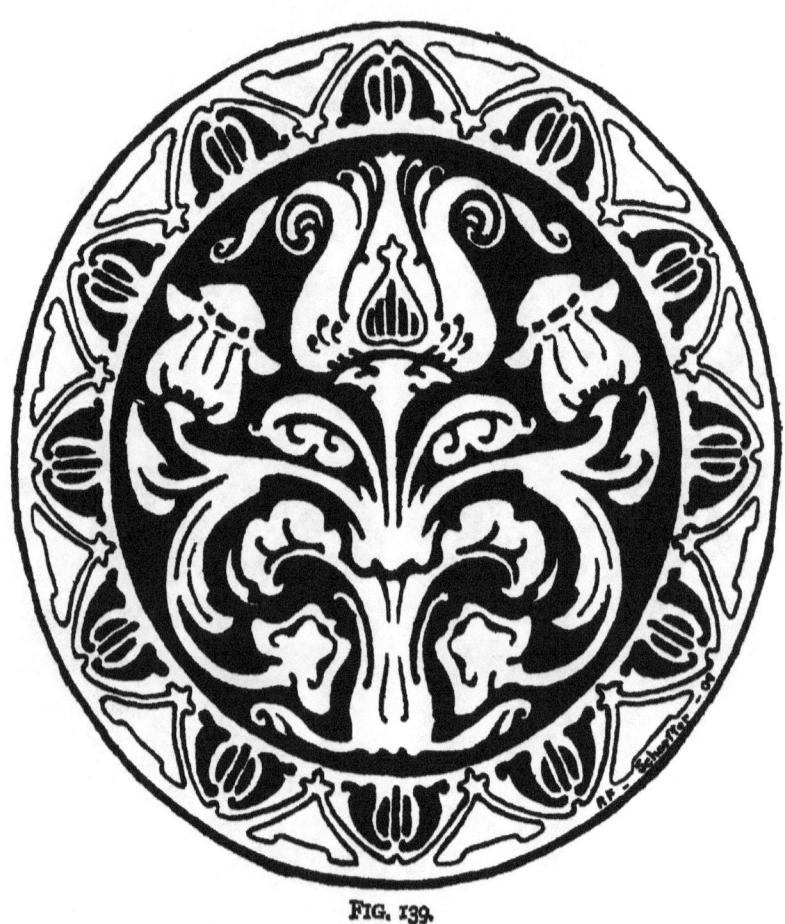

FIG. 139.

elasticity, the parts of the design should be in about the same state of completion at a given time, — not a carefully wrought detail in one place, with chaos and indecision elsewhere. And in the end there should be,

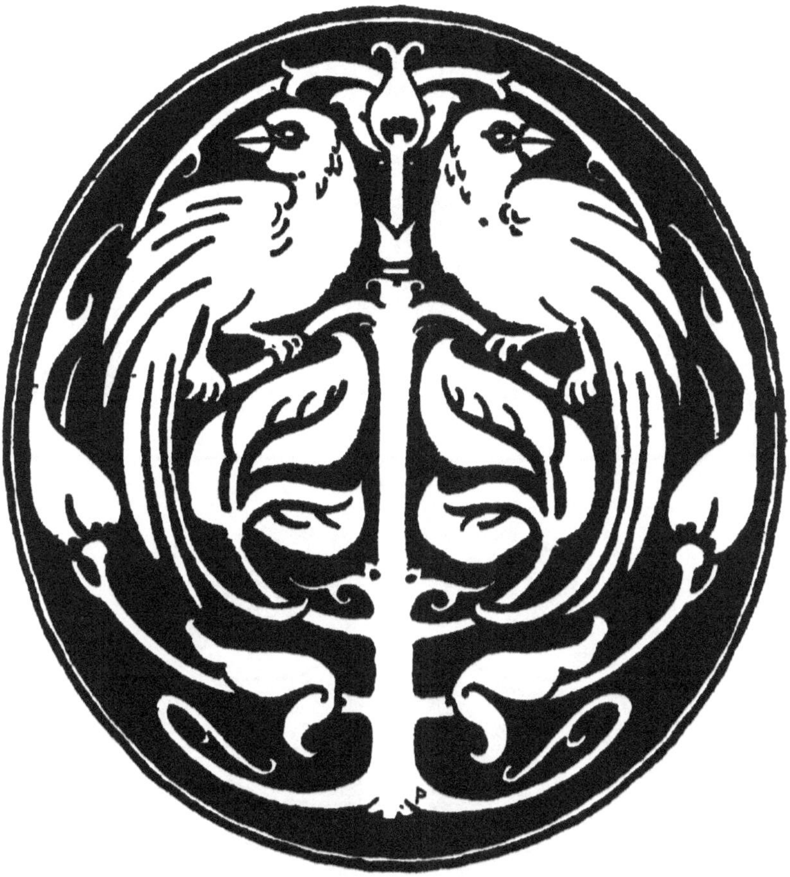

FIG. 140.

as always, a clear, definite, unmistakable statement.
Figures 137, 138, 139, 140 show various solutions of the

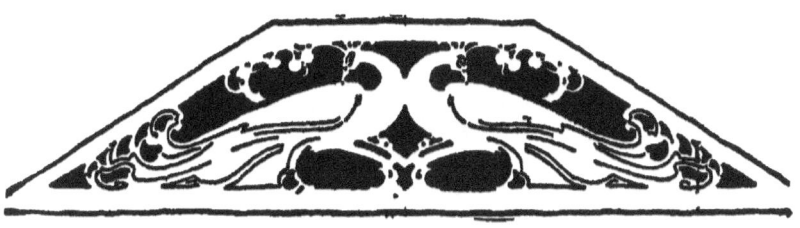

FIG. 141.

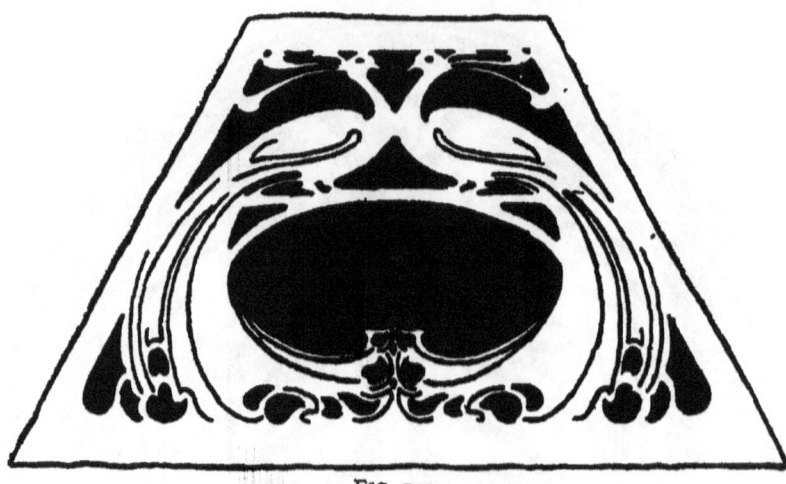

FIG. 142.

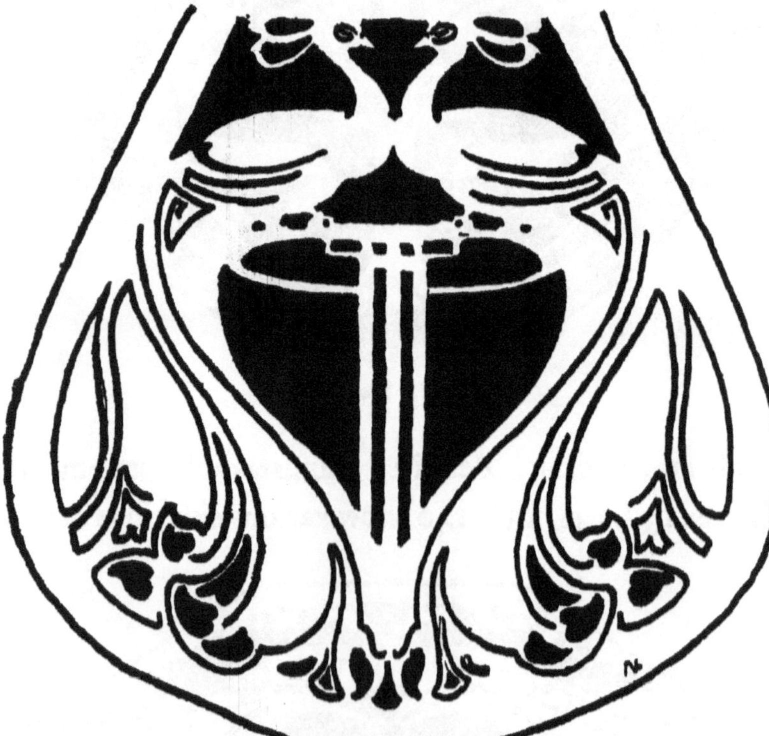

FIG. 143.

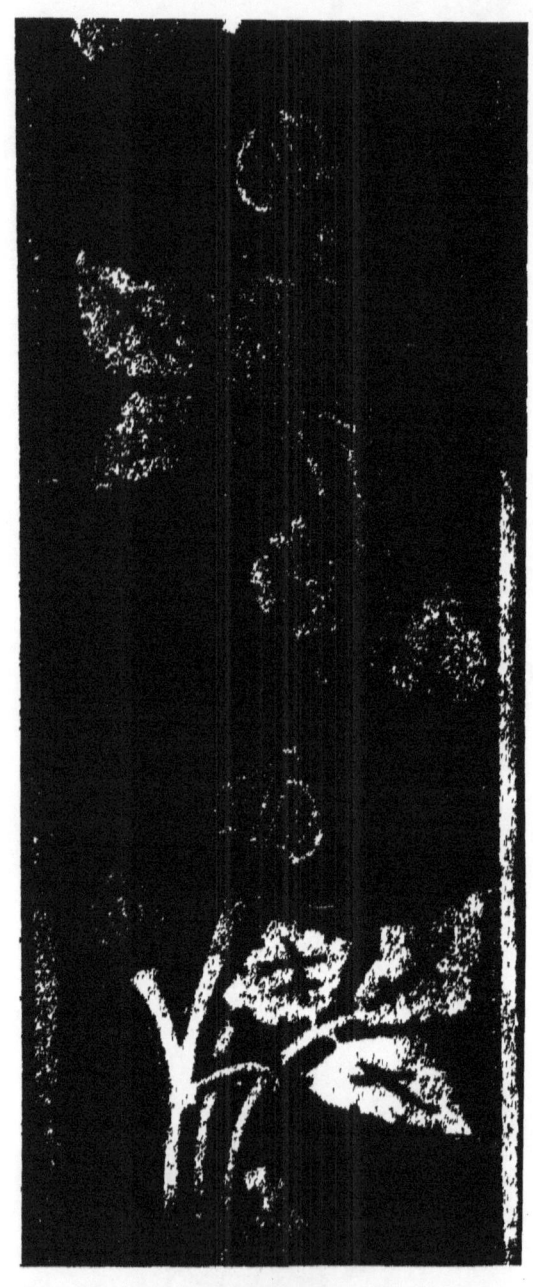

PLATE 62.
ABSTRACT NATURE FORMS.

problem as suggested, — with a slightly different solution though from the same point of view in Plate 62.

PROBLEM. This, the final problem of the series,

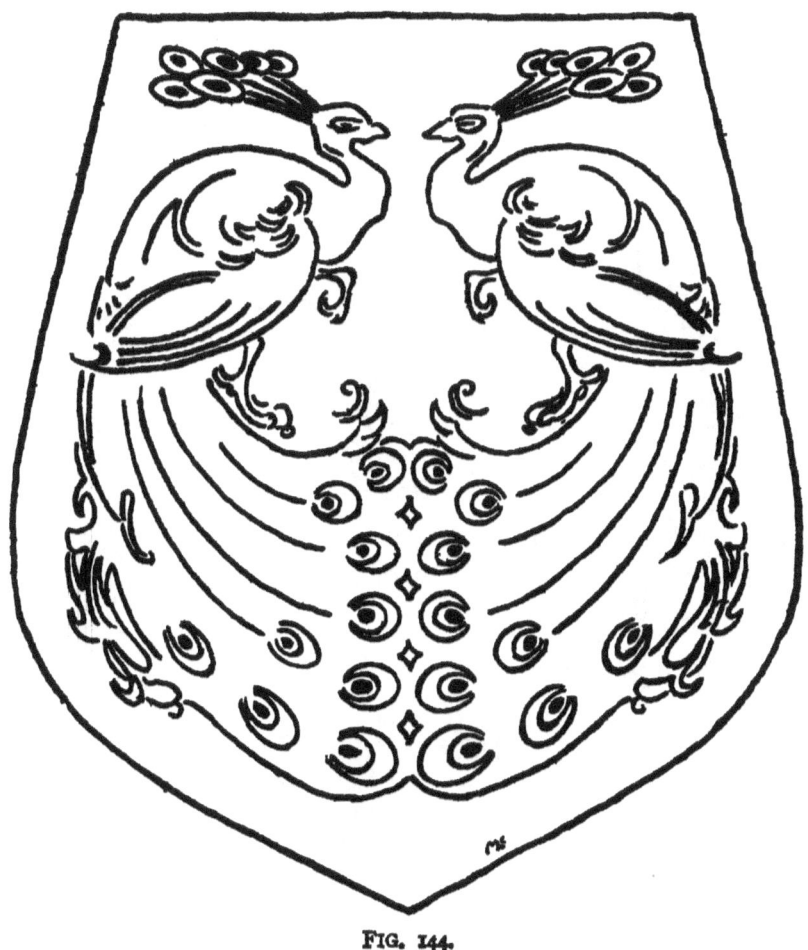

FIG. 144.

is more fully illustrated than any of the others because
it represents a test of ability to apply the principles
outlined in this book to the organization of an idea

involving many and real difficulties. The results are by pupils who have conscientiously followed work along the lines indicated through this book, and go to show

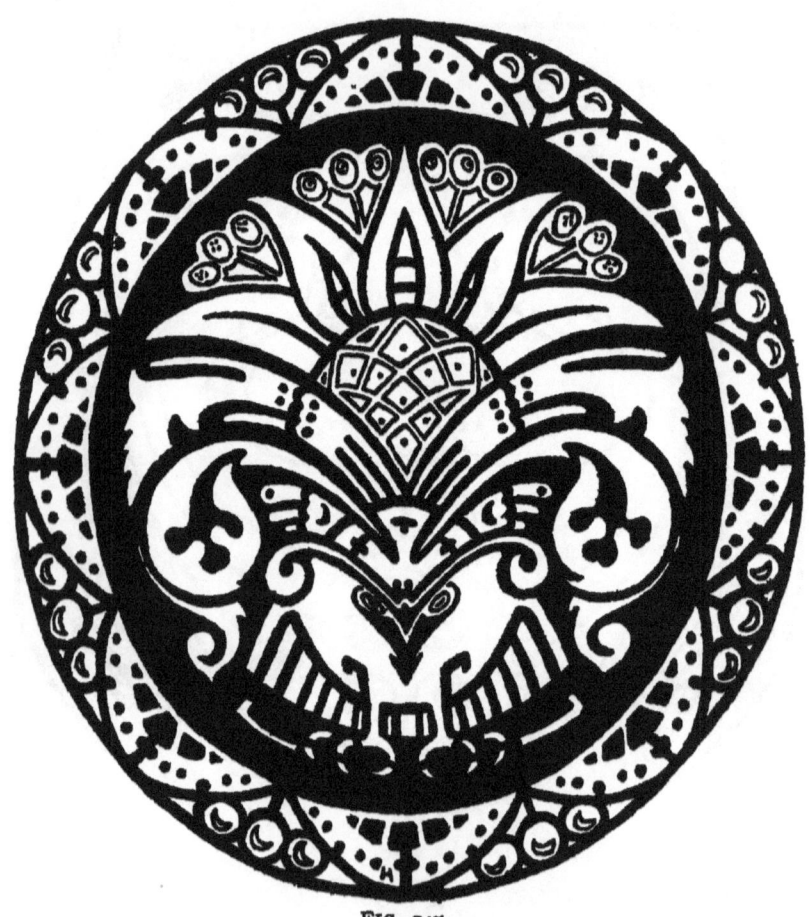

FIG. 145.

an intelligent, individual expression of a thought in terms of design. The motif suggested was —*peacock*. Whether or not the expression of the motif should approach the specific character of this bird or pass into a highly organized arrangement more or less abstract in character was left to the personal choice of each pupil. The results in Plates 63, 64, 65, and

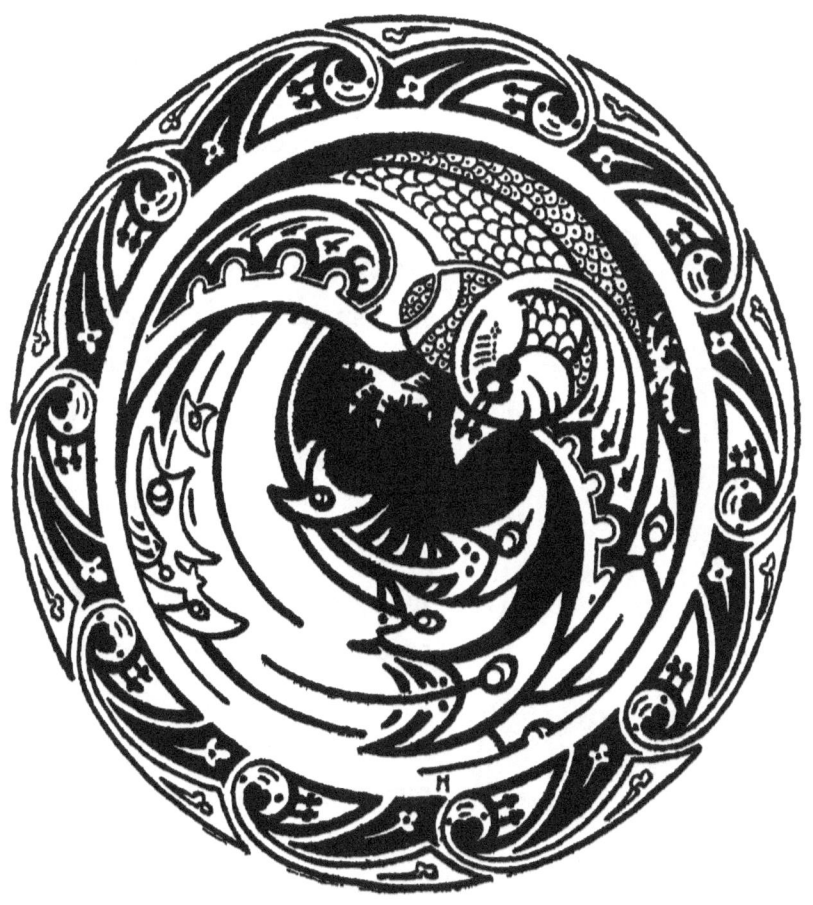

FIG. 146.

in Figures 141 to 145 inclusive stand as a summing up in graphic form of the principles defined and the problems through which they have been presented.

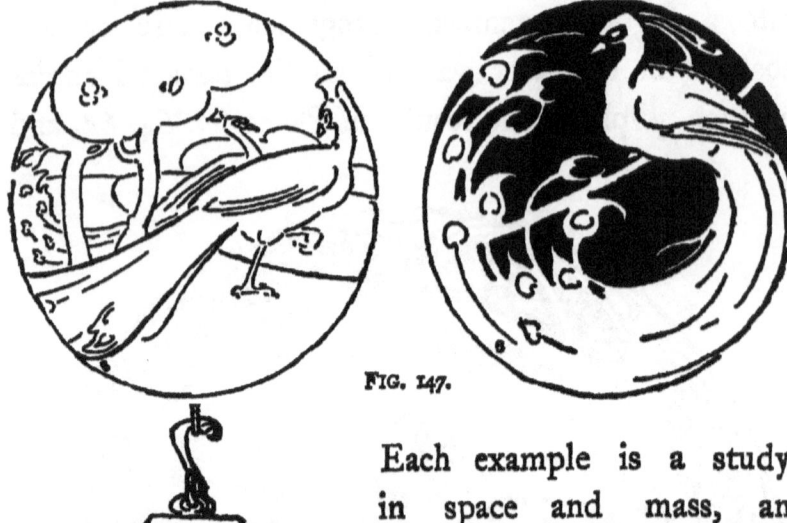

FIG. 147.

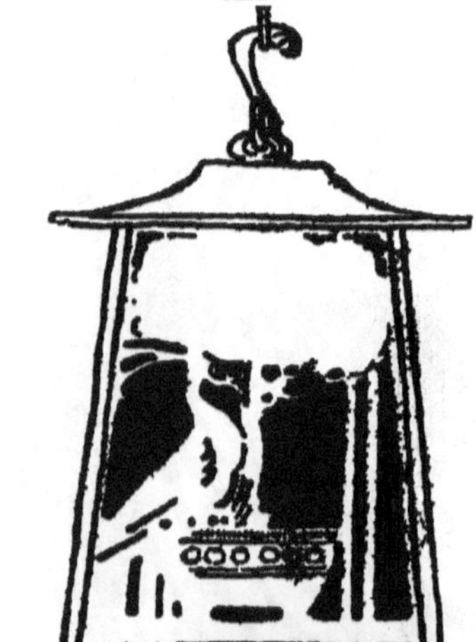

Each example is a study in space and mass, an adjustment of lines and forms. Note the reciprocal relations of details in each; the ways in which unity with variety, harmony with contrast, has been secured. Each detail is part of an organic whole, in which all superfluous elements have been eliminated. Figures 146, 147, 148 represent variations of the problem without the symmetrical plan.

The most profitable field for the study of the peacock

FIG. 148.

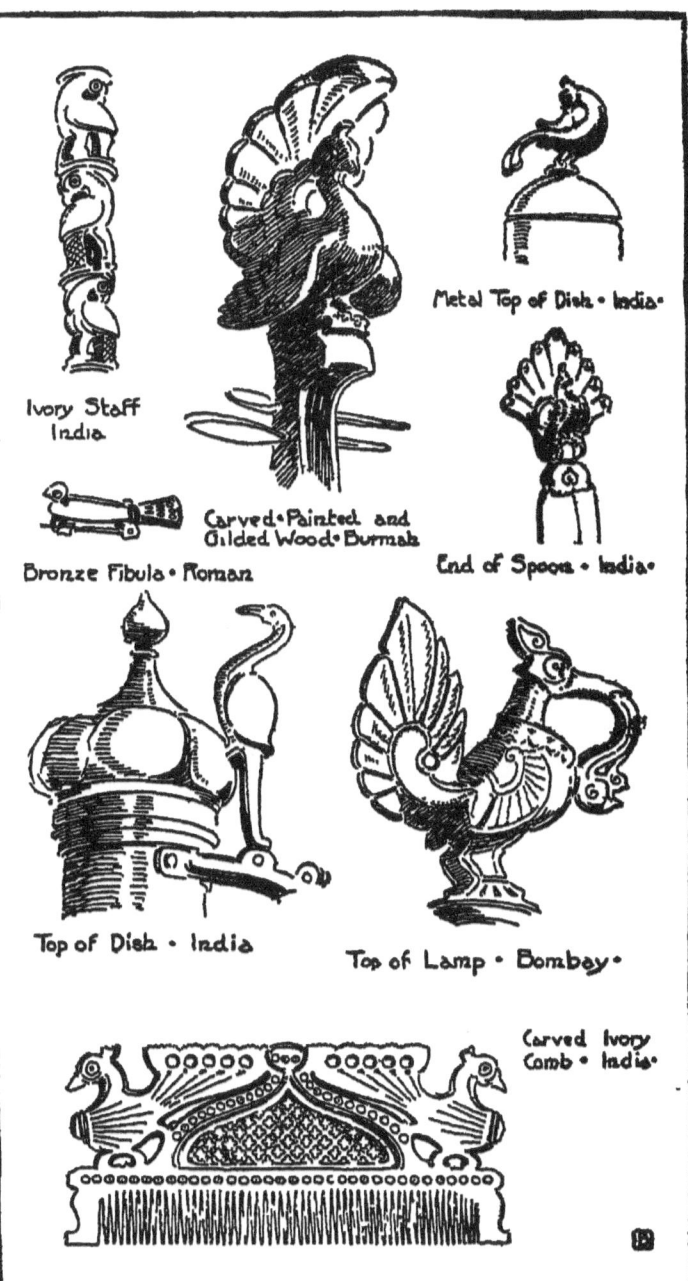

Ivory Staff
India

Carved·Painted and
Gilded Wood· Burmah

Metal Top of Dish· India·

Bronze Fibula· Roman

End of Spoon · India·

Top of Dish · India

Top of Lamp · Bombay·

Carved Ivory
Comb · India·

FIG. 149

in design is in the work of the Orient, particularly the work of Persia and India. In Figure 149 are a

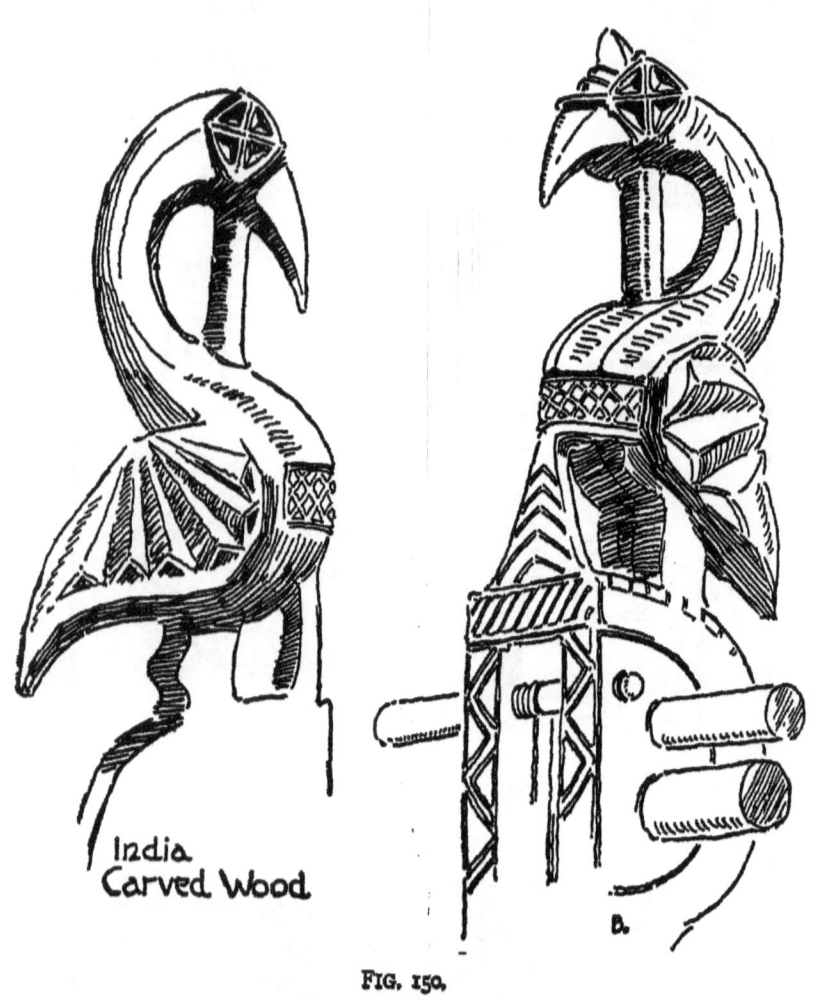

India
Carved Wood

FIG. 150.

number of sketches showing the form adapted to various purposes. In Figure 150 are two sketches of the

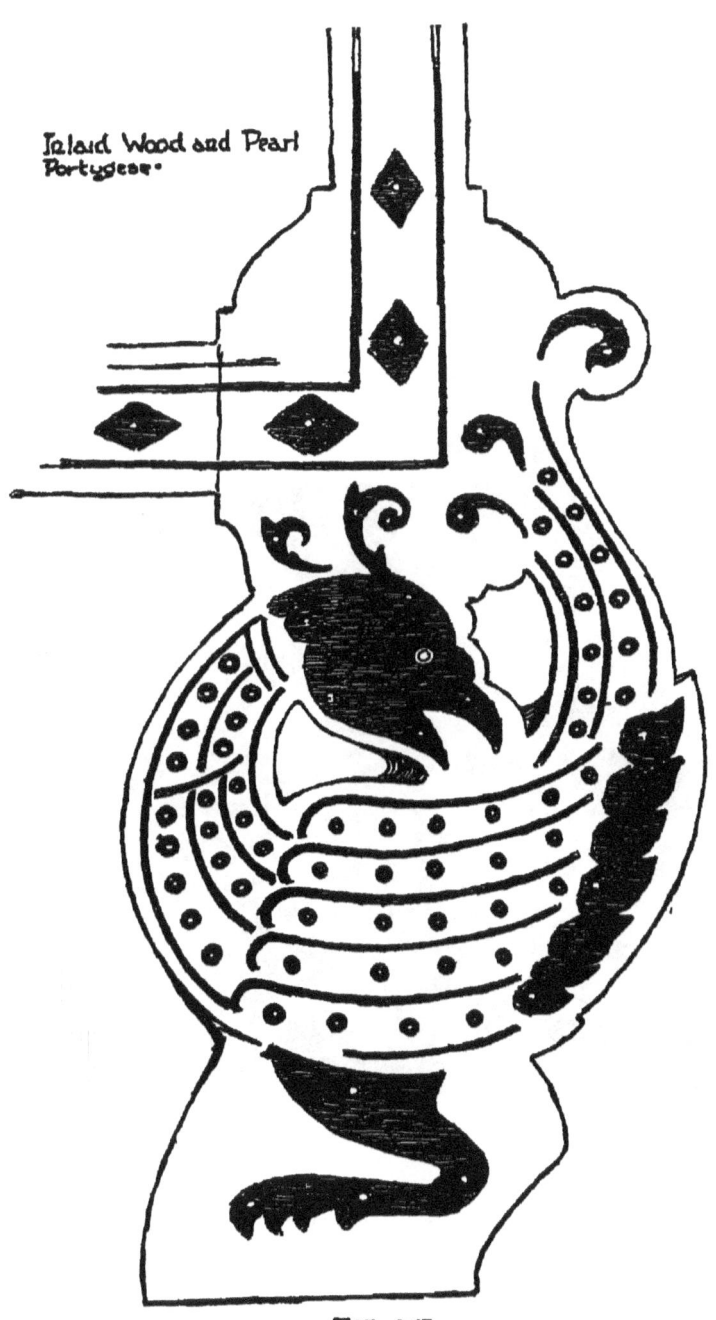

Inlaid Wood and Pearl
Portuguese.

FIG. 151.

same form from the end of a musical instrument. In Figure 151 is an inlaid foot of a table leg made in India, though of Portuguese workmanship. Figure 152 is

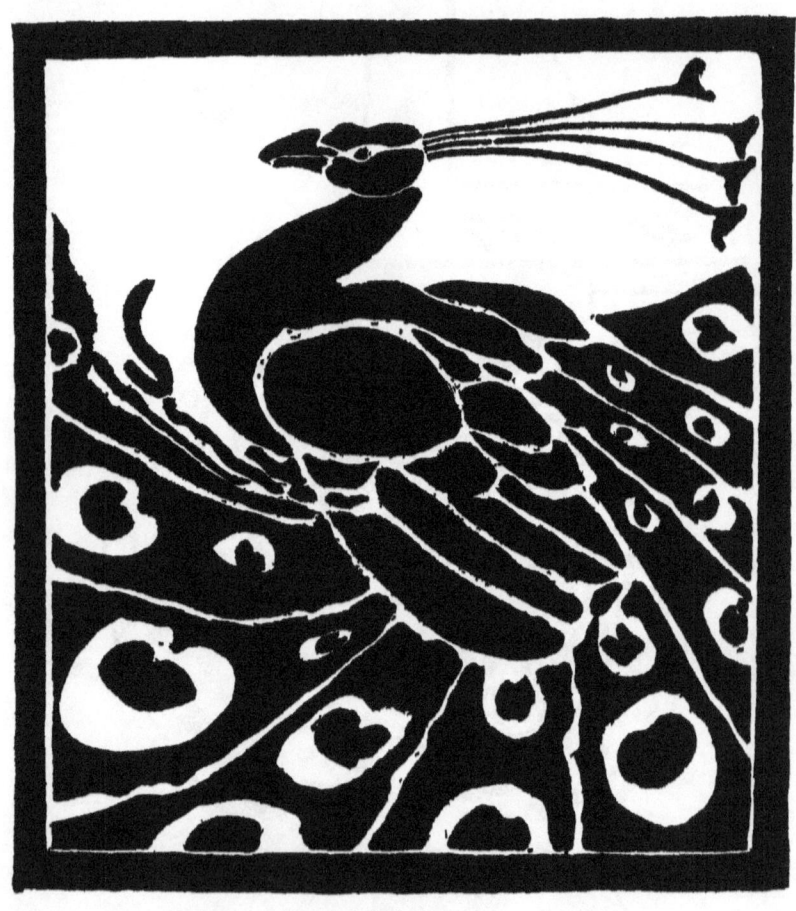

FIG. 152.

from a modern wall paper, — designer unknown to the writer, — an interesting treatment of this motif. In Plate 66 is a symmetrical expression of the idea in

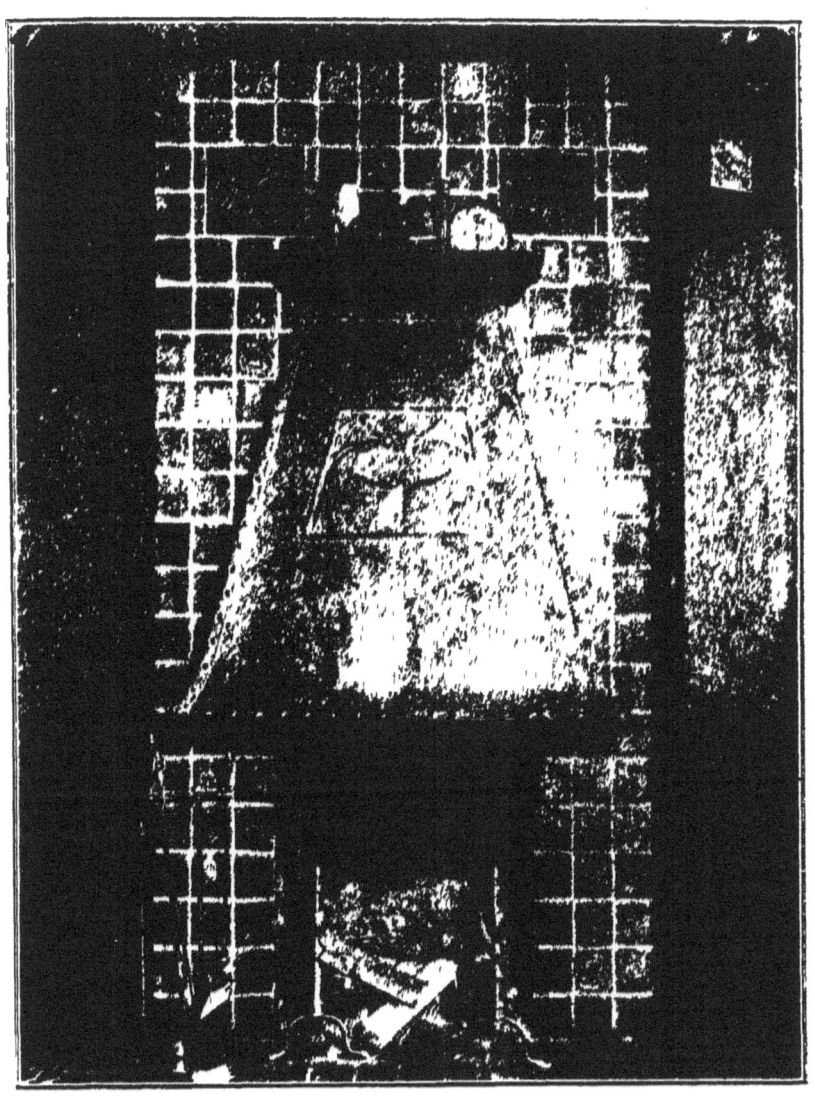

PLATE 66.

CONSTRUCTIVE APPLICATION OF MOTIF.

beaten copper adapted to the environment in which it appears and to the form of which.it is a part. The two last illustrations (Figures 153, 154) form a fitting

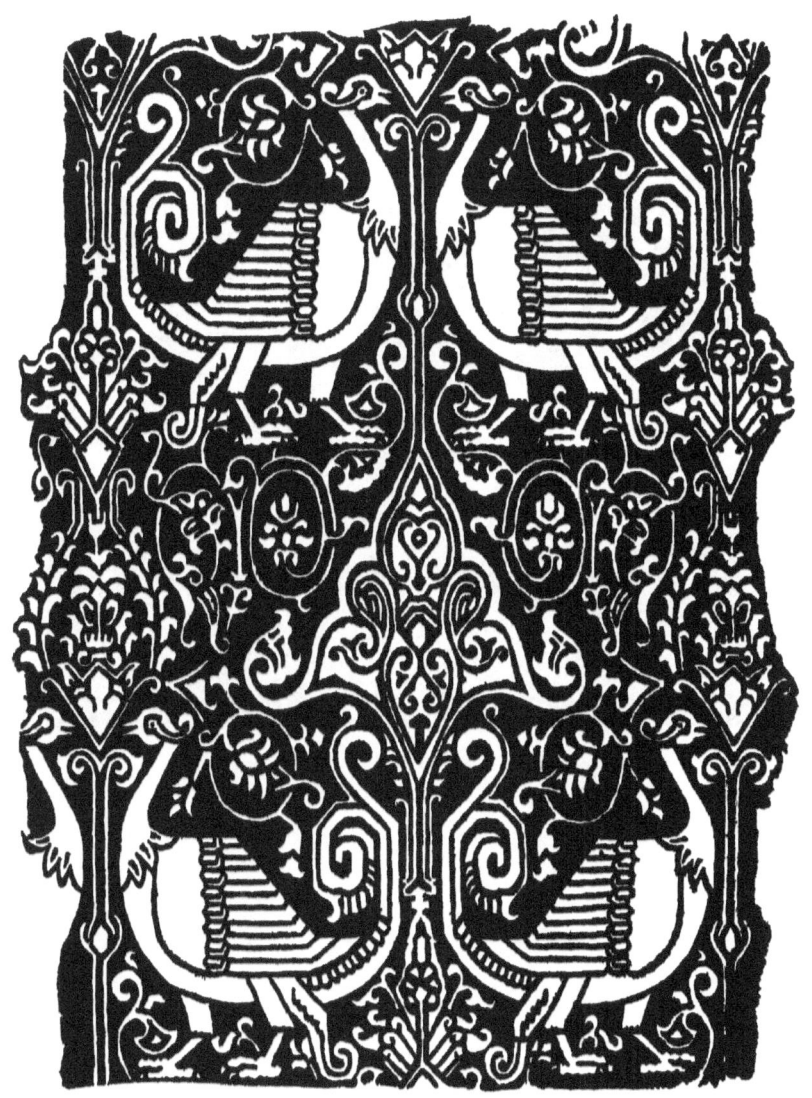

FIG. 153.

climax to our work and may well serve as a final source of inspiration in the study of and practice in the æsthetic principles of design.

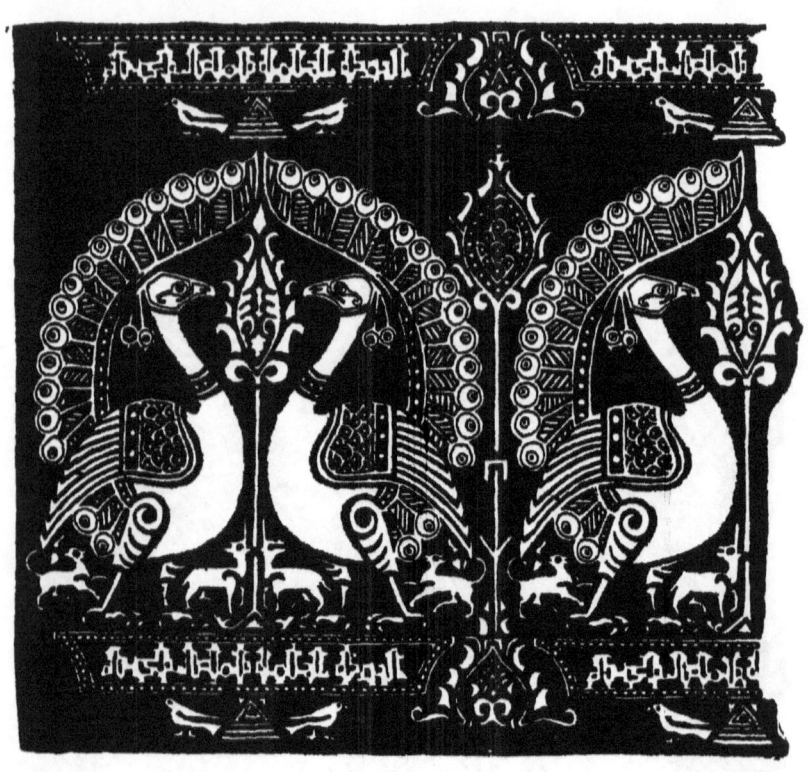

FIG. 154.

CHAPTER XIII

CONCLUSION

"It does not follow, even when our minds . . . are stored with the terms and the motives of Design, that we shall produce anything important or remarkable. Important work comes only from important people. What we accomplish, at best, is merely the measure and expression of our own personalities." — DENMAN ROSS.

IT is apparent that the most interesting work in design was achieved at periods when workmen were designers, when builders were architects. There was no such word or thought as architect until after the sixteenth century. This combination, the faculty to design and the skill to execute, lends interesting and fascinating charm to primitive work, to the peasant industries, now fast disappearing under pressure of modern factory methods, to the best products of the Orient, and to the work of the mediæval craftsmen.

The conditions have now radically changed. Workmen have ceased to be designers; builders have ceased to be architects; and the intimate personality which seems to be the very life of fine industrial work is seldom found. This evolution, the separation of art from industry, was of gradual development; it is only from the height afforded by time that we can note the subtle steps involved in the transition.

The early centuries of mediæval history were in a period of reconstruction, when all men were groping toward an expression of new ideals. In later centuries, with traditions acquired through hard-earned experience and with ideals more clearly in sight, with judgments strengthened and technical difficulties lessened, workmen with greater ability and taste than their fellows became known for the excellence of their achievements. Their presence was sought wherever important work was under way. From one town to another they wandered, leaving behind them a trail of noble churches, palaces, fountains, pulpits, and frescoes. And as these men did more of the thinking, their fellows did less. Still later, with the revival of classical traditions, an increase of luxury, and a consequent shifting of standards, the pathway to artistic renown ceased to lead through the workshop. But for a long time, during a period of notable production in the early days of the Renaissance, there was still a bond of intimate sympathy between the artist and the artisan. Old ties and traditions were not easily severed. Gradually, however, the men who practiced art began to depend more and more upon a theoretic knowledge of tools and materials, while the men who knew much about technical processes and methods of construction concerned themselves less and less with the abstract ideals, the principles and modes of expression of the artist. It has been left for us in modern times to add the final step in the transition, with arbitrary distinctions between fine and industrial art, and subdivisions of labor for purposes of commercial gain. One wonders if the skilled craftsman of old who gave mind, heart, eye, and hand to his work is to be entirely displaced by the "hand" whose function it will be to feed raw material into one end of a machine at so much per day, without questioning why or whence.

It is an odd commentary on the standards by which we measure our present civilization that our material progress, our tremendous strides in science and in mechanical invention, have contributed nothing to our æsthetic development ; even less than this, — have consistently contributed toward a lowering of artistic standards and the degradation of the skilled craftsman to the position of an unskilled operative. We have printing presses that are marvels of mechanical invention, insuring speed and accuracy of production; but it is seldom that we approach the artistic standards set by the old printers who struggled with their rude presses in the early days of the craft in Augsberg, Bamberg, and Venice. We have power looms that do everything but think ; yet we are scarcely within reach of the products that came from the looms of Persia, Sicily, and Italy, or of the old Flemish textiles. Science and mechanical invention have revolutionized metal working; we employ processes undreamed of by the mediæval craftsmen; yet they left behind them standards of beauty that make a comparison odious. Our builders have perfected devices unknown to the master builders of old; yet we never cease to measure and photograph the old churches and palaces with admiration and wonder.

Thus we find that the things now emphasized in the training of the artist are no longer essential to the productive efficiency of the workman. Art and industry are scarcely on speaking terms; whenever they meet they are mutually embarrassed because they have no topic in common for conversation. Between the shop-trained man and the studio-trained man there is ever a lack of understanding and sympathy. The artist deplores the lack of feeling and good taste on the part of the workman on whom he depends to execute his designs; the latter is impatient over the lack of practical knowledge shown by the artist. Both are right. The one approaches his problem with a superficial knowledge of technical limitations and possibilities; the other in the acquisition of technical skill is afforded neither opportunity nor incentive to cultivate a fine taste or an artistic judgment. Some day we shall have an art training that penetrates into the activities of daily life, based on the shop principles, though not necessarily on the methods, of the mediæval crafts. We shall think none the less of an art that seeks expression in terms of painting and sculpture : but we shall recognize the truth that art rests upon a basis broad enough to encompass all of man's activities.

In our study of design to-day we turn to the studio for our traditions rather than to the shop. We approach the subject from a point of view diametrically opposed to the development of design in its periods of finest production. We begin by drawing, painting, and modeling; we accumulate studies from Nature, and attempt to conventionalize this material on paper ; we study historic ornament, make careful copies from the various historic styles, and adapt motifs found through this process to our own needs ; we visit shops and factories (sometimes) and listen to interesting talks on the technique of carving, weaving, and metal work, on the relation of pattern to material ; we gather from practice in the "arts and crafts" a superficial idea of the tools and materials of many crafts, but have no thorough or practical knowledge of the technical demands of any one craft. We aim to produce studio-trained craftsmen. What we need most are shop-trained artists. The examples of industrial art which are so carefully treasured in our museums and galleries were the work of shop-trained men, not of studio-trained men.

A thoughtful study of the history of design would seem to indicate the futility of trying to teach designing through a paper product on a basis of theoretic knowledge or book-learned information as to tools, materials, and processes. We may hope to define elementary principles on paper, to appreciate and express an abstract beauty of line, form, and tone, to stimulate, in some measure, the imagination, to learn the value of clear and orderly thought; but if we wish to go beyond this abstract expression, let it be on a basis of practical experience in constructive work. With an experience that gives one command over the practical principles of a craft, the æsthetic principles learned through the solution of abstract problems may be given a real and vital application. The two should go hand in hand in order that there may be an immediate and effective correlation between them. Of one thing you may be sure: if you can impart character and interest to the lines and forms employed in the definition of elementary principles under the comparatively simple limitations of abstract design, you will find that much has been done to clarify your ideas when you attempt to speak through constructive work. The underlying principles of composition are not essentially different whether we weave an idea into cloth, beat it into metal, or carve it in wood.

It is well here to direct attention to some of the general points that have been emphasized throughout the book. It will, of course, be understood that a few typical problems only have been chosen to indicate a gradual development from simple beginnings to more complex questions. The step from one problem to another represents merely a new version under slightly varying conditions of the same elementary ideas. Each art rests upon principles peculiar to itself, inherent within the tools, materials, and constructive processes involved. The principles peculiar to one art are not necessarily applicable to another art. But somewhere beneath them all are questions common to them all. We sometimes speak of the principles of architecture as applied to the designing of — a book cover, for instance. The statement is misleading. The principles peculiar to architecture are not applicable to the designing of a book cover. Architecture is an art of wood, stone, brick, concrete, iron, developed through the acceptance of conditions that have given us types as widely divergent as the Parthenon, a California bungalow, and a Chinese pagoda. If there is any relation between an architectural composition and a book cover design, it must be sought in principles that are common to both, in abstract questions that belong to one quite as much as to the other. There is no infallible criterion by which beauty can be measured; and there will be an inevitable disagreement as to a definition of the most essential of the elementary principles. But if we eliminate the questions that are peculiar to each art in an effort to define æsthetic principles that are common to the practice of many arts, we shall find our discussions centering about the composition of lines, forms, and tones. Something, at any rate, has been done if we can find through practice that there is some common principle shared by the work of the primitive basket maker, the textile of the mediæval weaver, and the carving of the Japanese artisan, — that the product of each is an interpretation under different conditions and influences of the same principles of composition. The things that count for beauty in the vigorous expression of the primitive weaver occur again in the work of the Orient — but infinitely more subtle and refined.

We have always to accept with a grain of doubt the judgment of an individual when applied to the critical study of design. His opinion will probably be toned by his own practice and experience. We have likewise to question our own free choice. The things that appeal to us with most force may, indeed, narrow our judgment when applied to a broader field of criticism. Nor can we accept without reserve the general verdict of our day. There was a time when the best architects of England were building classic temples for use as town halls, — when Gothic was a term of derision. Even now there are those who profess to find neither interest nor beauty in the art of Old Japan.

The intent of a design should be clear; if it lacks interest, there is still hope through continued practice. An inarticulate, mumbled product is no more creditable in a design than in speech. A design is thought expressed in terms of line, form, and tone, because, perforce, it cannot be expressed in any other way. If the designer's thought is not clear to himself, he surely cannot hope to make it clear to others, and cannot expect others to interest themselves in a disorderly, mumbled result. A clear statement of an inferior idea is preferable to a vague, indefinite design that has to be reinforced by verbal explanations. An unexplained product is a fair index to a designer's thinking powers. If you feel that you have fine ideas, but that you are unable to give them adequate expression in terms of design, — try something else; Nature never intended that you should be a designer. It is safe to assert that Nature seldom endows a man with brilliant ideas without furnishing him some means for expressing them with clearness.

It is always important to know where to stop in

design, when just enough has been said. As with the painter, one's study in design is very much a question of eliminating the superfluous, of choosing that which is most essential. Those things which appear to be simple and spontaneous are often the result of years of training and persistent effort. Question the reason for every element that enters into a design; make each detail perform consistent service.

Learn the value of concentration; furnish the eye with a dominant thought and group other thoughts in subordinate relations.

Do not deplore lack of incentive, lack of interesting materials. The world is full of noble, inspiring ideas. The humble plant by your own doorstep, if you know how to use it to good advantage, may be given quite as much interest in design as the Persians gave to the pomegranate. Look about you, to your own environment, for motifs, not wander afar.

Last of all, do not be "clever." No term could be more of a reproach in art than this. Art is painstaking; it demands ceaseless work, toil, drudgery it may be. That which is easiest won is generally least worth while. The worker must ever be open-minded and watch against clever mannerisms as against a drought that dries up the river at its source.

INDEX

Printed in the United States of America.